Using Web 2.0 and Social Networking Tools in the K-12 Classroom

Beverley E. Crane

Neal-Schuman

Chicago

Don't miss this book's companion website!

To access curriculum examples from pioneering educators around the world; exercises and lessons in subject areas and grade levels not highlighted in the book; up-to-date information on interesting technologies; and Bev's Edublog, go to:

www.neal-schuman.com/webclassroom

Published by Neal-Schuman, an imprint of ALA Publishing
50 E. Huron Street
Chicago, IL 60611
www.neal-schuman.com

Printed and bound in the United States of America.

The paper used in this publication meets the minimum requirements of American National Standard for Information Sciences—Permanence of Paper for Printed Library Materials, ANSI Z39.48-1992.

Library of Congress Cataloging-in-Publication Data

Available at http://catalog.loc.gov

ISBN: 978-1-55570-774-3

For my grandchildren with love—
Natalie, Sam, Joe, Mikey, Bailey, Max, and Gavin,
the K–12 learners for whom this book is written.

Contents

Chapter 3. Using Wikis in Language Arts and Social Studies   39

Chapter 4. Experiencing History through Podcasts   65

Chapter 10. Bringing Web 2.0 and Social Networking into Elective Subjects   205

Chapter 11. Creating Community with Web 2.0 Tools and Social Networking   225

List of Illustrations

FIGURES

TABLES

Preface

Youth today, perhaps even more so than their teachers, are skilled in using computers and wireless devices for text-messaging, sending pictures, sharing music, reading books, and simply surfing from website to website. Thus, it is now more vital than ever that teachers use technology to engage their students' attention across the curriculum. Many teachers crave effective models for how, why, and when to use new Internet technology with daily lessons.

Using Web 2.0 and Social Networking Tools in the K–12 Classroom brings together the best of the best:

- Ideas and examples from educators who integrate Web 2.0 and social networking into innovative lessons, as well as into their daily lives
- Creative lesson and unit topics in science, social studies, and language arts—including earthquakes, the Middle East conflict, and plagiarism—and electives such as art, health, and government
- Web 2.0 tools and social media the educational community has deemed noteworthy for their value in offering students motivating lessons that adhere to educational and technological standards while providing opportunities to learn content
- A website (http://www.neal-schuman.com/webclassroom) and blog where educators can also learn outside the pages of this book

Using Web 2.0 and Social Networking Tools in the K–12 Classroom provides school librarians, technology coordinators, and teachers at the elementary and secondary levels with guidelines, models, and strategies for incorporating Web 2.0 and social networking as an essential part of the lessons and units they teach, as well as programs they develop. Parents, who in greater numbers are teaching their children at home, can use the unit plans to incorporate technology into writing, literature, science, and social studies. Pre-service teacher educators and library school program instructors may use the exercises and step-by-step instructions to provide their students with the knowledge and skills to meet state-mandated technology standards.

This book has four goals:

1. To describe Web 2.0 and social networking tools to educators new to the technologies so they can discuss them intelligently with students and other colleagues
2. To model Web 2.0 tools and social media through classroom examples
3. To explain to beginning users how to get started with each tool
4. To present practical unit and lesson plans illustrating the use of Web 2.0 and social networking in the K–12 content-area curricula

ORGANIZATION

Using Web 2.0 and Social Networking Tools in the K–12 Classroom is divided into 11 chapters. Chapter 1 introduces trends for the twenty-first century, provides teaching strategies using Web 2.0, and describes the framework for the model units that appear in the following chapters. Chapters 2 through 10 highlight Web 2.0 and social networking tools educators have identified as useful and motivating to student learning. Chapter 11 focuses on social media that help educators connect, take advantage of professional development opportunities online, and learn from one another.

Each chapter emphasizes one or more of the following:

1. Incorporating Web 2.0 and social media into the curriculum for communication, research, collaboration, and connections that will bring teachers and school librarians together
2. Activities that are varied, interesting, and achieve the fullest, most productive involvement of students
3. Instructional techniques that include independent, competitive, and collaborative learning
4. Interdisciplinary studies so that students will recognize the connections among subject areas

In addition to its focus on different Web 2.0 tools, each chapter also incorporates a different subject area, topic, and age level. Chapters build upon what educators have learned in previous chapters and often combine more than one Web 2.0 tool in the unit plans. For example, Chapter 2, "Enhancing Collaboration and Communication with Blogs," illustrates blogging in elementary English. A comprehensive lesson plan models ways educators can prepare students offline for blogging. Chapter 3, "Using Wikis in Language Arts and Social Studies," combines the use of wikis and blogs and collaboration in student reading and writing activities in literature and history to look at bullying, a real-life issue that affects students every day. By looking at "bullies" from history and literature, students can draw parallels to the modern era in which they live. In Chapter 4, "Experiencing History through Podcasts," upper elementary, middle, or high school students collaboratively explore events leading to the American Revolution through research, creating podcasts, and using other Web 2.0 tools. Chapter 5, "Opening Your Classrooms to the World via Skype," describes Skype videoconferencing's diverse uses. The detailed lesson plan engages students in writing responsive questions and comments for authentic audiences, skills vital to all subject areas at all grade levels.

Chapter 6, "Bringing the Social Networking Revolution to K–12 Classrooms," describes ways social networking adds to classroom learning. Examples illustrate creative projects using social networking tools, and the interdisciplinary unit plan explores the 2011 Middle East conflict, an issue not available in history books. Chapter 7, "Using Google in the Science Classroom—Tools That Work," introduces more tools for collaborating, creating presentations, exploring the earth, and much more. The unit for this chapter creates cross-curricular connections on the science topic of earthquakes, one that affects a large global population. The unit can be adapted for upper elementary, middle, or high school students. Chapter 8, "Creating Motivating Lessons with Video," incorporates digital storytelling to promote cultural awareness. The unit enables middle school students to focus on their preferred learning style as they create stories and incorporate video and audio into a digital story. Although designed for nonnative English speakers, Chapter 9, "Enhancing English Language Learning with Web 2.0 Tools," can be easily adapted for a mainstream classroom. The chapter unit introduces several Web 2.0 tools that let nonnative English speakers improve their reading, writing, speaking, and listening as they collaborate about migratory activities of whales with students in another country.

Chapter 10, "Bringing Web 2.0 and Social Networking into Elective Subjects," looks at resources currently available for the visual arts, music, health education, mathematics, and government. Lesson plans illustrate creative uses of Web 2.0 tools in these subjects. Finally, Chapter 11, "Creating Community with Web 2.0 Tools and Social Networking," introduces Web 2.0 and social networking tools to connect educators and create community. Building a personal learning network and a unit on teaching plagiarism through a mock trial conclude the book.

Most chapters have a similar three-part structure. Part 1: Ideas and Insights identifies and describes the Web 2.0 tool that is the focus of the chapter and illustrates—through a series of examples in specific content areas—how the tool integrates into the curriculum, as well as advantages for using it in the classroom. Part 2: Getting Started provides examples of one or more Web 2.0 tools and illustrates step by step how to begin using them. Part 3: Practical Applications includes practical unit-plan models in different content areas at both the elementary and secondary levels. The unit explains how the technology combines with broad-based examples in core content areas—language arts, social studies, and science. Educators can use the plans as they are presented or modify them to meet the individual needs of students and curricula. Exercises in each chapter offer opportunities for readers to practice what they have just learned, become familiar with Web 2.0 tools and social media, and reflect on the content of the chapter. Each chapter also contains a glossary of new terms and a list of websites that will be useful for the topic under discussion. The appendix describes the accompanying website.

In addition to this printed book, *Using Web 2.0 and Social Networking Tools in the K–12 Classroom* features a companion website: http://www.neal-schuman.com/webclassroom. The website provides curriculum examples from pioneering educators around the world, as well as exercises and lessons in subject areas and grade levels not highlighted in the book. A "What's New" section will keep readers up to date with interesting technologies and ones where space in the book prevented covering them. A link on the website provides access to Bev's Edublog so readers can share tips on technologies and innovative lesson ideas. Website notations in each chapter indicate places where the website might provide additional information.

Using Web 2.0 and Social Networking Tools in the K–12 Classroom is intended to encourage educators to learn more about and try Web 2.0 tools and social networking that many of their students are already using outside the classroom. The explanatory material, step-by-step explanations, examples, and model units and lessons should prompt teachers and school librarians to try these new technologies, and the accompanying website will continue to expand their knowledge and skills. All educators seek to motivate students to learn the content they are teaching, to think critically while learning, and to communicate on broad levels both inside and outside the classroom. Students are already using Web 2.0 tools and social media discussed in this book in their daily lives. Educators must take advantage of students' knowledge and skill to make learning that much more exciting and meaningful for them. A successful experience using Web 2.0 tools in the classroom can make all the difference!

Acknowledgments

This book is the result of the time and effort of teachers, school librarians, and IT educators who spent hours learning about Web 2.0 technology and, more important, integrating it into content-area lessons and libraries so that motivated students may learn the skills they will need for tasks and jobs in the twenty-first century. With the proliferation of social media, these same educators have shared their ideas, skills, knowledge, and creativity with novice technology users who desire to learn about Web 2.0 and social networking. A special thanks to those who gave me permission to use screenshots from their websites and blogs to bring examples in this book to life.

Thank you to Sandy Wood, my editor at Neal-Schuman, who provided valuable suggestions on content and organization of the book. She kept me on track. Thanks also to Betty Jo Hibberd, whose expertise made it possible to revise my website that accompanies this book. Finally, to my husband, I appreciate your patience with my long hours while writing and your help in assembling the final copies.

CHAPTER 1

A New Information Revolution

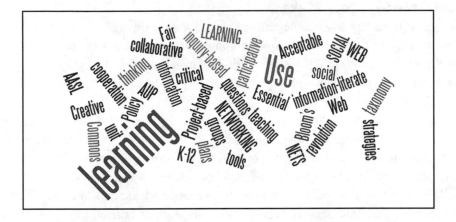

It is not the strongest of the species that survives, nor the most intelligent that survives. It is the one that is the most adaptable to change.

—Charles Darwin

The illiterate of the 21st century will not be those who cannot read and write, but those who cannot learn, unlearn, and relearn.

—Alvin Toffler, futurist, in *Rethinking the Future* (Gibson, 1999)

Think left and think right and think low and think high. Oh, the things you can think up if only you try!

—Dr. Seuss

PART 1: IDEAS AND INSIGHTS

Picture this: In one corner of Ms. Crane's classroom, one group discusses conserving water, a topic they plan to present at the Earth Day Fair. They have surfed the Internet and bookmarked on their Diigo page seven sites, including YouTube, blogs, and research sites. In the middle of the room another group is brainstorming possible ideas for recycling that their group can undertake. The scribe for the group is taking notes on their wiki so that the rest of the group can add comments and changes. Another group has Ms. Crane's eye as they squabble over who is playing which part in their podcast. Two students are studiously writing the script for the podcast on global warming. The most vocal group is creating their paper grocery bags to distribute to the local stores in town. These students are painting their grocery bags with recycling phrases and pictures while the other part of the group is writing a script for a VoiceThread to send to their partner class in Australia. Finally, off to the left three students are working on their Google Docs spreadsheet, itemizing the litter they collected for their pollution project.

(Continued)

(Continued)

The other half of the group is reviewing Google Maps to identify the areas where they collected the most litter to help eliminate pollution. When all groups complete their projects, Ms. Crane will hook up via Skype so students can present their results live to their partner class! Busy, busy, busy. While all of this activity is going on, Ms. Crane is circulating throughout the classroom, making comments and suggestions, answering student questions, and facilitating the process of learning in a Web 2.0 classroom.

What a Difference a Year Makes

Web 2.0 programs have rapidly become tools of choice for a growing body of classroom educators who are discovering that these tools provide compelling teaching and learning opportunities. Educators with no programming skills can publish their own journals, photographs, videos, podcasts, wikis, slideshows, and more. The web is now a two-way street. Everyday people are creating the content. Web 2.0 has taken over!

Web 2.0—or the Read/Write Web as some call it—is a breeding ground for creative and engaging educational endeavors. It is a two-way medium so that almost anyone can become a publisher or a "content producer." In Web 2.0, the creation of material or information on the Web is as much a part of the experience as the finding or reading of data had been in Web 1.0.

In 2011, Web 2.0 is a place to find people, to exchange ideas, and to demonstrate creativity before an audience. The Internet has become not only a great curriculum resource but also an important learning source for both students and educators. Students are creating online content, collaborating with other students around the world, and showcasing their work to a global audience. Educators gain new ideas and inspiration as they connect with other educators. Students and educators alike are on a learning spree, and Web 2.0 facilitates this networking. It provides authentic learning experiences for students, and it encourages global awareness, creativity, innovation, critical thinking, active participation, and collaboration. The knowledge our students gain from engaging with Web 2.0 technologies fosters communication and information literacy skills required in the twenty-first century.

Trends for the Twenty-First Century

As you read about some of the new Web 2.0 tools in the rest of this book, you will begin to see trends appearing that differ from the ways students have been taught in the past. As you read further, you will notice how these trends are already becoming part of more and more classrooms.

Based on extensive review of current articles, interviews, papers, and new research, the *2010 Horizon Report: K–12 Edition* examines emerging technologies for their potential impact on and use in teaching, learning, and creative expression within K–12 education (Johnson et al., 2010). The report identifies the following trends as key drivers of technology adoptions for the period 2010 through 2015:

- **Trend #1: Technology Is Empowering Students.** Increasingly, technology is recognized as a primary way to stay in touch and take control of one's own learning. Technology gives students a public voice and a means to reach beyond the classroom for interaction and exploration. It is a method for communicating and socializing and has become a transparent part of their lives.
- **Trend #2: A Tidal Wave of Information.** The publishing revolution is having an impact on the volume of content available that is difficult to even comprehend. There are over 100,000 blogs created daily, and Facebook has more than 500 million users as of July 2010, twice the

number of the year before. The amount of information presents a challenge to educators who must decide what information is worthy of their time and attention and how to teach their students to discriminate between the wheat and the chaff.

- **Trend #3: Everything Is Becoming Participative.** Technology continues to profoundly impact how people work, play, learn, socialize, and collaborate. Amazon.com is a good example of how the participative web works. Book readers write reviews of books that are a significant factor in readers' decisions to purchase a book. Moreover, Amazon takes the information of its users and by tracking their behavior provides data suggesting other books they might like to read. Other companies are following this same tack.

> ➤ *The website that accompanies this book (http://www.neal-schuman.com/webclassroom) will allow readers to participate with Web 2.0 as they read about it in this book.*

- **Trend #4: The New Consumers.** The new consumer combines "producer" and "consumer." New consumers not only acquire knowledge but also contribute to the production of that knowledge.
- **Trend #5: The Age of the Collaborator.** The age of the collaborator is here. The era of trusted authority (e.g., *Newsweek* or *The New York Times*) is changing to an era of transparent and collaborative scholarship (e.g., *Wikipedia*). The expert is giving way to the collaborator.

> ➤ *Join Bev's blog at http://bevcrane.blogspot.com/ to collaborate with other educators on topics of interest.*

- **Trend #6: An Explosion of Innovation.** The perceived value of innovation and creativity is increasing. Innovation is valued at the highest levels of business and must be embraced in schools if students are to succeed beyond their formal education. The methods of designing learning experiences must reflect the growing importance of innovation and creativity as professional skills. Innovation and creativity must not be linked just to arts subjects; these skills are equally important in scientific inquiry, entrepreneurship, and other areas as well. The combination of an increased ability to work on specialized topics by gathering teams from around the globe and the diversity of these collaborators should foster an incredible amount of innovation.
- **Trend #7: Social Learning Gains Headway.** We move from thinking of knowledge as an "answer" that is transferred from teacher to student to a more social view of learning. The model now includes students as contributors.
- **Trend #8: Social Networking.** Students today are using social networking sites such as Facebook, Twitter, and YouTube, among others, on a daily basis. Schools have still not caught up. Some educators are promoting social networking, if merely to communicate with their colleagues. These leaders are now introducing Web 2.0 into the classroom to their students. (Hargadon, 2008)
- **Trend #9: A New Publishing Revolution.** The Internet has become a platform for unparalleled creativity as educators and students create new content on the web. As well as locating information for research, Web 2.0 tools promote contribution, creation, and collaboration—often requiring only access to the web and a browser. Blogs, wikis, podcasts, video/photo-sharing, social networking, and more are changing how and why content is created.
- **Trend #10: Anytime, Anywhere.** No longer do students and educators communicate only in their classrooms, nor is the computer the only means to network. Smartphones, iPads, and other devices allow connection at home, in cars, at a basketball game, and more. Accessibility is at any time in any place.

Objectives of This Chapter

Chapter 1 provides an introduction to some of the Web 2.0 tools on the Internet, as well as teaching strategies, both of which are illustrated in the chapters that follow. After reading Chapter 1, educators will be able to:

- identify the importance of Web 2.0 tools for K–12 students;
- describe teaching strategies necessary for twenty-first-century learning;
- state how Web 2.0 tools enhance twenty-first-century teaching strategies; and
- formulate the framework of an Internet unit incorporating Web 2.0 tools.

Glossary

Each chapter provides a glossary of terms that may not be familiar to you. Review these words that appear in Chapter 1.

acceptable use policy (AUP): A written agreement, signed by students, their parents, and teachers, outlining the terms and conditions of Internet use.

Creative Commons: A nonprofit organization devoted to expanding the range of creative works available for others to legally build upon and share.

fair use: A doctrine in United States copyright law that allows limited use of copyrighted material without requiring permission from the rights holders.

information literacy: A set of competencies an informed citizen of the twenty-first century ought to possess to participate intelligently and actively in society.

social bookmarking: A method for Internet users to store, organize, search, and manage bookmarks of webpages on the Internet using tags.

social networking: A means of communicating and sharing information between two or more individuals in an online community.

VoiceThread: An online media album that can hold essentially any type of media (images, documents, and videos) and that allows people to make comments using text or audio.

Web 2.0 tools: A term associated with web applications that facilitate participatory information sharing, user-centered activity, and collaboration on the Internet. Examples include social networking, blogs, wikis, video sharing, and more. (Definitions of these terms appear in subsequent chapters.)

Becoming an Information-Literate Person in the Twenty-First Century

A mission of K–12 school librarians has been to help students become "information literate." In 2007, the American Association of School Librarians (AASL) revised its standards based on earlier guidelines in *Information Power: Guidelines for School Library Media Programs*, which provided a philosophical basis for developing library media programs. The result of this endeavor was a new set of standards titled *Standards for the 21st-Century Learner* designed toward information literacy in the twenty-first century (AASL, 2007).

Based on a common set of beliefs, the revised standards create four strands emphasizing that learners use skills, resources, and tools to:

- inquire, think critically, and gain knowledge;
- draw conclusions, make informed decisions, apply knowledge to new situations, and create new knowledge;
- share knowledge and participate ethically and productively as members of our democratic society; and
- pursue personal and aesthetic growth.

These new standards are aligned with state curriculum framework goals and form the basis for how the library and educators operate in K–12 education.

Web 2.0 tools make it easier to display information in different ways; they allow groups of people to work on a document or spreadsheet simultaneously while in the background a program keeps track of who made what changes where and when. In a Web 2.0 world, for example, instead of merely reading a newsletter, students might begin to publish one of their own.

In general, the key characteristics of Web 2.0 are the following:

- Web-based applications can be accessed from anywhere.
- Simple applications solve specific problems.
- Value lies in content, not the technology used to display it.
- Data can be readily shared.
- Distribution is bottom-up, not top-down.
- Students and educators can access and use tools on their own.
- Social tools encourage people to create, collaborate, edit, categorize, exchange, and promote information.
- Networking is encouraged; the more people who contribute, the better the content gets.

PART 2: GETTING STARTED—TEACHING STRATEGIES AND WEB 2.0 TOOLS

"Today's graduates need to be critical thinkers, problem solvers and effective communicators who are proficient in both core subjects and new, 21st century content and skills," according to *Results That Matter: 21st Century Skills and High School Reform*, a report issued by the Partnership for 21st Century Skills (2006: 21). These new skills include learning and thinking skills, information- and communications-technology literacy skills, and life skills. Students of today enter an increasingly global world in which technology plays a vital role. They must be good communicators, as well as great collaborators. The new work environment requires responsibility and self-management, as well as interpersonal and project-management skills that demand teamwork and leadership.

Web 2.0 Tools

Tim O'Reilly (2005), who helped coin the term "Web 2.0," offers this definition: "Web 1.0 was about connecting computers and making technology more efficient for computers. Web 2.0 is about connecting people and making technology more efficient for people." Web 2.0 continues to create new ways for large groups of people to collaborate and exchange information while reducing the importance of the computer itself as an information-delivery platform. As long as the applications and the data reside online, a variety of devices can function as information terminals whether they are smartphones, music players, or computers. Web 2.0 not only makes all this possible, it also makes it inexpensive and easy to deploy.

Philosophically, Web 2.0 is all about simplicity. It does not matter which device you use or where it is. Web 2.0 tools encourage free exchange of information and ideas between different tools and groups of users. Finally, because it encourages large-scale collaboration, Web 2.0 facilitates new forms of problem solving that can provide educators with valuable ideas and insights.

Web 2.0 Tools Covered in This Book

A myriad of Web 2.0 tools are available on the Internet today. It would be impossible to mention them all in this book, let alone cover them in detail. I have chosen representative tools from different categories: tools for collaborating, saving online pages, and networking; map tools; presentation tools; tools to aid learners whether they are auditory or visual learners; and tools for those whose first language is not English. Each chapter focuses on one type of tool; for example, in Chapter 2 you will learn about blogs. You will discover what the technology is and the benefits of using it with students. In order to get you started, several examples illustrate how the tool is being used in the classroom or library. Finally, you will view a sample, detailed unit plan in a specific subject area and grade level to use as a model so you can create your own lessons with your own students using this technology. A number of lesson plans throughout will demonstrate a specific use of Web 2.0, and "lesson clips" illustrate a teaching idea using Web 2.0.

Some of the tools covered in this book are blogs; podcasts; wikis; videos, VoiceThread and Skype for video conferencing; Google tools, including Google Maps, Google Earth, Google Docs, and others; social bookmarking; and social networking. One chapter highlights using Web 2.0 tools in elective courses and another with nonnative English speakers. Each chapter begins with a glossary that defines new vocabulary with which you may not be familiar. You may see some terms as you proceed through the book, and all are also listed in the index at the end of the book. A final chapter focuses on Web 2.0 to help educators collaborate, learn from one another, enhance professional development, and more.

Teaching and Learning Strategies

Although Web 2.0 tools energize and motivate students, teaching and learning strategies are equally or more important. Each of the teaching and learning strategies described next will be incorporated into unit and lesson plans in the following chapters.

Critical Thinking Defined

Critical thinking is a skill that can be taught, practiced, and mastered. It draws on other skills such as communication and information literacy to examine evidence, then analyze, interpret, and evaluate it. Revised in 2010, Bloom's digital taxonomy of the stages of critical thinking is now more relevant for twenty-first century learning in that it focuses on "doing," using verbs instead of nouns, and adds "creating" to higher-level thinking skills. Today's citizens must be active critical thinkers in order to compare evidence, evaluate competing claims, and make sensible decisions (see Figure 1.1).

Collaborative/Cooperative Learning

Research on collaborative learning by Johnson et al. (1984) and Slavin (1995) indicates that lessons structured around cooperative learning result in improvements in students' academic achievement, self-esteem, and positive social skills. These studies have shown that cooperative learning can foster:

- higher intrinsic motivation;
- a more positive attitude toward instruction and instructors;
- the development of leadership abilities;
- a sense of teamwork;
- improved self-esteem;
- greater acceptance of differences; and
- decreased dependence on the teacher.

In a cooperative environment, students must clearly articulate ideas through speaking and writing, work effectively with diverse teams, make necessary compromises to accomplish a common goal, and assume shared responsibility for collaborative work.

These researchers set up a structure with specified components for implementing cooperative learning in classrooms. The components include the following:

Figure 1.1. Bloom's Taxonomy Revised, the Visual Peacock

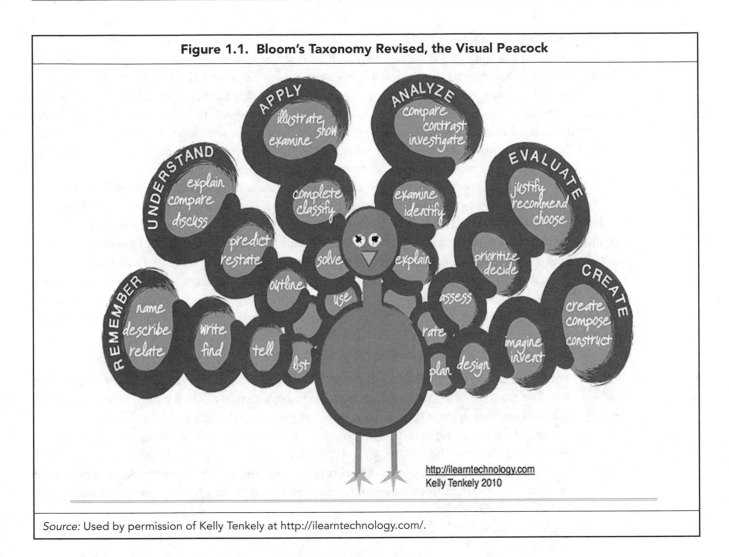

Source: Used by permission of Kelly Tenkely at http://ilearntechnology.com/.

- *Group heterogeneity* results in more critical thinking and greater perspectives when discussing material. This type of group pulls in varied genders, races, cultural and language differences, problematic behaviors, and past academic achievement.
- *Positive group interdependence* is the feeling among group members that no one is successful unless everyone in the group succeeds, for example, task interdependence, in which each student's task is necessary to complete the product.
- *Individual accountability* usually ensures that each student contributes to the group. Students must know in advance what they will be responsible for attaining, and teachers must be able to monitor what each student has contributed and the level of mastery of required skills.
- *Group processing* requires that teachers and students discuss and evaluate the functioning of the groups.

Making sure these components are part of each cooperative-learning activity helps ensure the success of the activity. Through collaboration, children acquire social skills, experience different viewpoints, and learn how to work together with people who are the same and with those who are different from themselves. For example, working with students from another country can instill in students a real excitement for school, thus motivating them to work on their activities. These principles contribute to social networking today and are vital to incorporating Web 2.0 tools into instruction.

Project-Based Learning

Project-based learning is a dynamic approach to teaching in which students explore real-world problems and challenges, simultaneously developing cross-curricular skills while working in small collaborative groups. Because project learning is filled with active and engaged learning, it inspires students to obtain a deeper knowledge of the subjects they are studying. Research (Thomas, 2000) also indicates that students are more likely to retain the knowledge gained through this approach than through traditional textbook-centered learning. In addition, students develop confidence and self-direction as they move through both team-based and independent work.

Projects are an important part of the elementary curriculum because they allow children the chance to ask questions that guide an investigation and make decisions about the activities they plan to undertake. Activities may include drawing, writing, reading, recording observations, and interviewing others. Dramatic activities can help children express new understanding and new vocabulary. Project work provides a context for applying skills the students have learned in the more formal parts of the curriculum and lends itself to group cooperation. It also supports children's natural impulses to investigate things around them. Even at the secondary level, project work can be a conduit for students to explore topics, resolve conflicts, share responsibility for carrying out tasks, and make suggestions—all skills necessary for living and working in today's society.

Project-based instruction can be divided into three phases:

1. Phase 1 is devoted to selecting and refining the topic to be investigated. At least some of the students should have knowledge of the topic, which should allow for integrating a range of subjects, such as science, English/language arts, and social studies.
2. Phase 2 focuses on fieldwork, which is the direct investigation of objects, sites, or events. Sources of information can be primary, such as live or virtual field trips and interviews with experts, or secondary, such as information acquired from research. As a result of the information obtained from these sources, students can make observations from which they can draw conclusions.
3. Phase 3 contains culminating and debriefing events that include preparing and presenting results.

Inquiry-Based Learning with Essential Questions

As all educators know, an effective questioning strategy by teachers is required to promote thinking by students to increase their understanding of a problem, topic, or issue. Essentially, these questions should: (1) direct the course of student research and require that students spend time pondering the meaning and importance of information they acquire; (2) engage students in real-life applied problem solving; and (3) usually lend themselves well to multidisciplinary investigations. These "essential questions" promote investigation, exploration, quest, research, pursuit, and study. As such, essential questions are powerful, directive, and commit students to the process of critical thinking through inquiry. Ultimately, the answer to an essential question will require students to craft a response that involves knowledge construction. This new knowledge-building occurs through the integration of discrete pieces of information obtained during the research process. Answers to essential questions are a direct measure of student understanding.

There is no "right" or "wrong" answer to an essential question as long as the answer is based on the data gathered and can be reasonably justified. Before students proceed very far, they list suppositions, pose hypotheses, and make predictions—many of which will be revised as they gather information. This thought process helps to provide a basis for constructing meaning. In order to solve the problem or propose an answer to an essential question, students need to ask themselves, "What do I need to know about that topic to solve this problem?" The questions they come up with must be answered before they can solve the problem. Subsidiary questions give students a direction and the data they will need to find an answer to the essential question.

Teaching approaches that are inquiry-based, constructivist, project-based, or student-centered foster essential questioning. While varying in specifics, these approaches all emphasize the importance of students exploring ideas, conducting hands-on investigations, engaging in projects on topics they choose, working collaboratively, discussing their ideas, gaining conceptual understanding, and evaluating their results. In general, these approaches view knowledge as something individuals construct for themselves through action, reflection, and discussion, not as something that is simply transmitted from teachers or books to students. Thus, educators need to organize courses not around answers but around questions and problems to which "content" represents answers.

The teaching and learning strategies discussed and Web 2.0 tools go hand-in-hand to focus on twenty-first-century skills identified earlier in this chapter.

Other Issues

Other issues besides content bear investigation when Web 2.0 tools are included in the curriculum. Two of the main issues are copyright and safety.

Copyright: Creative Commons

A new way of looking at copyright has unfolded with the advent of Web 2.0. *Wikipedia*, a user-produced encyclopedia, describes Creative Commons as a nonprofit organization devoted to expanding the range of creative works available for others to legally build upon and share (*Wikipedia*, 2011). The project, founded by Lawrence Lessig, provides several free licenses known as Creative Commons' licenses that copyright owners can use when releasing their works on the web. Owners keep their copyright but allow others to copy and distribute their work provided they give credit, with conditions specified by the owner that restrict only certain rights (or none) of the work and are less restrictive than traditional copyright. Some types of works protected by copyright law are books, websites, blogs, photographs, films, videos, songs, and other audio and visual recordings. Creative Commons' licenses are irrevocable. Although owners can stop offering their work under a Creative Commons license at any time, the rights associated with copies of their work already in circulation under a Creative Commons license will not be affected.

In 2009, there were an estimated 350 million works licensed under Creative Commons. You can search for material or sites licensed under Creative Commons at their website (http://wiki.creative commons.org/CcSearch). Google and Yahoo! also enable searching for Creative Commons' content, for example, pictures at Flickr (http://www.flickr.com/creativecommons/). Much more information about Creative Commons is available on their website (http://creativecommons.org/).

Fair Use

Fair use, a doctrine in United States copyright law, allows limited use of copyrighted material without requiring permission from the person who holds the rights. Examples of fair use include commentary, criticism, news reporting, research, teaching, library archiving, and scholarship. Fair use provides for the legal, nonlicensed citation or incorporation of copyrighted material in another author's work under a four-factor test.

1. *Character of the use*—Uses such as nonprofit, educational, and personal are more available for fair use than a commercial use.
2. *Nature of the work*—Published facts lean more toward fair use and usually do not need permission.

3. *Amount of the work used*—Lengthy quotes from a work that is deemed "educational" or a teacher copying an article for students in a class would be more likely allowed without permission. However, making multiple photocopies of whole articles, for instance, can violate fair use.

4. *Widespread use*—If a piece competes with the original by taking away sales, it can violate fair use restrictions. For example, if the use is widespread, it might have an effect on the market for the original.

Acceptable Use Policies

Educators who use the web for research and now for communication and collaboration must be cognizant of student safety and appropriate use on the Internet. Many school districts employ "acceptable use policies" (AUPs), a document that outlines schools' intended uses of the Internet and establishes dos and don'ts for online student behavior. Areas to address are cyber ethics, cyber safety, and cyber security. An AUP or some safety awareness program should be in place prior to using the Internet for classroom lessons. Many districts, educators, and school committees have created acceptable use policies that can serve as samples for new educators who incorporate Web 2.0 tools into their curriculum.

Educators and administrators are aware of the great potential for online communication and collaboration that social networking tools such as blogs, podcasts, or wikis may provide as part of learning activities; however, they also recognize the potential dangers of such tools. Educators are also creating separate AUPs that protect the rights and privacy of students and educators when using social networking.

The following webpages contain AUPs useful as models:

1. http://docs.google.com/View?docid=dfqjmd6d_24dfbht8d4. This AUP begins with personal responsibility when using Web 2.0 tools and provides AUP components and sample forms.

2. http://projectinterconnect.org/filters/aupintro.htm. The Project Interconnect site suggests components to AUPs and shows samples from a number of schools.

3. http://www.mcvsd.org/aup/MCVSD_AUP.PDF. Monmouth County Vocational School District provides a sample AUP.

4. http://www.doe.in.gov/olt/aup/aupmod.html. This AUP is a model from the Indiana Department of Education.

5. http://edubuzz.pbworks.com/w/page/11239900/socialmediapupil. This wiki has self-publishing and social networking guidelines for students.

PART 3: PRACTICAL APPLICATIONS

The term "unit" is one that is often used rather loosely. An instructional unit can comprise anything from a few days of concentrated study to a whole course. Units range from a five-day writing workshop to a year-long study of Mexico. A teacher may have several units going at the same time. For example, a social studies teacher can be exploring a map-study unit while studying Latin America. In one week a language arts class may work on a writing unit on Fridays and a drama unit Monday through Thursday.

The Unit Plan

In this book, model units contain the teacher's preplanning of the unit; the body of the lessons, including how the topic fits into content standards and achieves goals and objectives; a series of activities to meet the objectives before, during, and after the unit; and evaluation of the unit. In addition to the unit plans, you will see examples of lesson plans and lesson clips (short ideas for lessons) throughout this book.

The teaching of any unit depends on the needs, interests, and abilities of the students for whom it has been designed. Building a unit should be based on the teacher's assessment of what a class can and cannot do. Educators will get the most out of the practical models in this book by envisioning their own curriculum and students and how the models in each chapter can be adapted with their own content to fit their particular students. The units contain activities for individualized instruction, as well as small- or whole-group learning. This allows teachers to adapt those plans that fit their own teaching styles or to experiment with another type of unit in their own classrooms.

When creating Internet units incorporating Web 2.0 tools, teachers will follow steps similar to building most instructional units. Each unit is based on content, not on technology. One or more technology tools that are the focus of each unit are included to enhance instruction, whether in social studies, science, language arts, or second-language learning. The following steps serve as a model for the subject-specific units in subsequent chapters.

Step 1: Connect to the Standards—What Should Be Taught?

What areas should plans include in a subject area and at a specific grade level? National standards and state frameworks for teaching established by content-area curriculum development committees provide the road map. Each state has its own guidelines and has outlined knowledge and skills for students to achieve at each grade level. The California History/Social Sciences framework, for example, requires that history and social science courses begin in kindergarten and work toward:

> Knowledge and Cultural Understanding, incorporating learnings from history and the other humanities, geography, and the social sciences; Democratic Understanding and Civic Values, incorporating an understanding of our national identity, constitutional heritage, civic values, and rights and responsibilities; and Skills Attainment and Social Participation, including basic study skills, critical thinking skills, and participation skills that are essential for effective citizenship. (California State Department of Education, 2005: 10)

The framework also stresses specific themes and attributes such as communication, reasoning, personal development, and civic responsibility. This material helps schools focus on broad goals as they create their own programs of study, and it provides clear goals for student learning that form the basis of teachers' units and lesson plans.

Some concepts and skills cross all subject areas. In fact, currently 41 states have adopted core standards in English language arts and mathematics so that learning goals are common throughout the United States. As an example, in California, standards from language arts, social sciences, and science emphasize achieving the following goals:

- Students will work collaboratively. State standards emphasize the importance of environments that encourage shared learning. Since most businesses today emphasize the team approach to completing projects, working cooperatively is a skill students need to attain before they finish school. Web 2.0 tools present an especially good environment for collaboration, one in which students work together creating presentations, sharing information with other students around the world, and more. These types of projects require learning teamwork and shared responsibility.
- Students will become aware that communication takes many forms. For example, writing is a means of clarifying thinking and is a process that embodies several stages, including prewriting, drafting, receiving responses, revising, editing, and postwriting activities. Using information gathered from a variety of sources—including Internet sites such as blogs and wikis and students worldwide, to name a few—enables students to practice their writing about meaningful, far-reaching topics for an authentic audience. Oral responses to questions, analysis of information, and synthesis of data from various types of sources help students to acquire and

use higher-order thinking skills in all subject areas. Students no longer are bound by the walls of their classrooms.

- Teachers and school librarians will encourage and help students to use all technological resources. Students must see how Web 2.0 tools enhance learning and prepare them for responsibilities in the twenty-first century.

The American Association of School Librarians' updated *Standards for the 21st-Century Learner* (see page 4) and other guidelines, including *Standards for the 21st-Century Learner in Action*, which provides examples showing how to apply the learning standards at different grade levels, and *Empowering Learners: Guidelines for School Library Programs*, which defines future directions of school library programs, offer vision for teaching and learning with technology. Because the Internet provides a rich variety of media through which to learn, teachers can adapt their instruction and accommodate different learning styles by providing stimuli for visual, auditory, and kinesthetic learners. These standards should also be part of unit plans using Web 2.0 tools.

Another set of standards has been created by the International Society for Technology in Education called *National Educational Technology Standards for Students* (ISTE, 2007). These standards incorporate (1) creativity and innovation; (2) collaboration and communication; (3) research and information fluency; (4) critical thinking, problem solving, and decision making; (5) digital citizenship; and (6) technology operations and concepts. These standards should also be integrated into a unit plan using Web 2.0 tools.

Integrating content, technology, and library standards provides the framework for learning, combining subjects such as English, social studies, and science, as well as incorporating technology, the arts, health, and physical education into lessons and unit plans to excite students about learning. The goal is to hit them where they live with technology they use daily and ingrain in them the skills and knowledge they need to achieve in the twenty-first-century workplace.

Step 2: Design Unit Goals and Create Specific Lesson Objectives

Because broad content and skills are often described for teachers by state and national standards and frameworks or by local or school curriculum committees, general goals for instruction can be "givens" or fixed parts of the curriculum. However, teachers can create units that incorporate these mandated goals within their own list of unit goals and objectives.

An objective is a statement of what the learner will have attained once the learning experience has been successfully completed. Objectives define where the teacher is going with instruction, and they communicate these expectations to the students. When writing objectives, select a verb that is active and meaningful, such as calculate, analyze, or create. These verbs generate measurable demonstrations of the learning. Prepare sample outcomes to show students models.

Objectives can be stated in a number of ways:

- As a list of skills or processes the student will master
- As a list of course activities that the student will read, talk about, or write about
- As a description of products—for example, creating a podcast
- As a list of activities the student will be able to perform at the end of the unit

Step 3: Decide on Materials and Resources

Good materials enhance and reinforce good instruction. They can help a lesson have a stronger impact and improve learner motivation. Thus, teachers need to select the media—whether it is a blog, wiki, podcast, Google maps, or other resources—so the tools reinforce the lessons they plan to teach. Keep a separate notebook page for different subjects and types of tools. For each subject enter the topic you plan to teach, annotated URLs that fit the topic, learning strategies you will use, and tools that will reinforce the learning.

Step 4: Plan the Instruction

After creating the goals and objectives and gathering the materials, educators must plan the instruction, as well as determine Web 2.0 tools they plan to use. They must choose a sequence of materials and activities that meet the unit objectives and provide an interesting mix of tasks to accommodate small group instruction, peer learning, different learning styles, individual work, projects, and a variety of technological tools to enhance instruction.

Learning experiences should pose questions to stimulate deep critical thinking with time for students to talk and listen to one another. Every lesson must have a clear purpose that is comprehensible to the students. Making powerful connections to past, present, and future learning as well as to individual students and the community is vital. Connect one lesson to other lessons within the same day to integrate the curriculum and instruction, and examine the topic and issues from multiple perspectives.

Step 5: Prepare for Teacher- and Student-Based Assessment

No matter what is taught, it is important to evaluate how well students are progressing to make sure they are learning what teachers assume they are. Research (Thomas, 2000) could not be clearer that increasing formative assessment is the key to improvement on tests of all kinds, including traditional ones. More "authentic" and comprehensive forms of assessment provide not only significant gains on conventional tests but also more useful feedback because the tasks are more realistic.

What is meant by "authentic assessment"? It is simply performances and product requirements that are faithful to real-world demands, opportunities, and constraints. Students are tested on their ability to "do" the subject in context, to transfer their learning effectively. Students improve and are engaged when they receive feedback and opportunities to work on realistic tasks requiring transfer at the heart of learning goals and real-world demands.

Assessment can take many forms:

- *Monitoring by observation*. Process and lab skills or small-group projects can be monitored by observing students while they are engaged in activities.
- *Monitoring by student evaluations*. Students should be given opportunities to review and discuss cooperatively one another's assignments and projects.
- *Monitoring by examination*. A prepared list of questions tests students for understanding and application of the main ideas in the unit.
- *Monitoring by problem solving*. Exercises to test concepts taught in the unit require students to apply concepts they have learned.

Some specific assessment strategies to consider are:

- *Interviews*. Student/teacher dialogues in person or using Web 2.0 tools such as blogs or wikis can determine the approaches used in problem solving and students' views of what was learned.
- *Anecdotal records*. Teachers keep anecdotal records of the class and record student questions and behaviors. Blogs and wikis automatically keep track of students' work. Often the fact that all work is on one website makes evaluating less cumbersome.
- *Learning logs*. Students' comments using Web 2.0 tools reflect their thoughts and ideas about their learning.
- *Pictures/illustrations*. Students draw pictures, for example, using VoiceThreads or Storybird, illustrating their thoughts regarding a particular concept.

- *Active participation.* Teachers rate student involvement in active participation tasks and cooperative exercises. Rubrics make a good tool for this type of evaluation.
- *Role-play.* Students are asked to role-play parts of a process, for example, creating a podcast about concepts they have learned and sharing those concepts with other classes.
- *Student-taught lessons.* Students plan, research, and create a product they share with another class. They might use a podcast, Glogster, a digital story video, or other Web 2.0 tool to create the product.
- *Self-assessment.* Students rate their own progress and support their feelings.
- *Product.* Students are asked to create a product that demonstrates their knowledge of a content area. Many of the Web 2.0 tools covered in this book are useful to assess content-area knowledge.
- *Peer assessment.* Other students in a cooperative group rate the performance of the group's members.
- *E-portfolio.* Compilation of student work done during a specific year or on a particular project illustrates progress and competence.

These assessment techniques provide unique ways of evaluating student progress and assessing lessons teachers create at the same time. Many of the strategies will be used as assessment in the units in subsequent chapters.

Summary

Effective schools' literature shows that when teachers work together to build a coherent learning experience for students in all grades and within and across subject areas—one that is guided by common curriculum goals and expectations—they are able to improve student achievement (Lee, Bryk, and Smith, 1993). Effective instruction includes curricular goals and coherent learning experiences. The five steps just discussed form the basis for any good unit plan in any subject area. While teachers may emphasize one section more than another in their planning, each area is important to the learning process. Table 1.1 lists useful websites for this chapter.

CONCLUSION

This book is mostly about Web 2.0 and social networking and the student. *Using Web 2.0 Tools and Social Networking in the K–12 Classroom* focuses primarily on ways Web 2.0 tools can enhance the curriculum and improve student learning. There is a whole other aspect to Web 2.0, however: how educators can use these tools to further their own development, communicate with other teachers and school librarians, and have others listen to their personal voices. Chapter 11 provides a brief overview of tools educators can use that will allow them to get involved and create connections and conversations with other educators. Actively participating should make them more confident in using these new tools, thus enhancing their connections with their students.

> ➣ Use the accompanying website (http://www.neal-schuman.com/webclassroom) to expand your knowledge of Web 2.0 tools as you read about them in the chapters that follow.

With increasing numbers of free tools designed to meet educational goals and make students enthusiastic about learning, this is an exciting time to be an educator. Explore these new tools and include them in your toolbox of teaching strategies. According to educator and futurist Ian Jukes (2008), "We need to prepare students for THEIR future not OUR past." We need to replicate in the classroom the world in which students are living. If we teach today the way we were taught yesterday, we aren't preparing students for today or tomorrow. After all, when Rip Van

Table 1.1. General URLs	
URL	**Description**
http://www.youtube.com/	A video-sharing website where users can upload, view, and share video clips
http://www.technorati.com/	An Internet search engine for searching blogs
http://www.p21.org/index.php?option=com_content&task=view&id=254&Itemid=120	Partnership for 21st Century Skills
http://images.google.com/	Google Image Search
http://blogsearch.google.com/	Google Blog Search
http://www.graphic.org/	Graphic organizer
http://www.slideshare.net/NancyW1354/assessing-21st-century-skills?src=related_normal&rel=1625076	Formative assessment for twenty-first-century skills
http://www.iste.org/standards.aspx	ISTE *NETS Standards*
http://www.ala.org/ala/mgrps/divs/aasl/guidelines andstandards/learningstandards/tandards.cfm	American Association of School Librarians' *Standards for the 21st-Century Learner*

Winkle awakens, we want him to march into our schools and see that he is, indeed, in a new and different educational environment.

REFERENCES AND FURTHER READING

AASL (American Association of School Librarians). 2007. *Standards for the 21st-Century Learner*. Chicago: American Association of School Librarians. http://www.ala.org/aasl/sites/ala.org.aasl/files/content/guidelines andstandards/learningstandards/AASL_LearningStandards.pdf.

AASL and AECT (American Association of School Librarians and Association for Educational Communications and Technology). 1988. *Information Power: Guidelines for School Library Media Programs*. Chicago: American Association of School Librarians, and Washington, DC: Association for Educational Communications and Technology.

Anderson, L. W., and D. R. Krathwohl, eds. 2001. *A Taxonomy for Learning, Teaching and Assessing: A Revision of Bloom's Taxonomy of Educational Objectives: Complete Edition*. New York: Longman.

Bloom, Benjamin S., ed. 1956. *Taxonomy of Educational Objectives Handbook 1: Cognitive Domains*. New York: David McKay.

California State Department of Education. 2005. *History-Social Science Framework for California Public Schools, Kindergarten Through Grade Twelve*. Sacramento: California State Department of Education. http://www.cde.ca.gov/ci/cr/cf/documents/histsocsciframe.pdf.

Common Core State Standards Initiative. 2010. *Common Core State Standards for English Language Arts and Literacy in History/Social Studies, Science, and Technical Subjects*. Common Core State Standards Initiative. http://www.corestandards.org/assets/CCSSI_ELA%20Standards.pdf.

FNO.org, 1996. "II. Framing Essential Questions." *From Now On: The Educational Technology Journal* 6, no. 1 (September 1996). http://www.fno.org/sept96/questions.html.

Gibson, Rowan, ed., with a foreword by Alvin Toffler and Heidi Toffler. 1999. *Rethinking the Future*. London: Nicholas Brealey.

Hargadon, Steve. 2008. "Web 2.0 Is the Future of Education." *Steve Hargadon's Blog*, Classroom 2.0, March 5. http://www.classroom20.com/profiles/blogs/649749:BlogPost:115854.

ISTE (International Society for Technology in Education). 2007. *National Educational Technology Standards for Students*. International Society for Technology in Education. http://www.iste.org/standards/nets-for-students/nets-student-standards-2007.aspx.

Johnson, David W., Roger T. Johnson, Edythe J. Holubec, and Patricia A. Roy. 1984. *Circles of Learning: Cooperation in the Classroom*. Alexandria, VA: Association for Supervision and Curriculum Development.

Johnson, L., R. Smith, A. Levine, and K. Haywood. 2010. *The 2010 Horizon Report: K–12 Edition*. Austin, Texas: The New Media Consortium. http://wp.nmc.org/horizon-k12-2010/.

Jukes, Ian. 2008. "Ten 21st Century Education Quotes I Carry With Me." *The Innovative Educator* (blog), April 15. http://theinnovativeeducator.blogspot.com/2008/04/ten-21st-century-education-quotes-i.html.

Krathwohl, David R. "A Revision of Bloom's Taxonomy: An Overview." *Theory into Practice* 41, no. 4 (Autumn 2002). http://www.iowaascd.org/downloads/BloomRevised.pdf.

Lee, Valerie E., Anthony S. Bryk, and Julia B. Smith. 1993. "The Organization of Effective Secondary Schools." In *Review of Research in Education*, vol. 19, edited by Linda Darling-Hammond, 171–267. Washington, DC: American Educational Research Association.

McKenzie, Jamie. 2001. "From Trivial Pursuit to Essential Questions and Standards-Based Learning." *From Now On: The Educational Technology Journal* 10, no. 5 (February). http://www.fno.org/feb01/pl.html.

Newmann, Fred M., Anthony S. Bryk, and Jenny K. Nagaoka. 2001. *Authentic Intellectual Work and Standardized Tests: Conflict or Coexistence?* Consortium on Chicago School Research, University of Chicago. http://ccsr.uchicago.edu/publications/p0a02.pdf.

O'Reilly, Tim. 2005. "What Is Web 2.0? Design Patterns and Business Models for the Next Generation of Software." O'Reilly.com. http://www.oreillynet.com/pub/a/oreilly/tim/news/2005/09/30/what-is-web-20.html.

Partnership for 21st Century Skills. 2006. *Results That Matter: 21st Century Skills and High School Reform*. Partnership for 21st Century Skills. http://www.p21.org/documents/RTM2006.pdf.

Slavin, Robert. 1995. *Cooperative Learning: Theory, Research, and Practice*. Needham Heights, MA: Allyn and Bacon.

Thomas, John W. 2000. "A Review of Research on Project-Based Learning." Bob Pearlman/The Autodesk Foundation. http://www.bobpearlman.org/BestPractices/PBL_Research.pdf.

Wikipedia. 2011. "Creative Commons." Wikimedia Foundation. Last modified October 28. http://en.wikipedia.org/wiki/Creative_Commons.

CHAPTER 2

Enhancing Collaboration and Communication with Blogs

It Simply Isn't the 20th Century Any More Is It? So Why Would We Teach as Though It Was?

—Professor Stephen Heppel

PART 1: IDEAS AND INSIGHTS

As the Internet has evolved, Web 2.0 has become more about community. The web surfer negotiates the connections within a social or idea network, exchanges bits of content, creates something new, and then begins the cycle again. Because blogs are easy to create, classroom teachers are setting up their own blogs for different subjects from English to art. Educator groups are also creating blogs as a means to communicate among one another. No longer is the classroom teacher isolated behind his or her classroom door. Web 2.0 tools such as blogs and RSS feeds work together as part of this web phenomenon. Blogs or weblogs provide a communication space that teachers can utilize with students whenever there is a curriculum need, whether it is to develop writing, share ideas, or reflect on work undertaken in the classroom.

On blogs students own their learning, reflect and make connections about the knowledge they learn, and are motivated by their worldwide audience. What do students and teachers say about blogging? Some comments from teachers and students currently working with this technology in their classrooms illustrate why it is an important motivational tool for English/language arts.

"The shyest kid has become the most active blogger." (Greta Sandler, fifth-grade teacher in Argentina)

"I want to tell you the story about our blog. Now we have more than 120 posts and 1,500 comments. For me a blog is amazing." (Chino, student from Argentina)

"I love getting comments and I've met lots of different people from around the world, not just in Australia, and I've visited their blogs, too." (Emily, student from Australia)

"One thing we absolutely love is blogging!" (Third-graders in Los Angeles, CA)

"I feel important to my blog because I wrote things that I wanted to share with EVRY-BODY." (Dylan, a third-grader)

"Why would my students want to write on paper for their teacher to see, when they could write on their blog for the whole world to see?" (Kathy Cassidy, teacher)

These comments from educators and students give us a peek into the power of blogging illustrated in this chapter.

Objectives of This Chapter

This chapter is designed to be used by English/language arts educators and school librarians at both the elementary and secondary levels. By the end of the chapter, educators will be able to:

- state advantages of using blogs in the language arts classroom;
- describe a blog and identify characteristics and expanded uses of educational and English/language arts blogs in curricula and for educators;
- set up a blog and RSS feeds, as well as understand the necessary dos and don'ts of blogging;
- create a lesson plan incorporating a blog; and
- build an English/language arts writing unit that includes blogging.

An English/language arts curriculum has the responsibility to teach students to listen well, speak effectively, read and think critically, and write clearly and with purpose for a specific audience. To accomplish these tasks, English/language arts educators expose students to literature and require them to discuss and create meaning from texts they read. They also provide opportunities for students to speak in small groups and to the whole class. They create assignments that require students to write about their thoughts and experiences, and they ask them to work together and share ideas. Some of the new Web 2.0 tools lend themselves to use in English/language arts. One is blogging, the focus of this chapter.

Glossary

Review these new words in order to understand better the concepts that appear in this chapter.

aggregator: *see* RSS Reader.

Atom: A format similar to RSS; like RSS, the files may also be called feeds or channels.

blog or weblog (web + log): A website powered by software that simplifies publishing, organizing, and syndicating web content, usually maintained by individuals, groups of individuals, or institutions, containing regular entries of commentary, descriptions of events, or other material such as graphics or video. Entries are commonly displayed in reverse chronological order. Many blogs have RSS feeds.

Blogger: A Google blog-publishing service that allows private or multiuser blogs with time-stamped entries. Also may refer to a person who contributes to a blog by writing blog posts or comments.

blogging: Creating, maintaining, posting, and commenting on a blog.

blogosphere: The collective term encompassing all weblogs or blogs as a community or social network.

edublog: A blog written by someone with an interest in education on educational topics with educators as a primary audience.

folksonomy: The collaborative but unsophisticated way in which information is being categorized on the web or socially constructed taxonomies within Internet communities.

post: A message placed on the blog that may include text, images, video, and audio.

RSS: A family of web feed formats used to publish frequently updated content such as blogs, news headlines, and podcasts in a standardized format (RSS = Really Simple Syndication = Rich or RDF Site Summary).

RSS buttons (XML, RSS): A subscribe button to an RSS feed on a website.

RSS file or RSS feed or RSS channel: A list of items or entries, each of which is identified by a link. Each item can have any amount of other data associated with it as well.

RSS reader or news reader or RSS aggregator: A program that keeps a list of chosen feeds, checks those feeds regularly, and displays their contents in a readable format.

tag: A term associated with or assigned to a piece of information (e.g., a picture, article, or video clip), thus describing the item and enabling keyword-based classification of information and ability to find that information quickly.

tagging: The process of assigning meaning to a piece of information via keywords called tags.

Technorati: A blog search site that allows a user to find new blogs, and thus new feeds to subscribe to.

Introduction

More language arts educators are now using blogs in their classroom assignments for such tasks as creating literature circles to discuss books they are reading, writing for authentic audiences, and communicating with classmates and other school children around the world. As educators, it is also our goal to provide opportunities for students to speak in small groups and to the whole class about their experiences in literature and about the research they have conducted. Library media and computer specialists often provide advice and support to classroom teachers.

This chapter explores ways to integrate weblogs or blogs (a shortened form of weblogs) and RSS feeds into English and language arts content instruction. Blogs were one of the first Web 2.0 tools to command a strong presence for Internet users. In February 2007, statistics compiled by the Pew Internet and American Life Project showed that approximately 31 million Internet users, or 23 percent, had read someone else's blog; and about 12.2 million, or 9 percent, had created one (Lenhart and Fox, 2006). That's a lot of bloggers, and their numbers have continued to grow over the past few years.

Part 1 provides an introduction to blogging and examples of how teachers are using blogs in English/language arts. Part 2 suggests how to get started, including the technology and rules for using blogs and RSS feeds. In Part 3, a sample lesson plan illustrates an offline blog project in preparation for using blogs as part of a unit for a writing project at the secondary level.

What Are Blogs?

Weblogging, a term coined in 1997 by Jorn Barger, has been a popular and fast growing application (*Wikipedia*, 2011a). A blog is someone's personal dated "log" frequently updated with new information about a particular subject or range of subjects. Creating and maintaining a blog is called "blogging." If you have a blog, or contribute to one, you are a "blogger." Bloggers may form "online communities."

Not surprisingly, people have slightly different opinions about what exactly constitutes a blog, but there is a general acceptance that the format in which content is published matters, as well as the style in which the content is created. Additionally, blogs are usually defined by what they generally are, rather than trying to provide a specific definition.

According to a blog post titled "Blogging to Teach Reading," blogging is about reading first, especially about reading what is of interest to you, your culture, or your community (Richardson, 2007). It is also about your ideas. It is about engaging with the content and with the authors of what you have read—reflecting, criticizing, questioning, and reacting. If a student has nothing to blog about, it is not because he or she has nothing to write about or has a boring life. It is because the student has not yet stretched out to the larger world, has not yet learned to engage meaningfully in a community. For blogging in education to be a success, this first must be embraced and encouraged.

Weblogs could also be described as websites that are easily created and updated by those with even a minimum of technology knowledge. You don't have to know complicated codes because blog publishing is now almost as easy as sending e-mail. You just log in to your blog site from any Internet connection, enter the content in a typical Internet form, press a button, and your weblog is updated. Blogs can display not only text, but pictures, video, and audio, and can even store other files to link to such as Microsoft PowerPoint presentations or Microsoft Excel spreadsheets. To sum up, a weblog is a dynamic, flexible tool that is easy to use whether you're creating with it or simply viewing the results.

Characteristics of Blogs

A list of common characteristics of blogs may help you better understand the concept. Blogs:

- present content (called posts) generally in reverse chronological order with the most recent entry listed first;
- are usually informal and can be personal;
- are updated regularly; and
- don't usually involve professional editors in the process (that is, someone who is getting paid explicitly to review the content).

Beyond that, format, style, and content vary greatly. Some people post long essays, some just write short posts. Some talk about their work, others about their personal lives, and others only about politics or sports. There are numerous blogs that provide ways for small groups to share information efficiently within their schools' networks or to create a place to store projects. Some people post links they find interesting or humorous. Some add commentary to a post. Others only comment on blog entries written by others. Many blogs talk about technology. Some have a huge number of readers, others only a few dozen. Some are so personal they are read only by the person who writes them. A few public blogs are anonymous; however, most identify the author of the blog. Some are updated many times a day, others once a day, others a few times a week or less.

Blogs allow people to "share" in unique ways. Instead of simply using the Internet for reading information or to look something up on the web, blogs let people write, react, and share on the Internet. Bloggers, like any writers, need to know their audience. Successful bloggers aim their writing at that target audience.

Blog Components

Blog content ranges from text posts and comments—usually with links to websites, other blogs, or news articles—to blogs that are multiple pages with columns, videos, and pictures. In fact, many blogs now look like sophisticated websites, having the capability of showing images and videos as part of the blog itself. Review Figure 2.1 for the components of a blog listed here:

1. *Post Date*—date and time the post was published
2. *Title*—main title of the post
3. *Body*—main content of the post
4. *Link*—the URL of a complete, individual article referenced on a blog
5. *Comments*—reader comments in response to posts
6. *Tags or Labels*—categories or keywords the post is labeled with (can be one or more)
7. *Footer*—usually at the bottom of the post and often shows post date and time, author, tags, and statistics such as number of comments

8. *Posted by*—the person who created the post
9. *Icons*—symbols at the bottom of the post indicating the blogger can share the post to Twitter, Facebook, Google Buzz, or another blog, or can e-mail it to another person
10. *Blog archive*—previous posts listed in reverse chronological order in the sidebar.

Blog writers often "tag" or label their entries with keywords. According to *Wikipedia* (2011b), a "tag" is defined as "a non-hierarchical keyword or term assigned to a piece of information (such as an Internet bookmark, digital image, or computer file). This kind of metadata helps describe an item and allows it to be found again by browsing or searching." Tags have become an important tool for educators to find blog posts, photos, and videos that are related. A tag is like a subject or category. Another word used for tagging is folksonomy—an Internet-based information retrieval methodology consisting of collaboratively generated, open-ended labels that categorize content. The process of tagging is intended to make a body of information increasingly easier to search, discover, and navigate over time. Users who originate the tags and those who are the primary users of them now have a shared vocabulary that makes searching easier. Note the tags or labels in the sample blog entry shown in Figure 2.1.

Figure 2.1. Blog Components

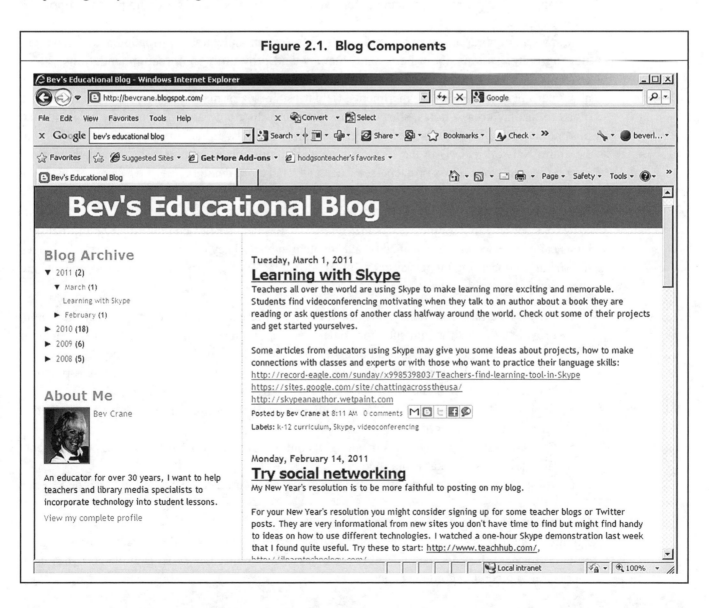

Blog Search Tools

A number of blog search tools—Technorati, Google Blog Search, Internet Public Library Blogs, Bloglines, Globe of Blogs, Blogdigger—enable the blogger to find content in the blogosphere. Other tools such as Google Reader, and Pageflakes exist to find, aggregate, and read blogs.

In summary, blogs offer a blogger the ability to archive content that is posted by date. The commenting feature of blogs allows for immediate feedback by those reading a post. The content posted to a blog can include text, images, files, audio, and video. Publishing posts to an intranet or the Internet can be done quickly and easily. Blogs are so simple to create and edit that they are ideal for the classroom teacher or school librarian.

Implications for Education

Blogs can be used in many aspects of education. For example, clubs and activities, sports teams, and parent groups use weblogs to post scores, meeting minutes, and links to relevant issues and topics. Blogs are also used by teachers to contact parents or for dialogue with other teachers and administrators. Blogs can contain notes to parents about classroom activities, meals, and vacations; a letter from the principal; a newsletter for parents by parents; and photo galleries of school events.

Many school librarians have realized their power in communicating information about resources, starting conversations about books and literacy, and providing book recommendations. Blogs enable teachers to initiate online conversations with their students, prompting thoughtful comments about current events, science experiments, field trips, books, or math problems. Many teachers use blogs to display course notes, showcase student work, distribute assignments, archive handouts, post homework assignments, and answer questions virtually. Educators often create a Personal Learning Network (PLN) in the form of a blog to communicate with and share everything from lesson ideas to global class projects (see Chapter 11 for more details).

Why Use Blogs in the Classroom?

Why consider blogging for the classroom? Here's why. Easy to use, fun, empowering, and inexpensive, blogs can be created and maintained by a technology novice. They offer a wide range of advantages in teaching and learning in the classroom, an important benefit being the ability to create student-safe sites. For example, blogs can:

1. Create a learning community, open 24/7, that is a different place than the traditional classroom.
2. Provide an authentic audience for student writing, including peers, parents, and a potential worldwide audience, while promoting a cross-curricular connection with other subjects.
3. Allow for feedback from the networked students, teachers, and other interested persons, making learning in a class blog setting a social activity.
4. Support differentiation. The blog can give some of the more verbally reserved students a forum for their thoughts.
5. Encourage reading. To make a meaningful comment, or to choose their favorite post, students first need to read what is out there.
6. Teach research skills prompting students to extend their research beyond the assigned work.

Encouraging Blog Comments

An important part of blogging is responding with comments to posts students create. But, how does an educator get others to respond? According to Greta Sandler, whose fifth-grade class has been successful in receiving comments on its class blog:

1. Set up a Personal Learning Network (PLN). The PLN is a support group that supports you, provides comments for your students, and is always there for you.
2. Comments for kids (http://comments4kids.blogspot.com/) is a place to enter your blog URL and receive comments from teachers and classes who sign up because they are willing to leave their comments.
3. Leave comments for others. If you want comments, you must leave them.
4. If your students leave new posts, tweet it and add the hashtag #commentsforkids and you will receive comments immediately.

Blogs are, above all, about expression. Blogs and the web in general allow students to look at many viewpoints easily, cross-reference them, or look for second, third, and fourth opinions. Peter Grunwald, who has studied the ways young people use web tools, says, "Kids are looking for opportunities for self-expression and to find their own identities. More and more students are becoming producers of information rather than passive consumers of it" (Grunwald, 2006). Teachers have been devising ways to treat learners as producers rather than products for a long while. The blog helps attain this goal.

Examples of Blogs in the Library and Classroom

Although surpassed by social networking sites such as Facebook (www.facebook.com) and Twitter (www.twitter.com), blogs still represent a large population of users in K–12 education. Many students are continuing to blog outside of school hours. Educators are becoming more aware of the benefits of blogs and are using them to their advantage in the classroom.

Students, teachers, and school librarians from elementary to high school are all creating educational blogs. One advantage of using blogs is the commenting capabilities blogging sites offer. Blogging also provides an authentic audience for student writing and allows for peer review. Whether learning about chemistry or physics, writing an essay, or reflecting on an article they read, a movie they watched, or an expert they listened to, students can use blogs for a variety of learning experiences.

Librarians and teachers from different subject areas often collaborate to educate students about using blogs in their classrooms. This partnership increases students' and teachers' awareness of the library and its usefulness, as well as helping teachers find examples of ways to incorporate this technology into the classroom. Students can write posts about any theme, topic, or content they are studying no matter what the subject. For example, a class of high school students maintains an Extreme Biology blog (http://missbakersbiologyclass.com/blog/), containing everything biology-related from podcasts on the animal kingdom to a guest scientist discussing his work on fruit flies. At the elementary level, Techie Kids blog (http://edublogs.misd.net/techiekids/) contains book recommendations, making connections through Skype videoconferencing, mammals, and much more. Their blog is full of comments on all of the interesting topics they have studied. Pirates of Room 4 (http://leakeysblog.edublogs.org/) display a math project of 3D shapes, a postcard project, and phonemic awareness. Kids globally in all grade levels and subject areas are learning to use blogs. Check out what one class has to say about its science blog at http://www.youtube.com/watch?v=bmVJRvjTecM&feature=player_embedded.

The following specific examples illustrate the use of blogs in both elementary and secondary classrooms and the library. Some are even award-winners.

Example 1: Blogging in Chemistry

Using Blogger, a tenth-grader in the United States created a blog titled "Chemistry: It's 'Element'ary" at http://www.hcchrisp.blogspot.com/, with content on both chemistry and physics, subjects about which he is passionate. His blog contains text, colorful photos, animated atoms, a video about molecular geometries and how they resemble household items, and more. Chris also incorporates other subjects (see Figure 2.2). For example, he wrote a haiku on why and how atoms form covalent bonds using electrons. There's so much on this blog that you could spend all day on it! Chris won first runner-up in the Edublog international blog contest for 2010. A teacher visiting Chris's blog had this to say: "Wow Chris…awesome video….I am a chem teacher and I plan on sharing this video with my students!" (see Figure 2.3).

Example 2: Mrs. Yollis' Classroom Blog

Mrs. Yollis' Classroom Blog (http://yollisclassblog.blogspot.com/) represents her third-grade class. Posts on the blog include activities with their blogger buddies from three other classrooms worldwide, their polygon project, and a new postcard project to connect with others around the world (see Figure 2.4).

Mrs. Yollis allows students to earn their own blogs if they demonstrate responsible work habits and regularly leave quality comments. Miriam's Magical Moment is an example of one of the students' blogs at http://victoria-miriamsmoments.blogspot.com/ (see Figure 2.5). Parents are the administrators of each of these student blogs. This class blog also won an Edublogs award for 2010, and they just hit the 50,000 visitor mark. What an accomplishment!

Example 3: Castilleja School Library Blog

A 2010 Edublogs library category winner, the library at Castilleja School (http://library.castilleja.org/?q=blog/7), a girls' school in Palo Alto, California, created an award-winning, comprehensive blog highlighting projects from writing articles in French to poetry activities to a peacemaker exhibit, to name just a few. The blog contains new books and student reviews, student-created videos, photos, and articles on food bookmarked on Diigo, a social bookmarking site. Special projects such

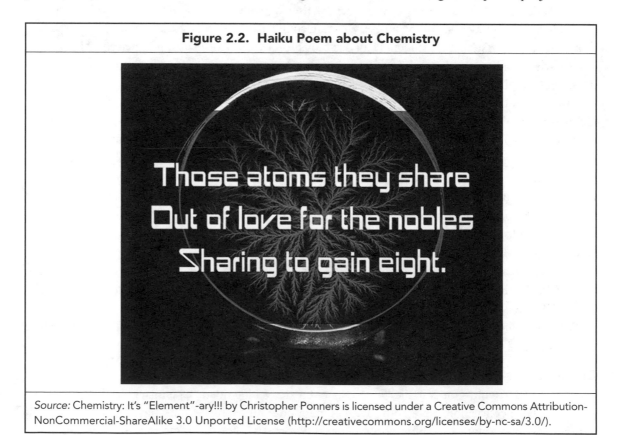

Figure 2.2. Haiku Poem about Chemistry

Those atoms they share
Out of love for the nobles
Sharing to gain eight.

Figure 2.3. Student Chemistry Blog

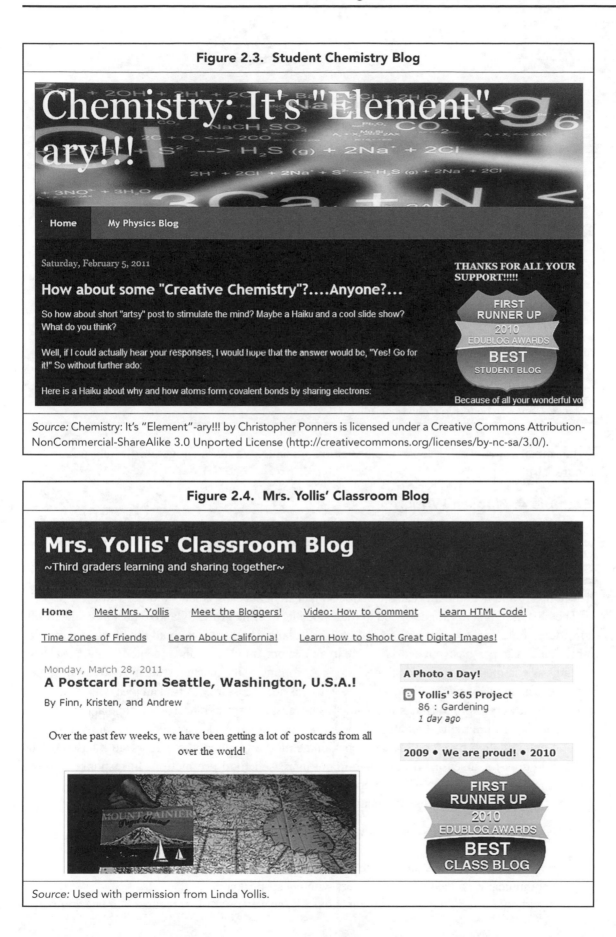

Source: Chemistry: It's "Element"-ary!!! by Christopher Ponners is licensed under a Creative Commons Attribution-NonCommercial-ShareAlike 3.0 Unported License (http://creativecommons.org/licenses/by-nc-sa/3.0/).

Figure 2.4. Mrs. Yollis' Classroom Blog

Source: Used with permission from Linda Yollis.

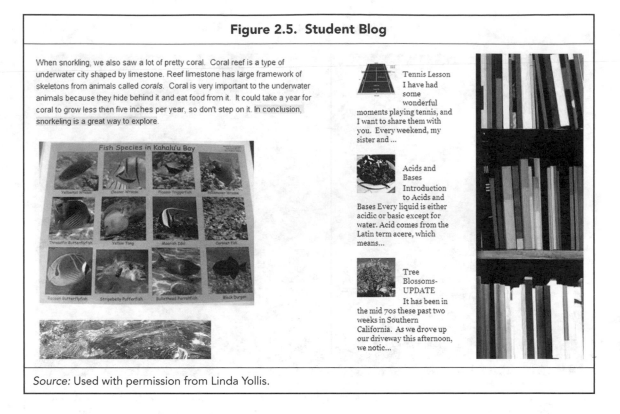

Figure 2.5. Student Blog

Source: Used with permission from Linda Yollis.

as the musical benefit for Japan are driven by students, who work together to help others (see Figure 2.6).

Example 4: Blogs in Writing

Example 4 is one teacher's method for using blogs as part of her students' writing assignments. This teacher requires that all assignments be turned in via blogs. She has found that the conversational nature of blog writing encourages students to think and write in more depth than traditional formal essays or short-answer assignments. Another advantage of receiving assignments in blog format is that both she and her students can subscribe so that students can see one another's work.

The blog assignments are designed to train students to think critically and to post informed, well-considered opinions. One classroom activity, for instance, had students read the blogged entries of others and write persuasive reactions—one in agreement, another in disagreement—and post these writings as comments to their classmates' blogs. According to the teacher, students initially struggled with the task, but they eventually learned the goal was not necessarily to find an idea with which they personally disagreed but to find another side to an idea and write persuasively from that perspective. For a genetics assignment, students assumed a range of positions—some that discouraged work in genetic manipulation based on security, cost, and ethics, and others that supported it based on the potential cures for disease, life extension, and increased food production. In response to these blogged assignments, the teacher also posted assessments in the form of comments.

Ideas specifically for English/language arts classes include:

- using blogs for real-world writing experiences (e.g., stem cell research, violence against animals);
- prolonging discussions outside the classroom;
- communicating questions and answers with guest speakers;
- providing teacher feedback to students quickly, as well as student feedback to one another;

Figure 2.6. Castilleja School Library Blog

Source: Used by permission of Jole Seroff, Director of Library and Academic Technology Services at Castilleja School.

- tracking student writing development;
- using peer networks to develop students' own knowledge; and
- updating new information such as homework and assignments.

Teacher Exercises: Now You Try It . . .
Review the following blogs to see how you might incorporate one of these ideas into your English/language arts class. Choose a blog that coincides with the age level you teach.

- http://theedublogger.com/check-out-these-class-blogs/. Select at least four blogs to review both at your own grade level and others. Make sure you check one at the elementary, middle, and high school levels. Describe which blog(s) were your favorites and why.
- http://kidblog.org/MrsLivnesClass/. Read several of the posts of different students and the comments. How would you rate the posts from 1–5 with 5 being the highest. Identify one or two characteristics of the comments that furthered the conversation. What suggestions would you make if they were your student comments?
- http://onlineroom25.blogspot.com/. View several posts by different students. Notice the technologies used in the posts. Do these visuals add to the posts? Why or why not?

Will Richardson is supervisor of instructional technology at Hunterdon Central Regional High School in Flemington, New Jersey, and known as one of the leading proponents of blogging in education. He writes:

> Blogging as a genre of writing may have great value in terms of developing all sorts of critical thinking skills, writing skills, and information literacy among other things. We teach exposition and research and some other types of analytical writing already, I know. Blogging, however, offers students a chance to a) reflect on what they are writing and thinking as they write and think it, b) carry on writing about a topic over a sustained period of time, maybe a lifetime, and c) engage readers and audience in a sustained conversation that then leads to further writing and thinking. (Richardson, 2004)

Blogging is a part of students' lives. It is now up to school librarians and teachers to make it a part of their education.

PART 2: GETTING STARTED CREATING BLOGS

There are many questions to contemplate as you think about setting up a blog for your classroom or library. One of the first considerations is your audience. Is the blog going to be public so others may view and comment on it? Is it private, just for yourself? Is it only for a specific class, for other teachers, for parents?

Considerations Before Setting Up a Blog

Blogs are easy to set up if you just follow a few simple steps. First, we'll look at some things to consider before setting up a blog.

Step 1: Choose a Service

Decide what blogging service to use for your blogs. There are many blogging hosts available and more being offered daily. Several used by educators are listed here:

- **Kidblog** (http://kidblog.org/), a free site designed for elementary and middle school teachers who want to provide each student with their own unique blog is simple, yet powerful, allowing students to publish posts and participate in discussions within a secure classroom blogging community. Teachers maintain complete control over student blogs (see Figure 2.7).
- **Blogmeister**, created by David Warlick with teachers and students in mind, is a good tool at the elementary level. It is offered free for classrooms, provides total teacher approval, and is usually not blocked by schools. Approximately 3,500 schools are using Blogmeister. The Landmark Project (http://landmark-project.com/) provides this free space for teachers as part of their mission to "redefine literacy for the 21st Century." To set up an account, the first person from your school must obtain a password. You can review how to get your password and sign up for the service at www.classblogmeister.com/. Go to http://legacy.teachersfirst .com/content/blog/tools2.cfm to see a chart of features.
- **Edublogs** (http://edublogs.org/) is another free blog site created by teachers for teachers, hosting more than 741,743 Edublogs. Everything you need to know about starting a blog is accessible at http://theedublogger.com/2010/01/05/week-1-create-a-class-blog/, along with ways to use your blog with students and how to use your blog to communicate with other educators (see Figure 2.8). View a chart of features at http://legacy.teachersfirst.com/content/blog/tools3.cfm.

Check these websites and others to determine which host you want to use for your blog.

Step 2: Select an RSS Reader

There are thousands of educational blogs alone. How does one keep track of all the information you are interested in? A second piece of equipment to help in your blogging is called an "aggregator" or RSS Reader. An aggregator enables you to read RSS content. (More on RSS in a moment.) Readers

Figure 2.7. Kidblog

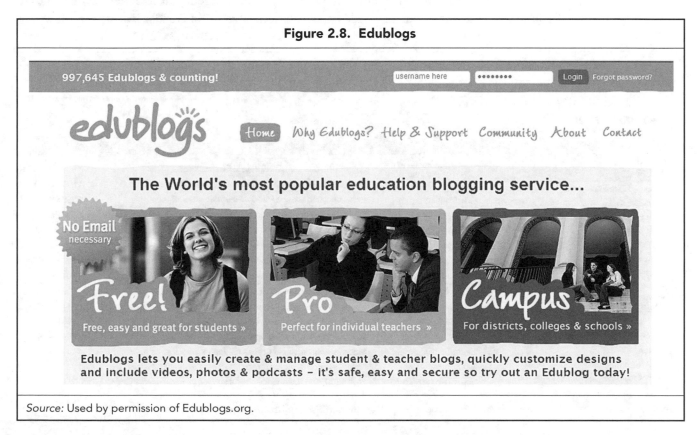

Source: Used by permission of Kidblog.org.

Figure 2.8. Edublogs

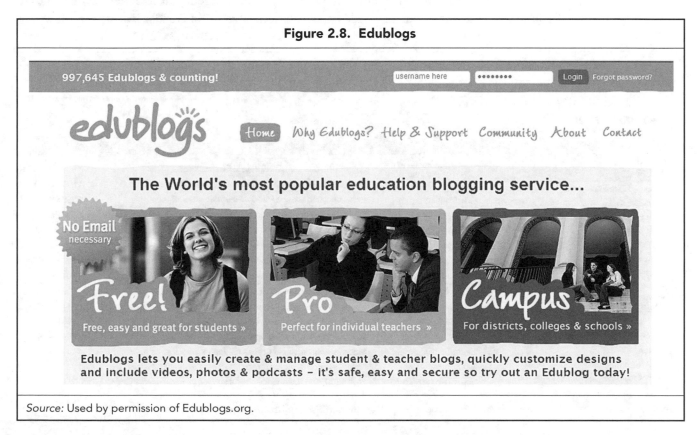

Source: Used by permission of Edublogs.org.

periodically check for new items in the RSS feeds you have selected on a time schedule that you have chosen. So, instead of looking for the news, it comes directly to you, saving you time and effort.

Basically, an aggregator is a piece of software designed to subscribe to sites through syndication and automatically download updates from websites and blogs. If the aggregator is running on your computer or other device, once you have the content you can either read it in offline mode or, if the aggregator is web-based, it will require connectivity to the Internet at all times.

There are two main categories of aggregators: "webpage style" and "e-mail style." Webpage style aggregators present new entries they have received as a webpage, in reverse chronological order so the result looks very much like a weblog put together by the software. E-mail style aggregators generally display new posts as messages, also in reverse chronological order, so you can click and view on a separate area of the screen.

Two other popular aggregators online are Bloglines (http://www.bloglines.com/), an online service for searching, subscribing, creating, and sharing news feeds, blogs, and rich web content and Google Reader (http://www.google.com/reader), free with a gmail (e-mail) account.

RSS Feeds

RSS and Atom feeds are a standard for sharing data between different web applications. RSS is an acronym that stands for Really Simple Syndication (version 2.0). A web feed is a way for websites to continuously "feed" you announcements of their latest content, with links to each new item. To instantly learn what's new on a site, just check its feed. Symbols used to identify that a feed is available on a particular website appear at the top of a page. RSS delivers information through podcasts, blogs, social networks, search agents, and peer-produced content, and the venues are increasing every day (see Figure 2.9).

Which is best for you depends on how you use RSS and how urgent you consider the messages to be. If you're only checking your RSS feeds once a day, then an online reader is just fine. However,

Figure 2.9. RSS via Google Reader

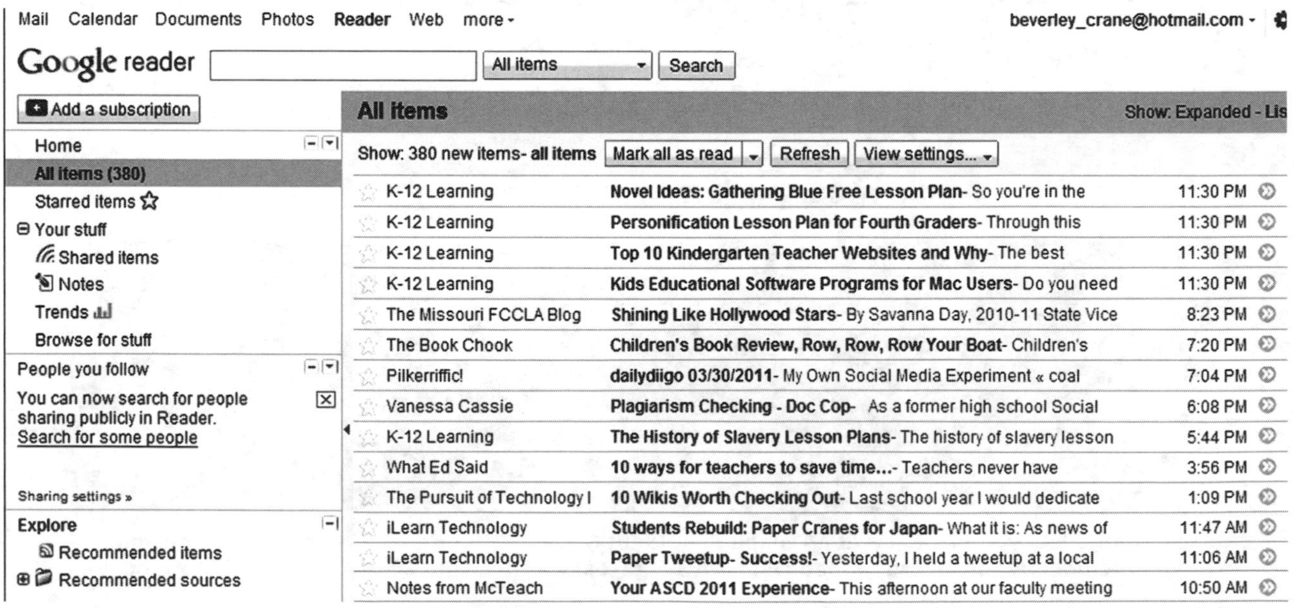

Source: Google Reader™ is a trademark of Google, Inc. Used by permission; http://www.google.com/.

if you check feeds constantly, then it is better to have the RSS software on your desktop. A complete list of feed readers is available from RSS Compendium at http://allrss.com/rssreaders.html.

Step 3: Set Up Your Blog

In many cases, the teacher sets up a blog account and then adds student accounts, which reside under the teacher's account. Teachers can decide whether student blogs will be public or private; they can also review student posts or comments on posts and leave online feedback for students to improve their writing. Thus, students' blog articles are published in a controlled environment hidden from public view.

Setting up a blog is very similar no matter what host you choose. Each host site illustrates how to use a blog, create one, and more (see Figure 2.10). Just follow a few steps:

1. Select "Create an account." Enter your e-mail address and a password.
2. Name your blog (e.g., Bev's Educational Blog) and enter a URL address (e.g., bevcrane .blogspot.com).
3. Choose a template for your blog. There are many on blog sites from which to select.
4. Your blog is created—it's that easy. Now you can begin to post entries to the blog.

Step 4: Blogging Guidelines

Before using a blog at your school, set up some very clear guidelines for your blog and students. Rules should be created, reviewed at the school site, and signed by both students in a blogging project and their parents.

Figure 2.10. Sample Blank Blog Entry Form

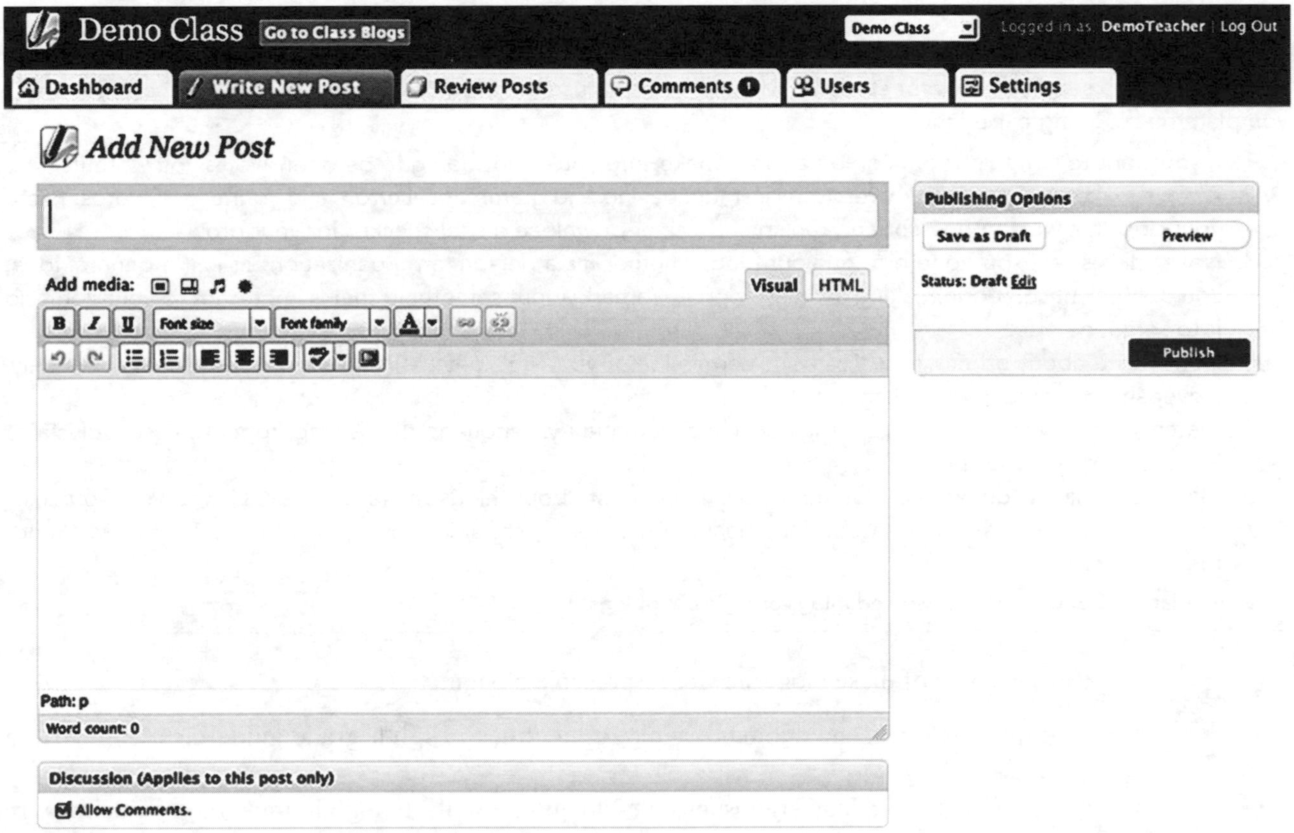

As part of your preparation for blogging, here are some sample guidelines:

- The principal is aware of the blog and has given his or her blessing.
- Parents sign permission forms for students to participate in the blog.
- Access to read posts and comments is by password only (shared with students and parents).
- All posting and commenting is monitored and approved by the teacher.
- Privacy is maintained; for example, no student names (use initials or pseudonyms instead), no student profiles online, no recognizable student images.
- Students must read and sign a blog user agreement.
- Students must sign a district's Acceptable Use Policy (AUP), if available, and recognize it is applicable even when they use the blog from home.
- Consequences for misuse of the blog are spelled out in advance and administered through the school's student disciplinary system.
- The blog is hosted on a reputable, established website.
- The district Internet filtering does not block the chosen blogging tool.

Figure 2.11 illustrates a sample contract you can modify. Other sample blog agreements can be found at:

- http://www.budtheteacher.com/wiki/index.php?title=Blogging_Rules. A blogging guide created by a Colorado teacher for his students.
- http://classblogmeister.com/bloggers_contract.doc. A blogging pledge created by Blogmeister blogging service as a sample.
- http://legacy.teachersfirst.com/content/blog/Sample%20Blogger%20Agreement.doc. A sample blogger agreement you may edit to fit your circumstances.

Rules for Writing Your Blog

It is important to set guidelines for students who are going to use the blog. Here are some rules to consider as you plan the blogging experience.

1. If you want to write your opinion on a topic, make sure you're not going to be offensive as you write it.
2. Always make sure you check over your post for spelling and grammatical errors and your use of words. Paste your post in a word processor and run spell check or download a spellchecker for your browser.
3. Never disrespect someone else on your blog, whether it's a person, an organization, or just a general idea. You don't want someone making an inappropriate remark about something that is important to you; don't do it to someone else.
4. Don't write about other people without permission; if you can't get their permission, use first names only. Never share someone else's last name.
5. Watch your language! This is part of your school community. Language that is inappropriate in school is also inappropriate on your blog.
6. Make sure things you write about are factual. Don't post about things that aren't true. Link to your sources.
7. Keep the blog education-oriented. That means you probably shouldn't discuss your plans for the weekend, the last dance, etc.

(*Source:* Adapted from http://patterson.edublogs.org/all-about-blogs/.)

Review some of these blog rules for responsible blogging:

- http://mrjorgensen.edublogs.org/blog-guidelines/. Eighth-grade guidelines from Brilliant Muskie Blog.
- http://hcato.edublogs.org/responsible-blogging/. Sixth- to eighth-grade blog guidelines from Endless Questions.

Figure 2.11. Blogging Contract

Purpose of the Blog:

_____

_____

_____

Safety:

_____

_____

_____

Terms and Conditions:

_____

_____

_____

Consequences:

_____

_____

_____

Signatures:

I agree to the terms and conditions of the class blog for (name of the class) for the (add dates) school year. I permit my student to participate in the blogging project.

_____   _____
Student Signature   Date

_____   _____
Parent Signature   Date

Parent Membership

I wish to be a registered member of the class blog. Please add me to the list:

_____

- http://legacy.teachersfirst.com/content/blog/rules.cfm. Rules from TeachersFirst for "gated" blogs including purpose, consequences, safety, terms and conditions, and signature page.

Teacher Exercises: Now You Try It...

Learn more about blogs by reading and commenting on several different types of blogs:

1. Read several blog posts in a subject area, topic, or issue of interest to you. Which of the blog posts made you want to comment and what was it about the post that engaged you? Here are some examples to try:

    http://primaryweb2.wikispaces.com/blogs—list of primary blogs

    http://jmsalsich.edublogs.org/—third-grade bloggers

2. Select a post that has inspired you to write your own post. What was it about the post that made you take action?
3. Edublogs, Kidblog, and Blogger host blogs. Compare/contrast their components. Which one would you use and why?
4. Set up your own blog at one of the blog sites listed in Part 2.

Once you have the blog set up, your next and most important consideration is how you will use it in the classroom to enhance student learning. Part 3 provides illustrations to show you how.

PART 3: PRACTICAL APPLICATIONS

Teachers have known for a long time that students develop better communication skills when they are authentically communicating. A number of educators are helping their students develop their writing skills by having thcm publish their work on blogs and then invite comments from other students in the class or students worldwide. Blogging can connect to every subject, and posts can be about any theme, topic, or content studied. Use your blog to connect students to what they have learned in the classroom, at home, or through another media.

Blog Clips

The following ideas from educators for blogging activities may help you get started.

- http://content.photojojo.com/tutorials/project-365-take-a-photo-a-day/. Project 365 blog. Every day of the year select one student to take a photo and reflect on it. Each morning a sign on the door lets the children know who the photographer of the day is. It is the student's responsibility to find something to take a photo of. Next, they write a reflection on why they chose to take that photo. They then have someone on hand to edit their writing and help them upload the photo to the blog and add tags. The students in grades 4–6 have a good understanding of the global audience they are writing for and have enjoyed the chance to reflect. Directions and suggestions on the site provide step-by-step instructions.
- http://studentchallenge.edublogs.org/. Created by Edublogs, the *Student Blogging Challenge* occurs in March and September each year and provides ten weeks of challenge activities designed to improve student commenting and blogging skills, as well as writing for a global audience.

Lesson Plan: Creating a Paper Blog

This lesson can be used as part of a unit to integrate blogging into your classroom. Creating a paper blog explains blogging to students without going online. You can use this lesson as an introduction before students blog online or if blogging is blocked at your school site.

Objectives

This lesson is designed to:

- help students understand the mechanics of blogging, questioning, and commenting on blogs;
- discuss appropriate uses for blogs; and
- practice safe blogging.

See Chapter 5 for a detailed lesson on questioning and commenting.

Materials

Collect the following material as you get started:

- A bulletin board (or if you have an online wiki—see Chapter 3 for more on wikis—you can use it for your posts)
- Magic markers in various colors
- Post-it Notes in different colors
- Stapler, tape, or pushpins for posting

Procedures

These tasks model the process students will go through when they actually blog online (see Figure 2.12):

1. Explain that students will practice writing on a blog before they actually go to an online blog.
2. Ask students to write a post of a paragraph or more on a specific topic and draw a picture to represent the post. A subject they are studying, a book they are reading, or a topic such as a favorite food are prime candidates.
3. At the end of the post, have students assign tags that tell what the post is about (e.g., food, dessert for a favorite food).
4. Show students where to post their blog entries on the bulletin board or wiki.
5. Ask students to select a post and comment on the content by writing their comments on Post-it Notes and sticking them near the original post. Give them some suggestions on commenting:
   a. Do they agree or disagree with the original post? Why or why not?
   b. What do they like about the picture the original writer drew?
6. Have students select two comments, add further comments, and post them with the original comments.

Evaluation

Several activities will determine how well students understand how to create and use blogs:

1. Have students review their own posts and comments on the wall blog. Ask students to assess their original posts and the follow-up comments and identify ones they think are best and the strengths and weaknesses of the posts and comments. Review the sample post in Figure 2.13 and use Figure 2.14 for students' reflections.
2. Ask students to write a final blog post on why they liked or disliked this activity.

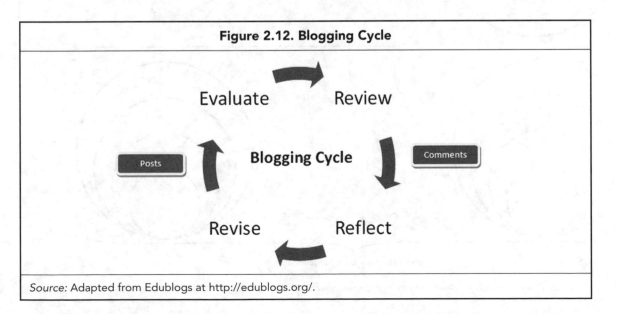

Figure 2.12. Blogging Cycle

Evaluate → Review

Posts

Blogging Cycle

Comments

Revise ← Reflect

Source: Adapted from Edublogs at http://edublogs.org/.

Figure 2.13. Blog Post

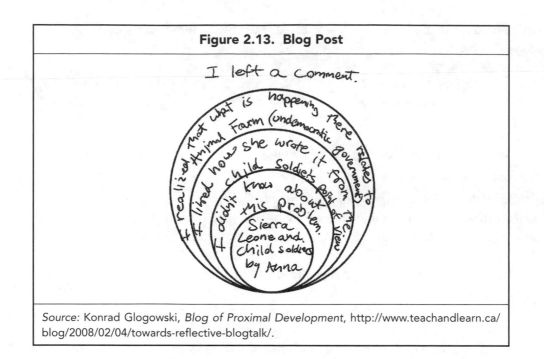

I left a comment.

I realized that what is happening there relates to

I liked how she wrote it from the

child soldiers point of view

I didn't know about this problem.

Sierra Leone and Child soldiers by Anna

Source: Konrad Glogowski, *Blog of Proximal Development,* http://www.teachandlearn.ca/blog/2008/02/04/towards-reflective-blogtalk/.

Figure 2.14. Template for Student Reflections

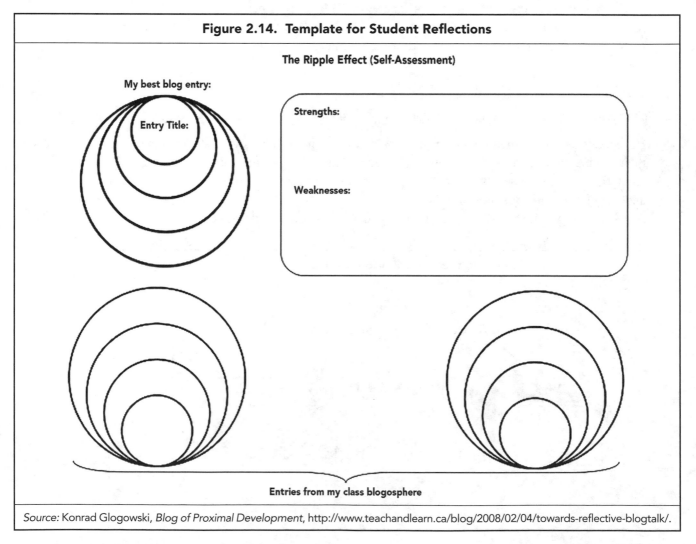

The Ripple Effect (Self-Assessment)

My best blog entry:

Entry Title:

Strengths:

Weaknesses:

Entries from my class blogosphere

Source: Konrad Glogowski, *Blog of Proximal Development*, http://www.teachandlearn.ca/blog/2008/02/04/towards-reflective-blogtalk/.

Follow-Up

After the lesson, try some of the following:

1. Explain to students that comments from readers can help the students consider new ideas and reflect on their own ideas in new ways.
2. Review netiquette for posting and commenting. Let students know all posts and comments will be reviewed.
3. Have students start writing on the online class blog.

Wall blogging is all about reading comprehension, writing, categorizing, comparing, contrasting, reflecting, documenting, and collaboratively exploring a topic. This activity uses visual, auditory, and kinesthetic aspects to engage learners with all learning styles, which makes this a fun activity for all. Students should now be able to transfer these skills to online blogging.

Teacher Exercises: Now You Try It...

To prepare to create your integrated plans using the Internet and RSS for research and blogs for communication, complete these exercises (see Table 2.1 for examples):

1. Do the following:
   - Sign up for an educational blog and post comments to a blog on a topic of interest to you.
   - Select a reader and add several blogs you want to follow to the reader.
   - Sign up for a blog at one of the sites listed in Part 2 if you haven't already done so.
2. Start your students out blogging by providing sample posts to which they must respond. This tests the concept before you create a complete lesson. Check the Blog Clips sidebar, p. 34, for ideas.

Table 2.1. General URLs on Blogging	
URL	**Description**
http://coolcatteacher.blogspot.com/2006/08/how-to-comment-like-king-or-queen.html	How to comment
http://teacherchallenge.edublogs.org/2011/03/13/student-blogging-activity-7-beginner-set-up-your-student-blogs/	Set up student blogs
http://teacherchallenge.edublogs.org/challenges-2/blogging-with-students/	Getting started blogging
http://www.youtube.com/watch?v=Vpe049Bx_jc&feature=related	YouTube blogging video student/teacher activity
http://langwitches.org/blog/2008/12/25/creating-an-outline-for-blogging-unit-plan/	Sample blogging unit at the elementary level
http://kidslearntoblog.com/the-literacy-act-of-blogging/	The literacy of blogging
http://theedublogger.com/2010/12/14/the-edubloggers-introduction-to-blogging/	Introduction to blogging
http://www.stevespangler.com/category/science-fair-secrets/	Steve Spangler Science Blog
http://mashable.com/2010/10/03/help-children-blog/	How to help your child set up a blog
http://21classes.com/shop/product	21Classes blog site
http://educational-blogging.wikispaces.com/	Ideas for using blogs from a classroom teacher

3. Brainstorm a list of possible topics students can write about or select a unit you plan to teach and add a blogging component. Use other class blogs as examples.
4. Set up mini-lessons on netiquette and commenting and try them with your class before the blog lesson.
5. Select a topic where you think a blog would be useful. Write a lesson plan including the components in this sample lesson and try it with your class.

CONCLUSION

Blogging offers incentives to write no matter what the subject with its emphasis on content, the possibility of speedy feedback, the option of working with both words and images, and the ability to link one post to another. Because students know they're going to have an audience, they often produce higher quality work for their blogs than students who write only for the teacher.

Blogging is one way of linking writing, reading, connecting information, and learning together. It also gives students the opportunity to be creators—rather than simply consumers—of online content. Now is the time for educators to expose students to safe practices and to academic uses of online spaces.

> ➤ *For additional examples, exercises, blogs in other subject areas, and more, go to Bev's website at http://www.neal-schuman.com/webclassroom.*

REFERENCES AND FURTHER READING

California State Department of Education. 2009. *English-Language Arts Framework for California Public Schools: Kindergarten Through Grade Twelve*. Sacramento: California State Department of Education.

Grunwald, Peter. 2006. "The Old Is New: Television, the Internet, and Students." FETC presentation March 23. In "Stats on Kids and New Media," *Moving at the Speed of Creativity: The Weblog of Wesley Fryer*, March 23. http://www.speedofcreativity.org/2006/03/23/stats-on-kids-and-new-media/.

Heppel, Stephen. 2008. "It Simply Isn't the 20th Century Any More Is It? So Why Would We Teach as Though It Was?" K12 Online Conference. http://k12onlineconference.org/?p=268.

Irwin, Tanya. 2008. "Study: Kids Are Master Multitaskers On TV, Web, Mobile." *Online Media Daily*. March 10. http://www.mediapost.com/publications/article/78118/.

Lenhart, Amanda, and Susannah Fox. 2006. "A Blogger Portrait." *Pew Internet and American Life Project Report*. The Pew Research Center. July 19. http://pewresearch.org/pubs/236/a-blogger-portrait.

Oatman, Eric. 2005. "Blogomania!" *School Library Journal*. August 1. http://www.schoollibraryjournal.com/article/CA632382.html.

Richardson, Will. 2004. "Metablognition." *Weblogg-ed: Learning with the Read/Write Web* (blog), April 27. http://www.weblogg-ed.com/2004/04/27.

Richardson, Will. 2007. "Blogging to Teach Reading." *Weblogg-ed: Learning with the Read/Write Web* (blog), January 20. http://weblogg-ed.com/2007/blogging-to-teach-reading/.

Wikipedia. 2011a. "Jorn Barger." Wikimedia Foundation. Last modified September 11. http://en.wikipedia.org/wiki/Jorn_Barger.

Wikipedia. 2011b. "Tag (Metadata)." Wikimedia Foundation. Last modified November 28. http://en.wikipedia.org/wiki/Tag_(metadata).

CHAPTER 3

Using Wikis in Language Arts and Social Studies

PART 1: IDEAS AND INSIGHTS

In Chapter 2, you read about collaborating using blogs and blogging. Teachers are also using wikis in the same way and are quite excited about their students' participation and enthusiasm for learning. When you use either blogs or wikis, the process becomes more interactive and transparent. Teachers show their enthusiasm about using wikis:

> "I have used countless technological tools—but I have never found a tool so useful in the educational process." (Vicki Davis, Westwood Schools)

> "I feel that this project was the most practical thing I've done for an English class in high school. In previous classes, the only multimedia form of presentation I have used has been PowerPoint, which has since become mundane for me. I enjoyed the creative aspect of being able to learn at the same time I helped to inform people from outside of my school." (Elaina, high school student)

> "There is just nothing out there so simple to use!" (Leigh Blackall, Blended Learning)

> "We needed to enhance opportunities for research, writing, and editing for a real-life audience in authentic situations." (Baltimore County Public Schools)

Wiki use has continued to increase in K–12 education. Wikispaces has given away 433,927 free educational workspaces, PBworks more than 300,000, to help teachers see how easy it is to use free educational wiki technology. Excitement among teachers, librarians, students, and now administrators about using wikis to meet educational goals has sparked the increased enthusiasm about introducing wikis into the classroom.

Objectives of This Chapter

This chapter explores ways to integrate wikis into English and language arts content instruction. It is designed to be used by English/language arts and social studies educators and school librarians at both the elementary and secondary levels. By the end of this chapter, in addition to content goals, educators will be able to:

- define a wiki and differentiate it from a blog;
- describe the characteristics of a wiki and why it is useful in the K–12 classroom;
- set up a wiki; and
- create a unit that includes the use of wikis to analyze a real-world topic.

English and language arts educators expose students to literature in the form of fiction, nonfiction, poetry, and drama. They require students to create meaning from texts they read. They also provide opportunities for students to speak in small groups and to the whole class about their experiences with literature. In addition, they create assignments that require students to write about their thoughts and experiences, and analyze ways literature provides meaning for their own lives. Now they are also adding wiki technology to their tools.

Part 1 of this chapter provides an introduction to wikis and examples of how teachers are using them as part of instruction. Part 2 suggests how to get started, including tools and rules for using wikis in education. In Part 3, a sample unit plan illustrates how to use wikis to analyze a problem in today's world in the realm of education. It crosses curricular areas from English/language arts to social studies at the secondary level.

Glossary

Review the following definitions to gain a better understanding of terms you may see in this chapter.

authentication mechanism: A user log-in to edit the wiki so every post or edit can be attributed to an individual student.

backchannel: An unofficial conversation taking place at the same time as an official discussion (e.g., watching a presentation online while conversing in a chat box at the same time).

backup feature: A wiki that backs up each night to prevent loss of data.

rollback feature: Used by administrators to repair any deletions of the wiki information or misuse as required.

sandbox: A place to try editing a wiki page created by others.

signature tool: A tool that creates a link to the wiki page of the user editing a wiki.

wiki: A collection of webpages designed to enable anyone who accesses it to contribute or modify content.

Wikipedia: An online encyclopedia with more than 200,000 contributors.

wikiword: Two or more words with initial capitals, run together. Wikiwords are topic names.

Introduction

Created as a tool to communicate among programmers, "wiki" is now a common term in our vocabulary. Wikis are being used in the classroom for everything imaginable. Group study guides, online lesson plans, classroom notice boards, collaborative essays—all come alive through wikis. As you explore this chapter, you will understand why the technology was given this name because a wiki is so simple to set up and easy to use.

What Is a Wiki?

A wiki is a collaboratively developed and updated website. Webpages are created and edited directly in the web browser (e.g., Firefox, Internet Explorer) by anyone who has been granted editing rights. Wikis can provide users with both author and editor privileges. This means that any authorized visitors to the wiki can change its content if they desire. A wiki is continuously under revision.

One of the wikis most known by librarians and teachers is *Wikipedia*, the online encyclopedia, with more than 200,000 contributors (see Figure 3.1). *Wikipedia*, however, has its share of both advocates and skeptics. Some educators worry about its quality and accuracy. One teacher comments on one of its strengths: "*Wikipedia* provides a teaching opportunity for teachers to talk to students about reliability and to teach them about being critical of sources and where information comes from."

What is the difference between a wiki and a blog? Chapter 2 provided comprehensive information about blogs. However, these terms are often confused. A blog or weblog shares writing and multimedia content in the form of posts and comments to posts. While members of the blog or the general public can comment on a post, no one is able to change a comment or post made by another. Blogs are a good forum for individuals to express their own opinions. Wikis, on the other hand, have a more open structure and allow others to change what one person has written. In fact, group consensus may override individual opinion.

Criteria for Selecting a Wiki

A teacher or librarian who is contemplating using a wiki should do so only after considerable thought. Following are some points for educators to consider when they decide to start a wiki.

- A host site without ads is best, if possible, so educators have full control over what information students are exposed to in their classrooms or libraries.
- Choosing a site that is easy for students to navigate lets them focus on learning the class topic rather than figuring out how to find the material or understand the technology.
- Some hosts offer the ability to use a wide range of learning media. For example, teachers and students should be able to easily incorporate text, color, images, video, and audio into their wiki pages to meet all learning styles.
- A monitoring capability is vital. Teachers need to be able to monitor what individual students are doing on the wiki. The classroom wiki must support individual log-ins for each member

Figure 3.1. *Wikipedia* Homepage

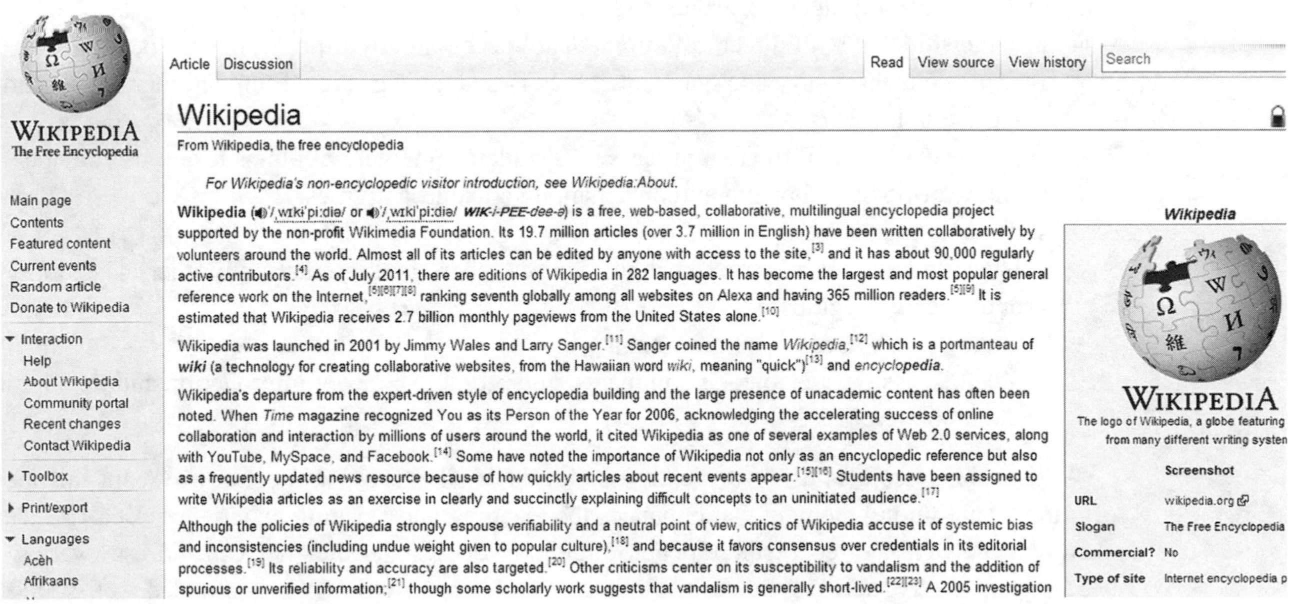

Source: Permission granted under Creative Commons Attribution/Share-Alike 3.0; http://creativecommons.org/licenses/by-sa/3.0/.

of the class, so that every edit made by students has their user names attached. This allows the teacher to track the progress on the wiki.

- Important also is the need for the wiki to be safe from intruders with good mechanisms for keeping out vandals and spammers. The educator can set privacy and decide who has access to the wiki's content.
- Students will work individually on some projects and collaborate in groups on others so separate areas should be available on the wiki site.
- Teachers will want to provide external web links as resources for students so that linking to external web resources is easy.
- Support from the wiki host should include an enthusiastic user community to help teachers share ideas on how to make the best of their classroom wiki. Viewing examples of educators using wikis for a variety of purposes is important when starting out.
- As part of the wiki, teacher aids are essential, such as notifying teachers by e-mail or RSS (see Chapter 2) when a change is made to the wiki, and keeping statistics about use by individual students. The ability to comment directly on students' wiki pages and calendars that lay out what is expected of students and by when are also important.

Of course, the best classroom wiki is free. A couple of free sites described later offer all or most of these criteria.

Why Use Wikis in the Classroom?

The question, then, is why should educators want to use wikis in their classrooms and why are students so excited to participate? Wikis, like any tool for learning, are limited in use primarily by the creativity of the educator. Ten reasons suggest the pedagogical importance of using wikis. Wikis:

1. encourage student involvement;
2. offer a powerful yet flexible collaborative communication space for developing content-specific areas;
3. provide a central place for groups to form around specific topics;
4. provide students with direct (and immediate) access at any time, from any location with an Internet connection to a site's content, which is crucial in group editing or other collaborative project activities;
5. show the evolution of thought processes as students interact with the site and its contents;
6. promote pride of authorship and ownership in a team's activities;
7. showcase student work;
8. expand students' horizons by enabling them to share and interact with other classrooms or groups locally or globally;
9. encourage collaboration on notes; and
10. enable discussions, encourage comments, and promote concept introduction and exploration on collaborative pages.

Wiki-enabled projects can provide various levels of site access and control to team members, offering a fine-tuning element that enhances the teaching and learning experience. Because wikis grow and evolve as a direct result of people adding material to the site, they can address a variety of pedagogical needs such as student involvement or group activities. Wikis are also well suited to reflecting current thoughts. In addition, wikis are helpful as e-portfolios, illustrating their utility as a tool for collection and reflection.

Classroom and Library Examples of Wikis

Teachers and librarians nationwide are using wikis in K–12 settings—and the possibilities appear endless.

Example 1: 2010 Flat Classroom Projects

The award-winning Flat Classroom Project (http://www.flatclassroomproject.net/all-projects.html), created in 2006 by Vicki Davis from the Westwood Schools in Georgia and Julie Lindsay, now at Beijing International School in China, was designed to challenge students to have a deeper understanding of the effect of information technology on the world (see Figure 3.2). Current Flat Classroom projects include the Digiteen Project: Global Digital Citizenship Collaboration and Education for middle and early high school students, 11 to15 years old and the Eracism Project (http://www.eracismproject.org/eracism-project-blog.html), a series of global collaborative debates for middle school students to promote awareness of racism on a global basis and ways to work together to solve the world's problems. Teams used VoiceThread (see Chapter 9) for their debates.

The Flat Classroom Project has four mandatory components for students:

1. An audio or video introduction posted as a blog post on the educational network (Ning) (see Chapter 11 for more on Ning)
2. A written collaborative report using a wiki where teams of students edit and discuss the topic on the discussion tab of the page
3. A personal multimedia response (e.g., digital story/video)
4. A post-project reflection in which students post their thoughts on the process during the project to the educational network (Ning)

Most recently schools from the United States, the Czech Republic, China, India, and the United Kingdom participated in an elementary school project for children 6–8 years titled "A Week in the

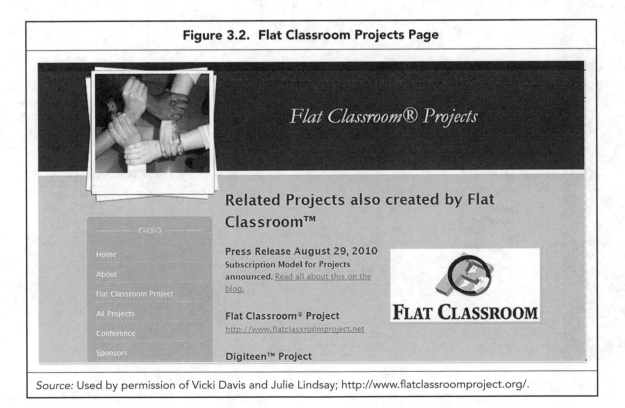

Figure 3.2. Flat Classroom Projects Page

Flat Classroom® Projects

Home
About
Flat Classroom Project
All Projects
Conference
Sponsors

Related Projects also created by Flat Classroom™

Press Release August 29, 2010
Subscription Model for Projects announced. Read all about this on the blog.

Flat Classroom® Project
http://www.flatclassroomproject.net

FLAT CLASSROOM

Digiteen™ Project

Source: Used by permission of Vicki Davis and Julie Lindsay; http://www.flatclassroomproject.org/.

Life" (http://aweekinthelife.flatclassroomproject.org/About+this+project). The project lasted approximately ten weeks with the goal of joining elementary school classrooms globally to explore life in each country. Through discussion and sharing, cross-classroom teams explored themes including school, clothing, leisure, sports, celebrations, and more. A final project using multimedia and documentation demonstrated what they learned.

A teacher in Houston, Texas, had the following to say about participating in a Flat Classroom Project: "I watched as these dynamic youth obliterated racial, ethnic, religious, and cultural barriers to build innovative collaborative projects . . . projects that, when realized, will address some of our world's most pressing social issues."

To learn more about Flat Classroom goals and activities, visit http://flatclassroomproject .wikispaces.com/Lesson+Plans. Read about the beginnings of the Flat Classroom project at http://flatclassroomproject.wikispaces.com/space/showimage/Flat_Classroom_LL_August07.pdf.

Example 2: Creative Cougars' Wikis

From first-graders to high school students, wikis can be used by all grade levels and in all subject areas. Mrs. Abernathy's fifth-grade "creative cougars" in Greenville, North Carolina, have put together several wiki projects that include multimedia. For social studies, students designed posters about each of the 50 states using the features of Glogster (see Chapter 8) (http://creative50states .wikispaces.com/), and placed them on their 50 states wiki. They also drew their own original pictures to interpret articles and amendments of the U.S. Constitution for their Constitution wikispace (see Figure 3.3). At the end of the project, colored copies of the book were made. Each student chose a

Figure 3.3. Creative Cougars' Wiki

Source: Used by permission of Jan Abernathy; http://creativecougarsconstitution.wikispaces.com/.

person to send a copy to—celebrities, politicians, and sports figures. After a lesson on how to write a business letter, students wrote and sent letters to their chosen recipients, including a copy of the Constitution book.

Students also created wikis to highlight a book they were reading in language arts, explorers for social studies, and a wiki dedicated to math concepts. Class members create the wikis, gather research, and add to it over time so that others will benefit from this information and edit it as needed. In fact, students even created fun multimedia wiki projects on topics such as synonyms/antonyms for language arts and polygons in math to help them study for the PSSA tests.

Example 3: Wikis in the Library

Librarians often use wikis to promote reading. On the Book Trailers for Readers wiki at http://www.booktrailersforreaders.com/, students create their own book trailers to tempt other students to read the books. Students from all elementary grades created videos after reading their books. This library wiki is an ideal way to show off student work (see Figure 3.4).

Example 4: Wikis for Different Subjects

On this social studies wiki, fifth-graders wrote about their favorite Civil War novels, including characters, plots, and why these books were their favorites. Review comments at http://crozet digikids.wikispaces.com/Civil+War+Novels (see Figure 3.5).

Figure 3.6 (http://crozetdigikids.wikispaces.com/Civil+War+Novels) illustrates one student adding to the wiki on his favorite book.

Students also have their own wikis that feature understanding of math concepts, discrimination, and a science review. Students can add, modify, or delete content to wiki pages on each topic.

Figure 3.4. Book Trailers for Readers

Source: Used by permission of Michelle Harclerode, Teacher Librarian, Diplomat Elementary School.

Figure 3.5. CrozetDigikids Wiki

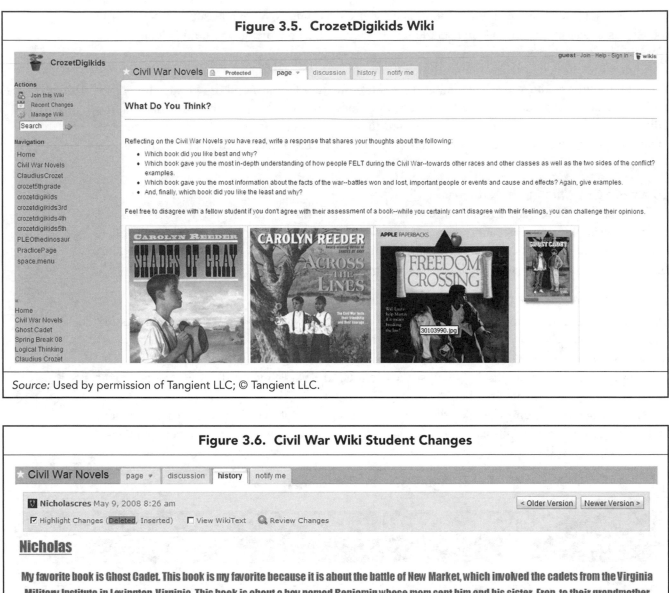

Source: Used by permission of Tangient LLC; © Tangient LLC.

Figure 3.6. Civil War Wiki Student Changes

Nicholas

My favorite book is Ghost Cadet. This book is my favorite because it is about the battle of New Market, which involved the cadets from the Virginia Military Institute in Lexington, Virginia. This book is about a boy named Benjamin whose mom sent him and his sister, Fran, to their grandmother that they have never met! Benjy's grandma happens to live in the city of New Market. Her house is only a little bit away from the Field Of Lost Shoes where the battle of New Market took place. While Benjy was visiting the battlefield he happened to meet a ghost. Benjy later found out that that ghost was Cadet William Hugh McDowell, who was one of ten cadets who died in the battle of New Market. Hugh tells Benjy about a watch that he lost the day of the battle and asked Benjy to help him find it. Will Benjy and Hugh find the watch? Read the book to find out. I recommend this book to all kids and adults. I hope you enjoy the book.

Brennan

Source: Used by permission of Tangient LLC; © Tangient LLC.

Wiki Ideas in Science

Some ideas schools have employed using wikis in science are listed here:

- Fifth- and sixth-graders' ACFT Science Lab wiki at http://acftscience.wetpaint.com/page/Student+Review+Videos features student-made videos on science projects.
- Littlewood's Nature guide wiki at http://littlewoodnatureguide.wetpaint.com/, created by fifth-graders, provides space for them to learn about and explore ecosystems.

- A high school biology class at http://mrsmaine.wikispaces.com/biology designs experiments and resulting lab reports on their wiki.
- Seventh-graders use wikis to keep track of their experiments and peer-edit information that is posted at http://mrsfranksciencewiki.wikispaces.com/Red+Group.

PART 2: GETTING STARTED WITH WIKIS

Using any technology tool requires thought, preparation, and experimentation prior to using it with students. Educators must advise administrators and parents and adhere to school policies. It is also a good idea to seek out other teachers and librarians who have been working with the new technology to hear about their experiences. Some basic questions the teacher or librarian must consider, to name a few, include: What service should I use? How will the tool fit into my curriculum or my library? Are my students capable of using it? Do the advantages outweigh the disadvantages? How is security handled?

Preparing for a Wiki

Before trying a wiki in your classroom, preparation is all important. The following steps will organize the process for the novice starting out.

Step 1: Keep the Administration Informed

Check your school's acceptable use policy (AUP) about using wikis and inquire about the following:

- Is it permissible to post student work to the web?
- What is the policy on posting student names? (Initials? First Names? Pseudonyms?)
- What is the policy on posting pictures of students or class scenes?
- What is the policy on posting any information that might identify the wiki class?
- Can these policies be met through security settings and parent and student agreements?
- Does the district filtering prevent access to the wiki tools from school? If so, will your administrator facilitate unblocking the wiki's exact URL?

The response of the administration will help you decide if a wiki has the capabilities and security you need for it to be successful for your classroom. It is also useful to set up short, simple usage guidelines, written in a positive tone. In addition, it is helpful to illustrate how other schools are using wikis in their classrooms to allay administrative concerns (see Figure 3.7).

Step 2: Make Basic Decisions about Setting Up the Wiki

An important aspect of any technology tool is its benefit to student learning. Before you start your wiki with your class(es), consider the following questions:

- How do you envision using the wiki? (How will you explain it to parents?)
- Who will be able to see the wiki? (Other schools? The class? Group members? Parents?)
- Who will be able to edit the wiki? (Other schools? The class? Group members?)
- Who will be able to join the wiki? (Students only? Parents? Invited guests? The public?)
- What parts of the wiki will you "protect" (lock from changes)?
- Who will moderate the wiki for appropriateness, etc.?
- Will you, as the educator, be notified of all changes?

Step 3: Choose a Host Using Specific Criteria

Consider criteria in selecting a service to host your wiki. These include:

Figure 3.7. Wiki Sample Contract

The following contract must be signed before students may participate in the class wiki.

Purpose of the Wiki

The members of [name of class] class at [name of school] will be participating in a class wiki for the purposes of [include all that apply, e.g., Practicing taking varied points of view on a topic]

_____

_____

_____

Safety

This wiki will be created using a wiki tool at [put in URL of wiki here]. The following instructions will protect students' safety.

_____

_____

_____

Terms and Conditions

Read the terms and conditions carefully before signing the contract.

- _____

- _____

- _____

Consequences of Violating the Contract

Any violation of the above terms and conditions shall make the violator subject to both immediate termination from the wiki, with all related sacrifice of points toward grades and to discipline through the school code of conduct, where applicable. At the teacher's discretion, a warning may be given in the case of minor infractions.

Signatures

I agree to the terms and conditions of the class wiki for (name of class here) for the (add dates) school year and permit my student to participate in the wiki project.

_____   _____
Student signature   Date   Parent signature   Date

- *Easy to use.* Ideally, how to add material to a wiki can be learned in a matter of minutes, even for young elementary students, as long as they can find letters on a keyboard.
- *Cost.* There are many free wiki hosts on the web, but some fund their existence through advertising that appears on the wiki pages. This can be very distracting or even inappropriate for students who inevitably click the enticing links. See if you can find a free host without advertising.
- *Appearance.* The wiki should be easily navigated so it is simple to find information within the wiki and the overall look can be adjusted. Video, audio, and images can be used as needed to add to the message. They should not be distracting but used where needed to further explain a topic.

- *E-mail addresses*. Some wiki hosts offer an easy way to set up student accounts in bulk without students needing an e-mail address.
- *Security*. The wiki should follow school policy. If the entire wiki needs to be in private view (visible and editable only by members), then it must be set up that way. You should be able to decide who has access to your wiki's content.
- *Usage guidelines*. The wiki should have short, simple usage guidelines written in a positive manner. The guidelines should encourage users to be considerate of others and be active and friendly in their wiki posts.

Step 4: Select the Wiki Host That Meets the Criteria

The following list provides two sample hosts on which to create wikis. Each service meets the criteria already discussed.

- *Wikispaces* (http://www.wikispaces.com/content/for/teachers) is a place where you can create a wiki to use in your classroom and your school. Wikispaces for Educators has given away more than 433,614 free, secure, advertising-free wiki spaces for K–12 education.
- *PBworks Basic Edition* (http://pbworks.com/content/edu-classroom-teachers) hosts over 300,000 wikis and serves millions of users every month. The service offers free, ad-free, secure wikis for K–12 education. In fact, more than 103,000 students and 8,000 teachers in Baltimore County Public Schools have wiki technology available to their classrooms to "enhance opportunities for research, writing and editing for a real-life audience in authentic situations." A case study at http://pbworks.com/content/casestudy-BCPS demonstrates the process they used (see Figure 3.8).

Note: These wikis also offer additional features at a fee.

Other sites on which to create wikis include:

- *Google Sites* (http://www.google.com/sites/overview.html). Free, ad-free hosting site.
- *Wetpaint* (http://wikisineducation.wetpaint.com/). Contains ads unless a fee is paid.

Figure 3.8. PBworks Education Page

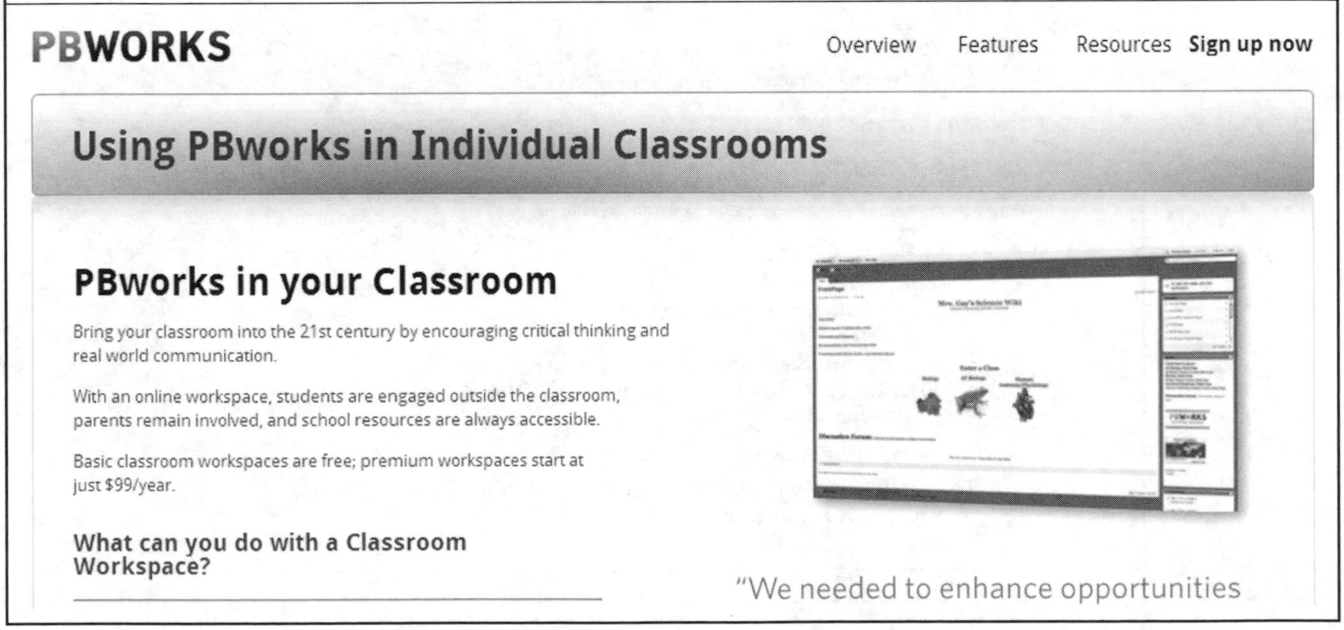

Setting Up a Wiki

An example using Wikispaces shows you how easy it is to set up a wiki. Other wiki hosts (e.g., PBworks) are equally easy to begin. With Wikispaces, setup requires six steps.

- *Step 1: Select a K–12 wiki. Name and describe your wiki.* The first step is to create a site name, a URL address, and a description of the wiki, and indicate who can view and edit the wiki.
- *Step 2: Select a style for the wiki.* There are a number of wiki templates available from which to choose. At this point you can preview and customize your wiki name.
- *Step 3: Preview the wiki.* Review the name and description of the wiki.
- *Step 4: Create a Wikispaces account.* Complete the screen entering data needed to set up the account (see Figure 3.9).
- *Step 5: Invite participants to your wiki site.* Identify the role you want them to play (e.g., writer, viewer) and enter their e-mail addresses. Once you have invited others to participate, click the link to set up the account (see Figure 3.10).
- *Step 6: Get going.* Your wiki is set up. Now you're ready to place some content on it and have others collaborate with you.

Figure 3.9. Create a Wiki on Wikispaces

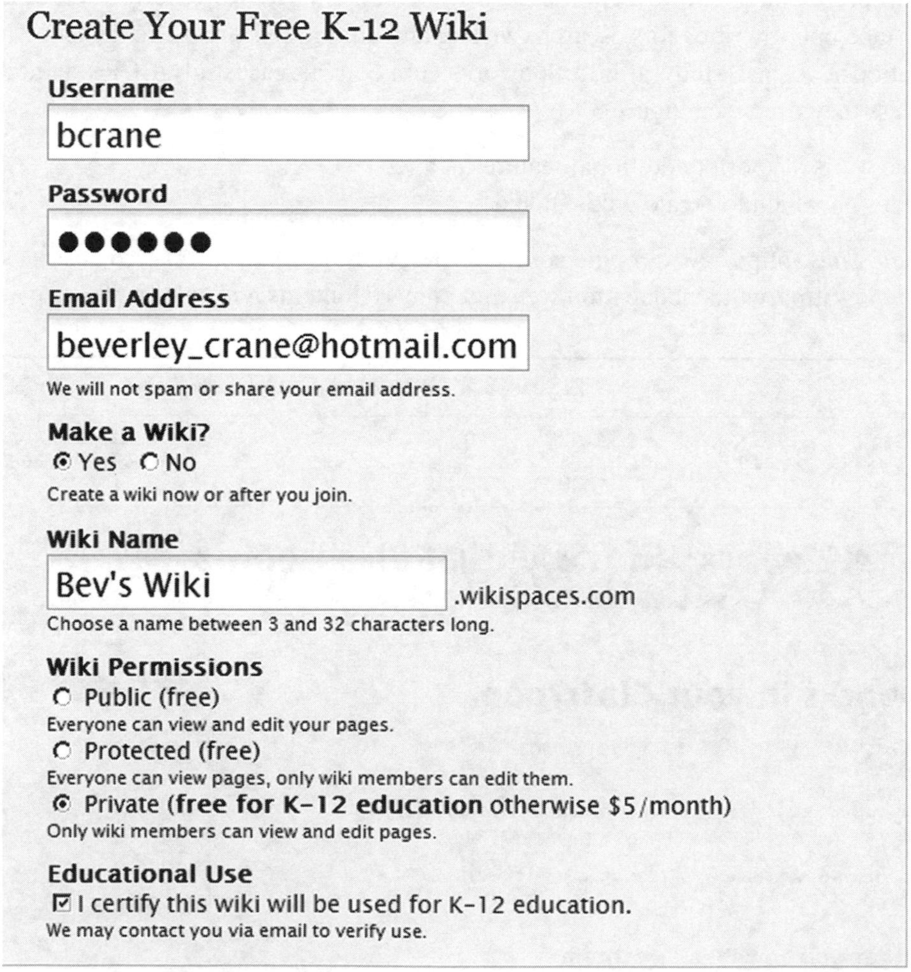

Create Your Free K-12 Wiki

Username

bcrane

Password

●●●●●●

Email Address

beverley_crane@hotmail.com

We will not spam or share your email address.

Make a Wiki?

◉ Yes   ○ No

Create a wiki now or after you join.

Wiki Name

Bev's Wiki   .wikispaces.com

Choose a name between 3 and 32 characters long.

Wiki Permissions

○ Public (free)
Everyone can view and edit your pages.

○ Protected (free)
Everyone can view pages, only wiki members can edit them.

◉ Private (**free for K–12 education** otherwise $5/month)
Only wiki members can view and edit pages.

Educational Use

☑ I certify this wiki will be used for K–12 education.
We may contact you via email to verify use.

Source: Used by permission of Tangient LLC; © Tangient LLC.

Figure 3.10. Invite Participants

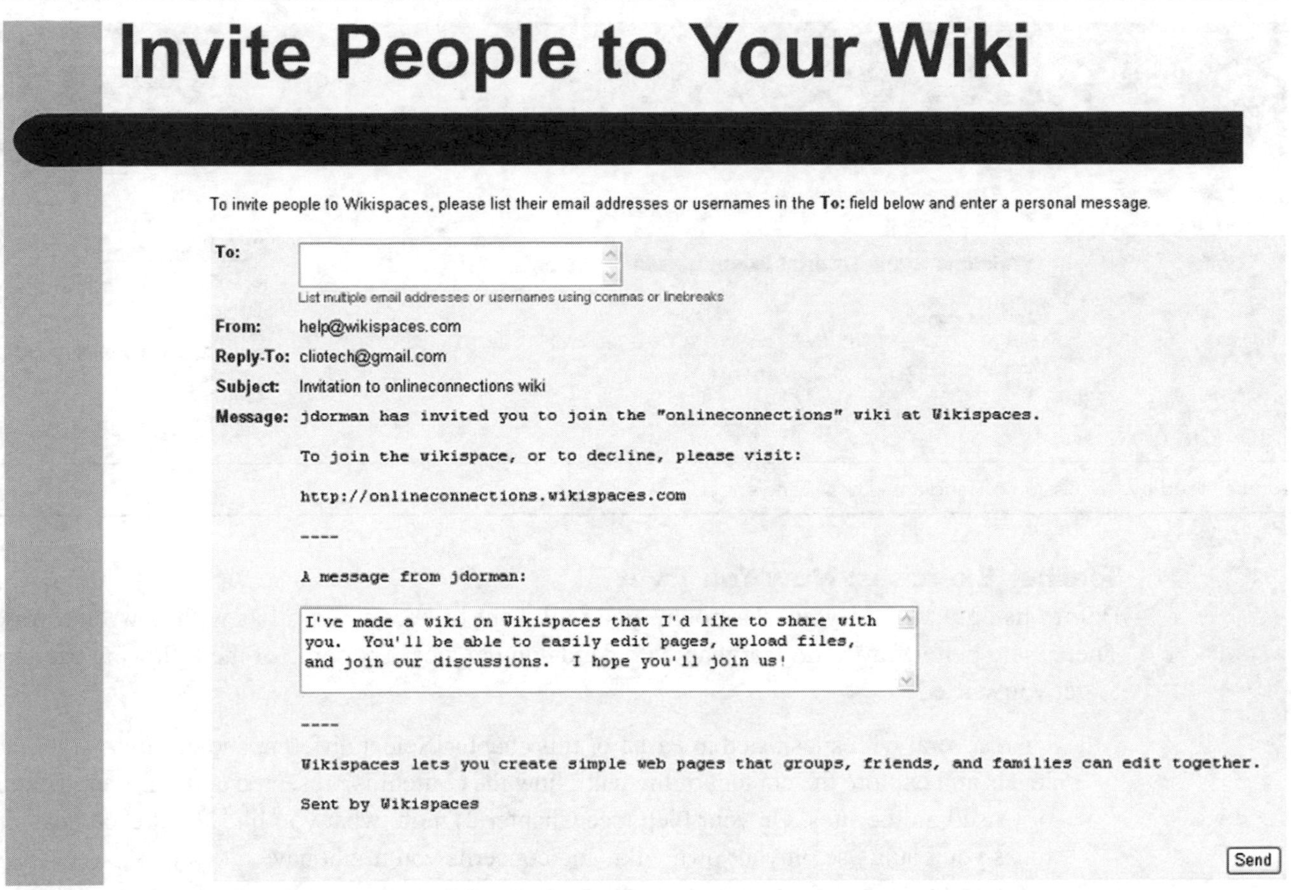

Invite People to Your Wiki

To invite people to Wikispaces, please list their email addresses or usernames in the **To:** field below and enter a personal message.

To:

List multiple email addresses or usernames using commas or linebreaks

From: help@wikispaces.com

Reply-To: cliotech@gmail.com

Subject: Invitation to onlineconnections wiki

Message: jdorman has invited you to join the "onlineconnections" wiki at Wikispaces.

To join the wikispace, or to decline, please visit:

http://onlineconnections.wikispaces.com

A message from jdorman:

I've made a wiki on Wikispaces that I'd like to share with you. You'll be able to easily edit pages, upload files, and join our discussions. I hope you'll join us!

Wikispaces lets you create simple web pages that groups, friends, and families can edit together.

Sent by Wikispaces

Send

Source: Used by permission of Tangient LLC; © Tangient LLC.

Decide How to Use the Wiki

Students can use wikis to create a set of documents that reflects the shared knowledge of the learning group. Wikis can also be used to facilitate the dissemination of information, enable the exchange of ideas, and encourage group interaction.

Wikis have two states, *read*, the default state, and *edit*. In the *read state* the wiki page looks just like a normal webpage. When users want to edit the wiki page, they must access the wiki's *edit state*. To edit a wiki, users click the edit button or link featured on each wiki page (http://help.wikispaces.com/Anatomy+of+a+Page) (see Figure 3.11). *Wikipedia* (http://www.wikipedia.org/), for example, provides a tab-style format at the top of each page, which contains a clickable link titled "edit this page" that users can click to access *Wikipedia's edit state*.

Other features shown as tabs at the top of wiki pages are important as well. The Discussion tab lets users communicate about a page without having to actually edit the page. For example, students can post new poetry on their pages, and others can offer "comments" in the discussion area. The History tab enables users to view changes that have been made to an entry, as well as return to a previous version of the wiki page, in case of accidental or intentional undesired changes. For formative evaluation teachers can use the "compare" feature to measure change over time in a student product. The Notify Me tab can save the educator time by keeping track of when someone makes changes to the wiki either via e-mail notification or through an RSS feed.

Figure 3.11. Wikispaces Edit Page

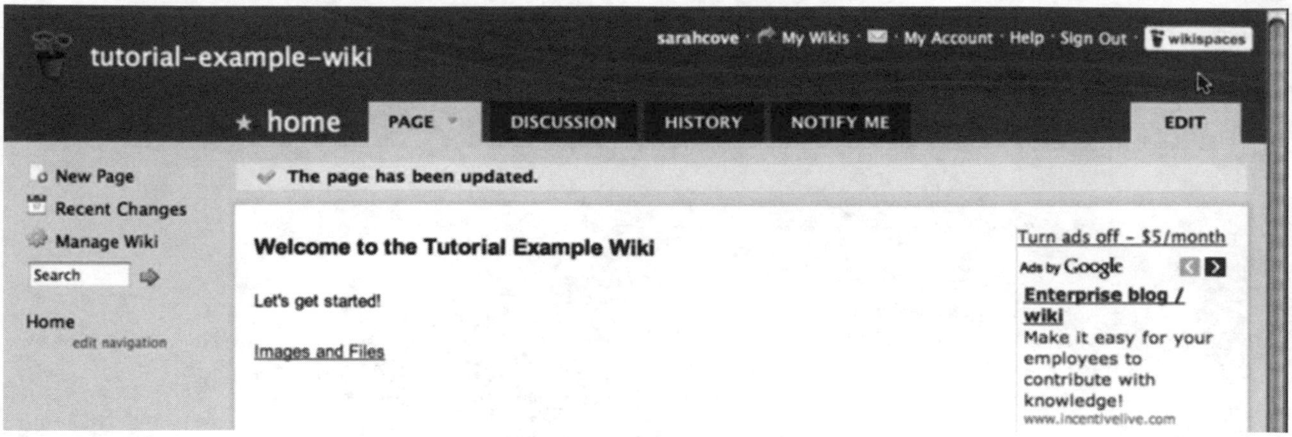

Source: Used by permission of Tangient LLC; © Tangient LLC.

Teacher Exercises: Now You Try It . . .

Before using a wiki in your classroom, you will want to become familiar with how one works. There is no better way to do that than with hands-on practice. Try some of the following exercises to get you started:

1. Visit several wiki sites listed in Part 1 of this chapter. Select different subject areas and grade levels and explore the content of the wiki: how the content is presented and different technology used on the sites. On your blog (see Chapter 2), note what you like about each host site, ideas you could use on your own wiki, and concerns you might have.

2. Now go to the websites for wiki services mentioned in Part 2 (e.g., Wikispaces, PBworks). Read the news, take a tour to see how they work, and compare the characteristics. Then write your comments on the Wiki Features Comparison sheet (see Table 3.1).

Table 3.1. Wiki Features Comparison		
Wiki Services	**PBworks**	**Wikispaces**
Embed media (video, images, links)		
Tracks edits and updates		
Personalize the wiki		
Privacy available		
Help		
Free for K–12		
Create student accounts without e-mail		
All changes reviewed		
Signature		

Note: Check the glossary at the beginning of this chapter for any words with which you are not familiar.

3. Go to Wiki Walk-Through created by TeachersFirst at http://www.teachersfirst.com/content/wiki/ and http://teachersfirst.pbworks.com/w/page/19849884/FrontPage. Review the basics and learn more about how teachers are using wikis in different subjects.

4. Now, if you really feel confident, start contributing to a wiki you find most meets your needs and with which you feel most comfortable.

Completing these tasks should give you practical experience in what you have been reading in Parts 1 and 2 of this chapter, and you will be ready to tackle Part 3—an actual example incorporating a wiki into a cross-curricular unit including English/language arts and social studies.

PART 3: PRACTICAL APPLICATIONS

In Chapters 2 and 3, you have learned about blogs and wikis and how they are being used in the classroom for collaboration, communication, improving reading and writing, and working together in groups. Team learning is an effective method for developing and strengthening content-area abilities. In Part 3 you will review a sample unit that combines the use of wikis and blogs and collaboration in student reading and writing activities in literature and history to look at a real-life issue that affects students every day. Before beginning the unit, you will need to create a classroom wiki and blog. In each chapter, Part 2: Getting Started has already described some of the details about setting up both.

An English/language arts curriculum has the responsibility of teaching students to listen well, speak effectively, read and think critically, and write clearly. To accomplish these tasks, English/language arts educators expose students to literature in the form of fiction, nonfiction, poetry, and drama. As students read and respond to literature, their abilities to think critically, interpret, and explain what is written will improve. As part of daily classroom activities, teachers provide opportunities for students to speak in small groups and to the whole class about their experiences with literature. They create assignments that require students to write about their thoughts and experiences and analyze ways that literature provides meaning for their own lives.

In social studies, teachers may have students explore varying perspectives about heroes, explorers, military commanders, and events of the past and present. Assignments may have students review information on historical events and personages ranging from the Revolutionary War era to the time of Abraham Lincoln to the Cold War. Students must think critically as they read a historical biography or delve into the events of a particular historical period. And, in conducting research, they may find conflicting viewpoints about figures in history, their characters, and their actions.

Many educators also incorporate technology into English/language arts and social studies classroom activities. Students search the web for sources for research projects, use tools such as Microsoft PowerPoint to create class presentations, and write their essays using word processing. Web 2.0 tools provide additional diversity so educators can craft assignments that will engage students as they work together and collaborate to produce the results for a project.

Multidisciplinary Unit Plan for English Literature and Social Studies

This unit offers students a way to investigate an issue that has become more prevalent in today's society, especially for students. Bullying has drawn the attention of educators from kindergarten through twelfth grade. By looking at "bullies" from history and literature, students can draw parallels to the modern era in which they live. Working independently and collaboratively, students assume roles that prompt them to report their findings from a unique perspective. All teams' work must fit together to make the culminating product a success and will be available for review through one central Web 2.0 tool—the class wiki. Groups will also use their blogs and group wikis to write about and comment on the issue of bullying. The unit is designed as a multidiscipline activity involving language arts, history, and technology to focus on a topic of importance in today's world.

This unit for grades 9–12 identifies and analyzes characters who are looked upon as bullies in literature and history. By reading novels and biographies whose characters mimic bullies in personality and actions and reviewing news articles about current world figures, students can find similarities and differences between these persons and people they associate with every day. The activities in this unit model the types of tasks that educators can create for their own classes.

Note: This unit can also focus on characters in children's literature and be modified to use at the elementary school level.

Step 1: Connect to the Standards—What Should Be Taught?

This unit supports *Standards for the English Language Arts*, created by the National Council of Teachers of English (NCTE) at http://www.ncte.org/standards/commoncore. It also builds on Standards for Social Studies. The unit encompasses the use of print, oral, and visual language and addresses six interrelated English language arts: reading, writing, speaking, listening, viewing, and visually representing as follows:

- Research will illustrate interdisciplinary connections between literature, history, and technology.
- Students will read a wide range of literature from many periods in many genres to build an understanding of the many dimensions (e.g., philosophical, ethical, aesthetic) of human experience.
- Activities, including gathering information and using the Internet, will develop students' research skills.
- Students will use analysis and synthesis to think critically as they research modern-day comparisons to the characters of a novel or figures in history.
- Students will read a wide range of print and nonprint texts to build an understanding of texts, of themselves, and of the cultures of the United States and the world; to acquire new information; to respond to the needs and demands of society and the workplace; and for personal fulfillment. Among these texts are fiction and nonfiction, classic and contemporary works, and online reading.
- Students will apply a wide range of strategies to comprehend, interpret, evaluate, and appreciate texts. They will draw on their prior experience and their interactions with other readers and writers.
- Students will conduct research on issues and interests by generating ideas and questions, and by posing problems. They will gather, evaluate, and synthesize data from a variety of sources (e.g., print and nonprint texts, artifacts, people) to communicate their discoveries in ways that suit their purpose and audience.
- Students will develop an understanding of and respect for diversity across cultures, ethnic groups, geographic regions, and social roles.

The unit will also reinforce the technology standards from the International Society for Technology in Education (ISTE), which include:

- improving familiarity with and use of Web 2.0 tools; and
- incorporating Web 2.0 technology into classroom content projects.

Step 2: Identify General Goals and Specific Objectives

In addition to content standards, the goals and specific objectives that follow form the basis for the content and skills of this unit.

Goals

When searching for information on the characters in their novels or past and modern-day historical figures, students will:

- participate in groups, during which they share their ideas and views about stories they read and history they interpret, gain new insights from their peers, and collaborate to clarify meaning;
- make personal connections to fiction and nonfiction by writing and telling about a time when they experienced a similar situation or emotion as one of the characters or figures of history;
- locate, gather, analyze, and evaluate written information for a variety of purposes, including research projects, real-world tasks, and self-improvement;
- build critical thinking skills by analyzing and synthesizing collected research; and
- interpret character traits based on the context of the entire novels to show how character analysis plays a part in understanding a reading.

Objectives

More specifically, as part of each goal, in the area of Content Objectives in English and History, students will:

- draft, revise, and edit their writing as part of the writing process;
- write with a command of the grammatical and mechanical conventions of composition;
- gather and use information effectively for research purposes;
- apply a variety of response strategies, including rereading, note taking, summarizing, outlining, and relating what is read to their own experiences, actions, and feelings;
- read critically and ask pertinent questions regarding characters in the novels, biographies, or news they have read;
- identify the characteristics of the bully, the bullied, and the bystander;
- synthesize historical research and draw conclusions from and evaluate real-life persons; and
- explore the connections between a character and the actions that character takes or doesn't take.

And, in the area of technology objectives, students will demonstrate competence in using a wiki for collaborative writing and a blog for communicating ideas.

Step 3: Gather Materials

Students will already have read at least one biography of a historical figure and one novel that identifies characters as bullies or those being bullied. Using their knowledge of characters in their readings of at least five news articles, they will research real-life persons whom students feel exhibit the personalities, hopes and actions, or other attributes of their characters. Some possible resources are listed in Table 3.2.

Step 4: Create the Activities

Literature that depicts bullying behavior provides students with the safe distance they need to begin to relate, and in some instances work through, their own experiences. Through the characters and events of a story, young people can begin to define bullying behavior and develop constructive responses for situations in which they are confronted with such an experience. By identifying bullies in history or modern times, students will see how others interacted and reacted to the actions of bullies.

This unit requires that students think about their novels, not in isolation, but by analyzing the characters and identifying characteristics they might see in a person they know or have read about elsewhere, such as political leaders, sports figures, entertainment personalities, and others whom

Table 3.2. Bullying Unit URLs	
URL	**Description**
http://stopbullyingnow.hrsa.gov/kids/seen_bullying/index.html	Describes bullying, signs, and what to do Tabs for kids, educators, and parents
http://stopbullyingnow.hrsa.gov/topics/cyberbullying/index.html	Cyberbullying
http://en.wikipedia.org/wiki/School_bullying	School bullying on *Wikipedia*
http://www.ehow.com/info_7859861_types-bullying-school.html	Types of bullying at school
http://www.ehow.com/how_7861809_deal-school-age-bullying.html	Article about dealing with school-age bullying
http://www.bullying.org/htm/main.cfm?content=1096	Presentations about bullying
http://pbskids.org/itsmylife/friends/bullies/	PBS site on all types of bullying and activities to deal with it

they might know more personally. Tasks students must now complete will require them to employ increasingly higher levels of critical thinking as they analyze the characters from the novel, compare their traits with real-life persons, and synthesize the material into a product.

In addition, students will be working in small groups on the class wiki. They will read and comment on one another's writing about their characters and add comments and questions to other groups' characters. Students will also use their blogs to write reflective pieces about their group work, the characters they are researching, and what they are learning from these collaborative activities.

Activities to Introduce the Unit

One goal of this unit is to reinforce what students learned from literature and emphasize the value and relevance that literature and history have for their own lives. These initial tasks require students to think about novels as they relate to characters. Students should also be able to look at world events and compare and contrast the actions of leaders, politicians, and well-known figures and the effects they have on people's lives.

Group wikis. To draw upon their prior knowledge, students in groups of three or four will compile information about bullying on their group wiki. They will:

- discuss their knowledge about bullying and describe their experiences with bullying by answering questions such as: What is a bully? Why do persons bully? What does it feel like to be bullied? Have you ever been a bully? A victim? A bystander when bullying took place? What do you do in such a situation?
- complete the bully chart—are the comments myths or not? Explain why and give an example (see Figure 3.12).
- brainstorm a list of personality traits and actions of the bully, those being bullied, and bystanders. Have one person start the wiki list and have others add to the initial list.
    Note: The teacher should model an example of personality traits and actions of a famous person most students would recognize, such as Hitler during World War II or Saddam Hussein in Iraq.

- write a draft analysis of a bully, victim, and bystander. Other students in the group will delete/expand on the information compiled on these personality types.

Figure 3.12. Bully Chart		
Myths about Bullies	**Yes/No and Why/Why Not**	**Give an Example**
Bullies are rejected by their peers and have no friends.		
Bullies have low self-esteem.		
Bullies appear to have healthy mental lives.		
Bullies are easy to spot.		
Myths about Victims		
Victims are below average in physical size and strength.		
Victims are passive and tend to be more anxious, insecure, cautious, quiet, and sensitive.		
Victims dominate others.		
Victims have many close friends at school and are socially acceptable.		
Victims love to go to school.		

The Class Wiki. The class wiki will be the central repository for all of the information collected by each group. Each group will:

- collect their notes about their famous persons;
- choose at least three other groups' bullies, victims, and bystanders to read about and add at least three comments and/or questions on those persons to the group wiki;
- collect photos and other artifacts that represent their person's traits and actions;
- discuss the notes about their persons made by other classmates, then write a draft analysis of each person (bully, victim, bystander);
- review at least three groups' draft analyses and—based on their own knowledge from research and discussion—add to, delete, and modify the analyses of other groups; and
- write final analyses of their own famous figure, taking other students' revisions into consideration.

Activities during the Unit

During the introductory activities, students reinforced their knowledge of bullying by researching famous persons who exhibited characteristics of bullies, victims, and bystanders. A successful character analysis demands that students infer abstract traits and values from literal details contained in a text. They must now complete a number of tasks to compile sufficient information to convince class members of the similarities between characters in literature or history and the real-life persons they researched.

In groups of four, students will:

- form literature response groups during which they share their ideas and views about a book they have selected to read together. The book should have characters who meet criteria for bullies, victims, and bystanders (e.g., *The Chocolate War*, *The Outsiders*, *Lord of the Flies*, *A Separate Peace*, *To Kill a Mockingbird*, *Oliver Twist*). Interaction as a group invites the readers to extend their thinking about the characters and prolong their involvement with the text.
- review characters in the novel and select a character who fits the characteristics of a bully, a victim, and bystanders who help or ignore the interaction. For example, in Golding's *Lord of the Flies* you might select Jack, Ralph, Piggy, and Maurice as examples of each type.
- write blog posts about these characters as they read each chapter. Analyzing the different posts, the group leader will start listing ideas from their discussion on the group wiki. This often helps to provide further clarification. As readers, they need to draw a conclusion about the character's traits (*to infer them*) from what the character says, thinks, and does.
- analyze their characters:
  - think creatively about how they would respond, think, and speak, depicting changes in the person, his/her actions, feelings, etc., and create blog entries from one of the characters' point of view;
  - use examples to illustrate the changes;
  - discuss how they felt at the end of the reading and what they learned from their experiences in the novel; and
  - write blog comments identifying similarities and differences among the different types.
- create blog posts to make personal connections to the story by writing about a time when they experienced a situation or emotion similar to that of one of the characters.
- brainstorm a list of persons the group thinks fits the description of their characters using the Character Analysis Log (see Figure 3.13). Note page numbers and quotes that they think exemplify their character's traits.

Figure 3.13. Character Analysis Log

Instructions. On your wiki use this form to identify personality and physical traits of the main characters from the novel your group has selected. Also include quotes from the novel to support selected character traits.

_____ (name of character)

Example: Piggy (*Lord of the Flies*)

Character Trait	Adjectives	Quote to Support Trait	Actions

- brainstorm three adjectives about physical appearance, three adjectives about personality, three adjectives about emotions, one quote from another person about the real-life person, and one quote by the real-life person that is indicative of his/her personality; place all on the wiki. Create a Character Trait Map of the real-life person (e.g., personality, characteristics, accomplishments, actions, etc.) See Figure 3.14 for an example.

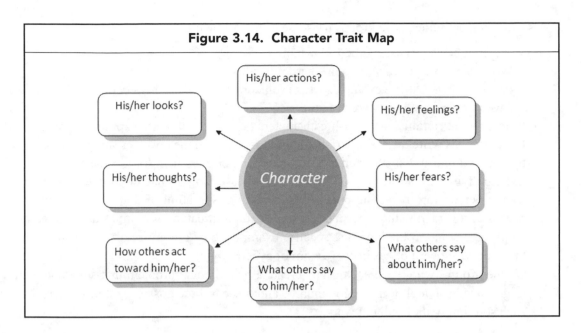

Figure 3.14. Character Trait Map

His/her actions?

His/her looks?

His/her feelings?

His/her thoughts?

Character

His/her fears?

How others act toward him/her?

What others say to him/her?

What others say about him/her?

The Group Wiki. Throughout this part of the activity, groups will use the wiki to keep track of all information that represents the real-life person. Groups will do the following:

- Divide their wiki space in half using one side for traits of their novel character and the other side for the real-life person, making sure supporting page numbers and quotes or URLs are listed.
- Collect the group's notes on the wiki, have teams read the notes and add to them, and begin writing the character sketch of the real-life person.
- Have each group review the character sketches of other groups, making their changes and suggestions on the wiki.
- Write a final draft character analysis of their real-life person, incorporating other students' suggestions.

Note: It is a good idea for each student in the group to assume a role (e.g., *research coordinator* assists others in finding key quotes, pictures, primary sources, etc.; *archive manager* uploads all files to the wiki page, etc.).

The Product. This task will encompass all learning that has taken place during the unit.

- Divide the class into three groups, and have each group create a Glogster poster (www.glogster .com) (see Chapter 8) representing the role of the bully, the victim, or bystanders to educate other classes about bullying issues. Place the poster on their blog for the rest of the school to view.
- Explain why bullying is unacceptable and how it affects others by illustrating bullying behavior through the characters of the novel they have just read.
- In groups of four have pairs each create a hypothetical problem that someone their age might face in school or in the community and role-play the situation, each with a different resolution. Discuss the resolutions and decide which solution is best and why.
- Reflect on their experience with this project. Submit a written statement describing their thoughts and feelings about bullying.

Activities to Be Used as Follow-Up

Now that students have educated themselves, let them spread the word and help educate their peers about bullying. As they have learned, one way to decrease bullying is to build supportive relationships among students, because friendships protect students from bullying.

As extension activities, have groups try some of the following:

- Write blog posts discussing the following:
  - Why do people get caught up in a herd mentality?
  - Provide some real-life examples where someone has bullied them but they're the ones who have to hide, as if they were at fault.
- Role-play the fictional and real-life characters they wrote about to capture personality traits. Have students write their own scripts for various scenes in the novel, creating two outcomes— the original one and an alternative. They can then perform them for the class.
- Cyberbullying takes a variety of forms, such as assuming a false online identity in order to trick a person into revealing personal information, spreading lies about a person, posting photos of a person without permission, and sending threatening or intimidating messages to another person. On the blog, list specific examples they are aware of where someone they know or have heard of has been a victim of cyberbullying.
- On the group's wiki, have each group create a hypothetical problem that someone their age might face in school or in the community, and present three possible solutions. Explain why each solution will or will not work.

Step 5: Evaluate What Was Learned

It is important to evaluate both students' work (the product) and students' working (the process). For this unit evaluation will be based on:

1. Assessment of the analyses of the characters from the novel and the real-life persons (see Figure 3.15).

\				
Figure 3.15. Wiki Rubric				
Category	**4 points**	**3 points**	**2 points**	**1 point**
Content	Covers topic in-depth with details and examples. Subject knowledge is excellent.	Includes essential knowledge about the topic. Subject knowledge appears to be good.	Includes essential information about the topic but there are one to two factual errors.	Content is minimal or there are several factual errors.
Organization	Content is well organized, using headings or bulleted lists to group related material.	Content is logically organized for the most part.	Connect uses headings or bulleted lists to organize, but the overall organization of topics appears flawed.	There was no clear or logical organization but a lot of facts.
Contribution to the group	Contributes greatly to the development of the group and class wiki.	Contributes adequately to the development of the group and class wiki.	Contributes moderately to the development of the group and class wiki.	Contributes minimally to the development of the group and class wiki.
Accuracy	No misspellings or grammatical errors. No broken links or missing images.	Three or fewer misspellings and/or mechanical errors. No more than two errors in the student's contribution to the wiki.	Four misspellings and/or mechanical errors. No more than four errors in the student's contribution to the wiki.	More than four misspellings and/or mechanical errors. More than five errors in the student's contribution to the wiki.

2. Collaboration among team members in reviewing and revising their own fictional character analysis and real-life character descriptions and those of other groups on the wiki. See Figure 3.16 for a collaborative rubric.
   a. Thorough research on the real-life person as compared to the character in the novel
   b. Participation in creating the wiki content

Figure 3.16. Group Participation Rubric

Name: _____

Date Observed: _____

Feature	Mastered	Developed	Developing	Not Developed
Time on Task	Always on task	Mostly on task	Sometimes on task	Completely off task
Verbal Response	Elicits others' opinions	Accepts others' opinions	Ignores others' opinions	Rejects others' opinions
Participation	Actively participates in group goals	Occasionally participates in group goals	Sometimes participates in group goals	Does not contribute to group goals
Interaction	Listens and gives nonverbal feedback	Exhibits attention to others	Exhibits inattentive behavior	Exhibits rude behavior
Attitude	Encourages participation of others	Accepts participation of others	Discourages participation of others	Ridicules others

3. Have students complete the Wiki Self-Evaluation Checklist (see Figure 3.17).

Figure 3.17. Wiki Self-Evaluation Checklist

Category	Beginning	Developing	Accomplished	Exemplary
I can distinguish wiki sites from other websites.				
I can describe several key characteristics of wikis.				
I can create a wiki page and/or create my own wiki.				
I feel confident about creating a wiki as part of my assignment.				

Use the Wiki rubric to evaluate the work students accomplished throughout this unit on bullying in which they used the wiki as an integral part of creating material, collaborating with classmates, and presenting the finished product.

Summary

This unit used characters in young adult literature as a starting point to make students think about literature as it relates to their own experiences. They used listening, reading, writing, and researching to accomplish the tasks of this unit. They incorporated some of the latest technology—creating and using a wiki—for easy collaboration, revision of their writing, and presentation of their projects to classmates, and blogs for commenting on specific topics related to bullying. As a result, they improved their critical thinking and saw how literature relates to their own lives. Finally, students are now familiar with using a wiki for collecting information, talking about and revising writing, and publishing their work, and blogs for stating their opinions about a specific topic.

Teacher Exercises: Now You Try It . . .

To prepare to create your own lesson using a wiki, complete the following exercises:

1. Visit at least three or four general wiki URLs from Table 3.3. Click links and add those of interest about wikis or blogs to your own wiki or blog. Go to http://teachersfirst.wikispaces .com/ and select at least two wikis in your subject area and grade level to review. Select a third wiki that appears to have a different purpose (e.g., an administrative site). Write a brief description of the sites on your blog and reflect on how a wiki can be used in your classroom.
2. Search for a subject that interests you discussed on a wiki and add a comment to it. (*Hint:* Add the word wiki to your keyword search.)
3. Write a short description explaining how you would incorporate a wiki into one of your lessons. How/what would the wiki add to your class?
4. Create a wiki with content using a free wiki-hosting website.
5. Reflect on the following questions about wikis:
   • How might you use a wiki in your instruction?
   • How would using a wiki benefit your students?
   • What hurdles might impede your using a wiki?
   • How is it possible to remove the hurdles?
6. Create a personal wiki that you can use to reflect on the Web 2.0 tools that you are learning about in this book. Invite colleagues to participate.

CONCLUSION

When starting out with your wiki, keep the activity very simple, whether you have seniors or second-graders. At first have students access the wiki in class. See what other educators who are using wikis in their lessons are doing:

• From a Minnesota high school, Mrs. Wolfe's Course Wiki (105.wikispaces.com) showcases student work in U.S. history, world cultures, U.S. government, and constitutional/criminal law.
• At Trinity Grammar School in Sydney, Australia, a drama teacher commented: "The public nature of the wiki is an inspiration for students because they learn from each other as they can see, access and comment on each other's page. I've had three reluctant 'pen and paper' students who have written more in two weeks than they did in an entire year."
• At a high school in Texas, a teacher and his students built what they think is a comprehensive, ever-changing, dynamic health science website that is their constant classroom companion. To quote the teacher, "If you are a teacher and want something that you can't, in my opinion, live without, create your own wiki. You will be glad you did!"
• Grandview Library for K–3 is a diverse wiki created by the school librarian. Projects range from kids' news to Readers' Theater, storytelling, student projects, and much more. Visit this site at http://www.grandviewlibrary.info/ to see how a wiki can be used in K–12 education.

Review other URLs for wikis to learn more (see Table 3.3).

Table 3.3. General Wiki URLs	
URL	**Description**
http://spacewithapurpose.wikispaces.com/Wikis+Home	All about wikis—Mini Camp Wiki
http://www.youtube.com/watch?v=-dnL00TdmLY&feature=player_embedded	Wikis in Plain English—video
http://www.teachersfirst.com/getsource.cfm?id=7237	Wiki Walk-Through, including K–12 wikis
http://infolibrarian.wikispaces.com/Research+Projects+K-12	Wiki projects
http://educationalwikis.wikispaces.com/Examples+of+educational+wikis	Examples of educational wikis
http://teacherleaders.typepad.com/the_tempered_radical/2010/01/part-one-teacher-tips-for-wiki-projects.html	Teacher Tips for Wikis
http://greetingsfromtheworld.wikispaces.com/	Best Wiki of 2010 from Edublogs

> ➤ *Additional examples, URLs, exercises, and using wikis in different subject areas can be seen on Bev's website at http://www.neal-schuman.com/webclassroom.*

REFERENCES AND FURTHER READING

The American Heritage Dictionary of the English Language, 4th ed. 2000. Boston: Houghton Mifflin Company.

California State Department of Education. 2009. *English-Language Arts Framework for California Public Schools: Kindergarten Through Grade Twelve*. Sacramento: California State Department of Education.

Davis, Michelle R. 2007. "Wiki Wisdom: Lessons for Educators." *Digital Directions*. September 12. http://www.edweek.org/dd/articles/2007/09/12/02wiki.h01.html.

Friedman, Thomas L. 2006. *The World Is Flat*. New York: Farrar, Straus and Giroux.

ISTE (The International Society for Technology in Education). 2007. *National Educational Technology Standards for Students*. Eugene, OR: The International Society for Technology in Education. http://www.iste.org/standards/nets-for-students/nets-student-standards-2007.aspx.

ISTE (The International Society for Technology in Education). 2008. *National Educational Technology Standards for Teachers*. Eugene, OR: The International Society for Technology in Education. http://www.iste.org/standards/nets-for-teachers/nets-for-teachers-2008.aspx.

Oatman, Eric. 2005. "Make Way for Wikis." *School Library Journal*. November 1. http://www.schoollibraryjournal.com/article/CA6277799.html.

Sheehy, Geoffrey. 2008. "The Wiki as Knowledge Repository: Using a Wiki in a Community of Practice to Strengthen K–12 Education." *TechTrends* 52, no. 6 (November/December). http://www.springerlink.com/content/y2w08p64281248h4/.

Wikipedia. 2011. "Wiki." Wikimedia Foundation. Last modified October 24. http://en.wikipedia.org/wiki/Wiki.

CHAPTER 4

Experiencing History through Podcasts

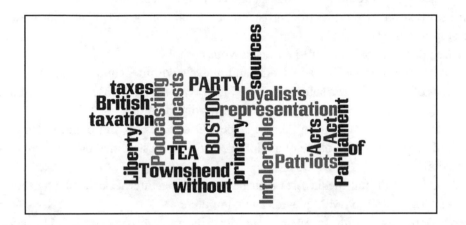

PART 1: IDEAS AND INSIGHTS

Although videos and social networking have joined with podcasts as popular K–12 learning technologies, nonetheless, podcasting is still alive and well in the K–12 classroom. Because it is easy to create podcasts and little equipment is involved, educators can include podcasting in the curriculum without much expense.

Objectives of This Chapter

This chapter is designed for use by educators at both the elementary and secondary levels, especially in social studies. Teachers in other subject areas can adapt the unit plan in Part 3 to their subject. After reading Chapter 4 and working through the exercises, teachers and librarians will be able to:

- guide students in Internet research and transform the research into a product;
- understand the basics of podcasting and why to use podcasts;
- find and listen to podcasts on the Internet; and
- create a unit using podcast technology.

Many educators today are familiar with conducting research on the Internet and, if they are not, most of their students are. Information from different sites reveals many different viewpoints on the same historical figure or event and requires students to think critically about the validity and bias of the information. In addition, schools can now take advantage of technology and analyze and synthesize their research into new formats employing audio and video, thus enhancing instruction for all learning styles.

> ➤ *For examples in other subject areas and different grade levels, go to Bev's website at http://www.neal-schuman.com/webclassroom.*

Glossary

Review the following terms before starting the chapter to fully understand the concepts discussed.

Audacity: A free digital audio editor application.

digital media player: A consumer electronics device that is capable of storing and playing digital media such as podcasts.

download: To transfer a file from the Internet or other computer to your own computer.

GarageBand: A software application that allows Mac users to create music or podcasts.

host: The person who introduces the podcast and each of its segments.

ID3 tags: Information such as the title, artist, album, track number, or other information about the file stored in the file itself.

iTunes: A free digital media player that runs on your computer.

Levelator: A free application that adjusts the audio levels within an audio segment.

MP3: A means of compressing a sound sequence into a very small file, used as a way of downloading audio files from the Internet. Popular format for digital audio.

MP4 (short for MPEG-4 or Motion Picture Expert Group 4): An audio and video compression standard that allows the storage of audio/video files to be streamed over the Internet or stored on media such as CDs or DVDs.

podcast: A series of digital media files distributed over the Internet using RSS feeds or Google Reader for playback on MP3 players and computers.

storyboard: A representation to present and describe interactive events, including audio and motion, for the purpose of previsualizing the final product.

upload: A file transfer from a computer to the Internet.

Introduction

A Web 2.0 technology such as the podcast can be an important tool in education because the technology is easy to use and allows students, teachers, librarians, administrators, and parents to share information at any time. Podcasts can be used in a variety of ways. Teachers can create a podcast of a lesson so that absent students can keep up to date with content they have missed. Podcasts provide the vehicle for keeping in touch with parents on their students' progress, homework assignments, and special events at the school. Administrators use podcasts for school announcements. Librarians create book talks as podcasts. Podcasts enhance the curriculum in a range of ways from broadcasting interviews to sending pen-pal letters, publishing oral presentations, and more. Video podcasts, to a lesser degree, are also used. Video will be discussed in greater detail in Chapter 8.

In addition, podcasts enhance cooperative learning, allowing students in small groups to interact with one another, learn from one another, solve problems together, and use one another as resources. The unit plan in Part 3 requires students to work together to organize the project and delegate tasks among group members. They will have to listen to one another's ideas and comments, ask questions of one another, respect the opinions of others, and share ideas and thinking. Only by helping one another can groups create successful podcasts.

Part 1 of this chapter examines podcast technology—what it is and why it should be used in education—and provides examples to illustrate its use in the classroom with today's curriculum. Part 2 contains tips on equipment, hosting services for podcasts that educators suggest, and steps to put together a podcast. Finally, Part 3 lays out a step-by-step unit plan with objectives, activities, and evaluation. Two sets of exercises are included. The exercise following Part 2 involves educators in practicing what they have learned about the technology, and the exercise following Part 3 has them formulate plans to create their own podcasts in a curriculum area. Tables containing websites for the unit and general websites to visit for more information on podcasts complete the chapter.

What Is a Podcast?

The word "podcast" combines two words to make a new word: (1) "pod" from the well- known music player iPod, or "playable on demand," and (2) "broadcast." Podcasts are one-way, noninteractive communications. According to *Wikipedia* (2011), "a podcast is a collection of digital media files which is distributed over the Internet, often using syndication feeds (e.g., RSS or Atom feeds) for playback on portable media players and computers." Once subscribed to, podcasts can be regularly distributed over the Internet or within a school's network and accessed with an iPod or a computer. The essential element of a podcast, what makes it "subscribable," is the RSS (Really Simple Syndication) feed. If you have a website or podcasting host that creates an RSS feed for you, you don't have to worry about this technical aspect of podcasting (see Chapter 2 for more about RSS feeds.). A podcast is an alternative learning form for students that may interest them more than just sitting and listening to the teacher lecture every day.

Why Use Podcasting?

There are many educational benefits of using podcasts for both teachers and students. Children acquire social skills by collaborating, learning to write, organizing, and delivering information when they have an authentic audience, and they enjoy themselves in the process. More specifically,

- Podcasting easily engages a population of diverse learners.
- Students can work together to script, record, and edit a podcast that can be stored and easily shared with a potentially worldwide audience. Knowing that there is a real-world audience gives students purpose and motivation to create a spectacular product.
- Students can edit and revise until what they say and how they say it is perfected.
- Students can save the podcast for other students, friends, and family members to listen to, learn from, and enjoy.
- For teachers, evaluating podcasts of the information students share can offer a very natural formative assessment tool. Teachers can assess student skills such as the effectiveness of the arguments, use of technology, and presentation skills.
- The process of putting together an audio recording is extremely valuable in that it brings together different curriculum areas, such as language arts, science, and social studies.

When students create a podcast to present an argument and provide the specific details to support it, they are learning to think, to be logical, and to process information effectively, as well as to communicate. They are also building twenty-first-century skills such as problem solving, collaboration, and the ability to gather and analyze data.

Classroom and Library Podcast Examples

An important aspect of beginning work with a new technology is to view examples of the tool being integrated into a lesson. This provides a model from which to get ideas for your own podcast. Review the following examples for different grade levels and subject areas. Kids now have a voice!

Example 1: Lunch Time Leaders

Since the fall of 2008, a group of students, with the help of their eighth-grade social studies teacher, has been interviewing experts during their lunch periods. Starting with candidates running for mayor of their city, they have expanded their interviews to people both near and far from local community leaders and business people to authors, educators, and even a firefighter. Many of the interviews are done using Skype (see Chapter 5) and broadcast live on their class wiki (see Chapter 3). You can visit their podcasts at http://lunchtimeleaders.podbean.com/ (see Figure 4.1).

Example 2: Portable Radio CA

Winner of Best 2010 Educational Podcast from Edublogs.edu, Podcasting from the Portables comes from Ottawa, Canada. The radio show is student-driven, with more than 250 kids participating to create regular episodes containing plays, mysteries, interviews, experiments, and more. The podcasts are placed on the class blog, and visitors can post comments. These fifth- and sixth-graders at two elementary schools are proud they have had almost 10,000 downloads. Listen to their podcasts (see Figure 4.2) at http://portableradio.edublogs.org/.

Example 3: ColeyCast

A pioneer in student podcasting since 1999, Mr. Brent Coley taught fifth grade at Tovashal Elementary School in California until 2011 when he became an administrator and has involved his students in creating podcasts on a number of topics in different subjects, including English settlements in North America, human body systems, facts about the United States, book trailers, and sentence structure, to name just a few. Check ColeyCast at www.mrcoley

> ➤ Find URLs for additional examples at various grade levels at Bev's website at http://www.neal-schuman.com/webclassroom.

.com/coleycast/index.htm for examples, as well as many tips to get started with podcasting. Notice the different podcasts in Figure 4.3.

Figure 4.1. Lunch Time Leaders

Source: Used by permission of Paul Bogush, Moran Middle School, Wallingford, CT.

Figure 4.2. Portable Radio CA

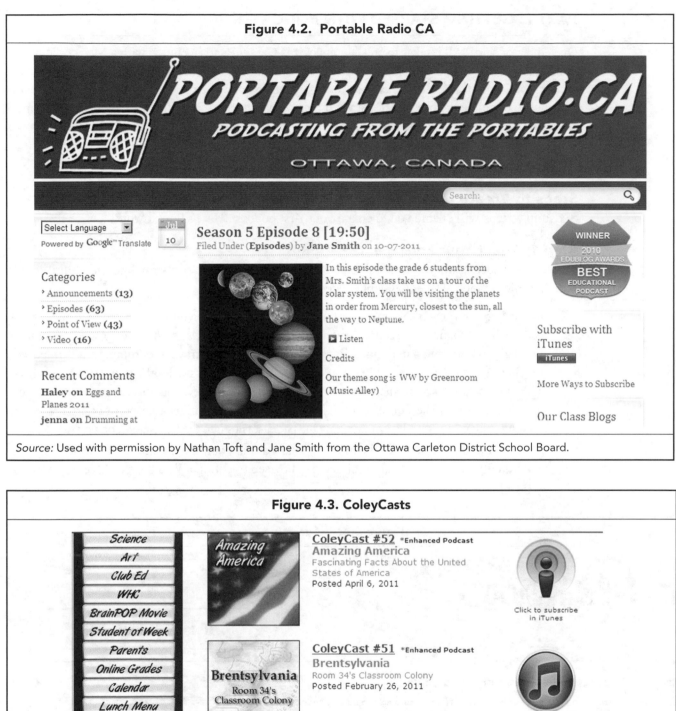

Source: Used with permission by Nathan Toft and Jane Smith from the Ottawa Carleton District School Board.

Figure 4.3. ColeyCasts

Source: Used by permission of Brent Coley; http://www.mrcoley.com/.

PART 2: GETTING STARTED WITH PODCASTS

One educator said, "All it takes to create a podcast is GarageBand (included with a Mac computer), a built-in microphone, and your students' creativity." Actually, although the technology is easy to learn, preparation is important. Educators must train students to know their audience, pick a theme, research their point, organize the presentation and, of course, practice. As in writing an essay, a podcast must have a beginning, middle, and end. Research may be necessary, and preparing the podcast requires students to work together. All of these tasks require students to think critically, communicate effectively, and collaborate with classmates—all learning activities unrelated to the technology!

Steps to Create a Podcast

Six simple steps will enable you to create your first podcast. Here's how it works.

Step 1: Select Your Equipment

To create a podcast, all you need is your own microphone, some software, and the ability to talk into that microphone. The equipment needed includes:

- *Recording equipment.* No matter what type of microphone you choose, try to find one that cancels background noise. A good microphone won't eliminate all of the background noise, but it will help to keep it to a minimum. Background noise can destroy a recording, so it is important to filter out as much as possible. Moreover, student presenters will talk at different volumes—some will be louder than others. One of the good solutions to level out discrepancies in volume is the Levelator from The Conversations Network (http://www.conversationsnetwork.org/levelator/). It is free and easy to use, by just dragging the podcast files into the Levelator icon on your desktop.
- *Editing equipment.* Some of the most popular editing equipment includes the following:
  - **Audacity** is a free software tool that can be used to edit in a Windows or Mac environment (see Figure 4.4).

Figure 4.4. Audacity

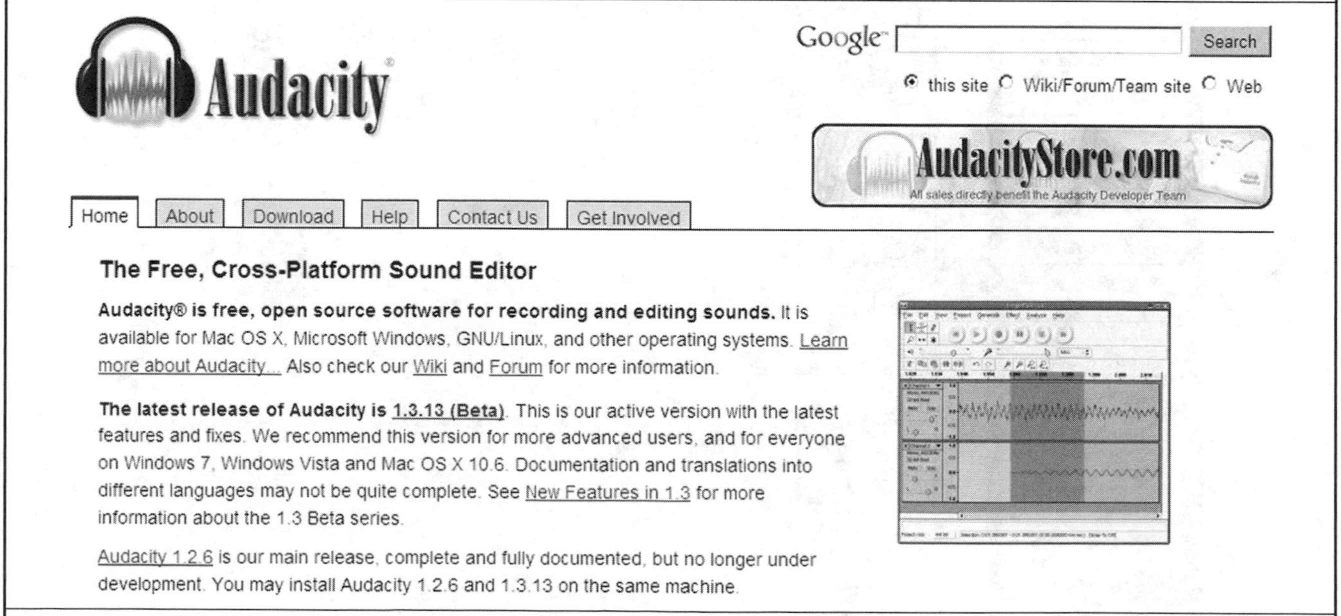

Source: Used by permission; http://audacity.sourceforge.net/copyright. "Audacity™" is a trademark of Dominic Mazzoni.

- **GarageBand**, popular with educators, comes free with Mac computers (http://www
  .apple.com/ilife/garageband).
- **VoiceThread**, also free, offers educators premium accounts with unlimited bandwidth and
  lets students comment from home, via audio or text, about pictures or documents
  (http://www.voicethread.com/). See Chapter 9 for more information.
- *Music.* Music can announce the introduction to your podcast, supply background, and provide
  transitions between different segments. Often, music is copyrighted and cannot be used without
  incurring cost. However, sites abound with royalty-free sounds, including Soundzabound
  (http://www.soundzabound.com/), and The FreeSound Project, a collaborative database of
  licensed sounds with a Creative Commons license (http://freesound.iua.upf.edu/index.php).
- Other equipment for uploading podcasts for distribution is also needed.
  - **Google Reader** (http://www.google.com/reader) lets educators sign up for RSS feeds and
    keep tabs on what is happening in any other classroom across the country, their subject
    area, teacher ideas, and more (see Figure 4.5).
  - **iTunes** (http://www.itunes.com/) for PC or Mac is a digital media player application for
    playing and organizing digital music and video files.

Step 2: Plan for Recording

Before students even think of stepping up to the microphone, much planning must be done. In fact,
preproduction may take over three-quarters of the time necessary to produce a podcast. Planning
puts the focus on learning, not on the technology. Several things need to be considered:

- *Consider the audience.* Who will listen to the podcast? Is it everyone in the school? Is it
  parents? Is it students in another state or at another grade level? Determining who exactly the
  audience is should help focus the podcast.
- *Name the podcast.* The podcast will need a name—the more creative, the better. Since listeners
  search podcasts on the Internet, an intriguing name can catch the eye of a prospective listener.
  Often names are added to each segment of the recording to emphasize the theme of the podcast.
- *Decide on the format.* Who will actually be heard in the recording? Should you have a host?
  What segments do you plan for the show? Will there be continuing episodes?

Figure 4.5. Google Reader

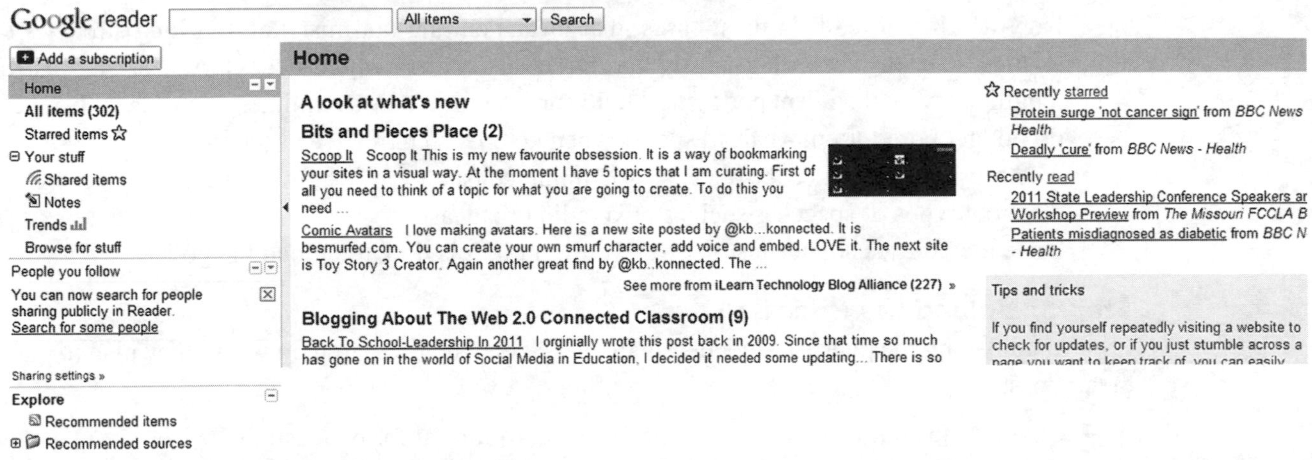

Source: Used by permission; http://www.google.com/. Google Reader™ is a trademark of Google, Inc.

- *Consider the length.* This will be based on your content and audience. Some teachers have everyone pair up in class. The pairs all write segments and present the segments to the entire class. The teacher and students then select which segments should be included in the podcast. This way everyone is involved, the podcast gets the best segments, and the recording will be an appropriate length.
- *Write a storyboard.* A script will allow students to know exactly what they are going to say, when they will speak, and whether they will speak alone or with a partner. Additionally, music and visuals should be planned at this time.

Step 3: Record the Podcast

While recording is the technical part of podcasting, preplanning before recording requires critical thinking, communication, and group work.

- Before students record, they should practice reading their scripts out loud, paying special attention to speaking loudly, clearly, and slowly. The speaker must learn to control his/her volume, speed, and fluency.
- Technically, speakers should start with a few sample recordings to test the software, adjust volume levels, and make sure everything works.
- Consider the following tips when recording:
  - Know your segment very well. Have it close to memorized.
  - Speak slowly and clearly so that your audience can understand you.
  - Do not touch or move the microphone. You will hear it on the recording.
  - Be quiet if you are not the speaker. The microphone is sensitive and will pick up any little noises in the background.
  - Avoid rustling your papers when at the microphone. Put the paper on the table if you need to read from it.
  - Be interested in what you are saying—your voice will show it if you're not.
  - Do not move around when speaking into the microphone; plant your feet.
  - Do not get too close to the microphone. It will distort your voice and your audience won't be able to understand you.

Step 4: Post-Process the Recording

The actual technical post-processing may be delegated to a small group of students, but all students working on a podcast should be listening and commenting on necessary changes.

- Now it's time to edit. In most cases, that means cutting out mistakes and long stretches of silence. Edit the recording wisely and rerecord sections where necessary. Check files for length, as typical student podcasts should run no more than 10 minutes at a time so listeners do not get bored. Remove dead spaces when no one is talking (see Figure 4.6).
- Add music to introduce the podcast. You might consider music between segments if there are different types of speeches such as on a radio broadcast.
- Once the podcast sounds just the way you want it, it is time to upload the podcast.

Step 5: Upload the Podcast

Prior to uploading the podcast, students should have done their research on where they plan to place the podcast.

- Convert the audio file to MP3 format, a standard format for podcasting.
- Upload the podcast files that include a description of your podcast, a link to the corresponding MP3 file, and other information. There are a number of websites that will hold your recording

Figure 4.6. Recording Wave

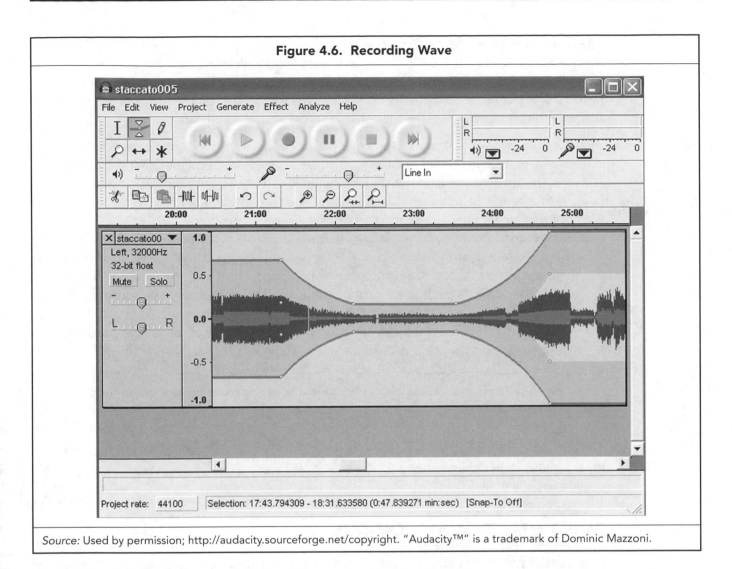

Source: Used by permission; http://audacity.sourceforge.net/copyright. "Audacity™" is a trademark of Dominic Mazzoni.

for free. Create a blog on a free website (e.g., Blogger, Google Sites) and post your material there so it is available for others. If your school has a website, this is another place to create a specific directory for the podcast. See Chapter 2 to see how to create a blog.

- An MP3 file contains information about the artist, album, genre, etc., stored in ID3 tags. Windows Media Player and iTunes use these tags to organize the MP3s, so you may want to add this information before uploading it.
- Test all files using any player to make sure they are ready for distribution.

Step 6: Publicize the Podcast

Now it's time for publicity for your podcast.

- Create a newsfeed for your podcasts. These are RSS files describing your podcasts that contain information about each and link to the MP3 files you have created.
- To help attract an audience to your podcast, submit your link to podcast directories such as iTunes or promote it on sites such as the Educational Podcast Directory (http://epnweb.org/). Such sites include links for downloading your podcast. By submitting your podcast to one of these directories, your podcast can be accessed by a large group of people.

> ➤ Review additional details about storyboarding and recording a podcast at Bev's website at http://www.neal-schuman.com/webclassroom.

Teacher Exercises: Now You Try It . . .

You have completed Parts 1 and 2 where you learned about podcasting technology and how it might help you teach your students. Take a moment now to get some hands-on practice with what you have learned. Complete the following exercises so you have a good understanding of the technology before putting it together with the educational aspects of creating a lesson.

1. Explore some of the tutorials for either GarageBand (http://www.apple.com/support/garage-band/) or Audacity (http://audacity.sourceforge.net/help/documentation). Write basic step-by-step instructions you and your students can follow to learn how to use the software.
2. Visit a couple of free music sites, listen to several clips, and note the names if they seem appropriate for introductory music. Try downloading a music clip.
3. Visit each of the example podcast sites in Part 1 and listen to the student podcasts, identifying what you like about the podcast, and what appears to be a good length (e.g., how long do you like as a listener?). Note the structure and what segments are used in each show. How do you think your students might react to participating in one and what might you do to prevent any unforeseen difficulties from arising? Reflect about these issues on your blog.
4. If you really feel confident, sign up using RSS to receive one of the podcasts that you find most meets your needs and with which you feel most comfortable.

> ➤ *More exercises are available at Bev's website at http://www.neal-schuman.com/ webclassroom.*

Now that you have had some personal experience with these technology tools, it's time to put them together with the important part, the educational value of integrating the technology with a content-based unit plan.

PART 3: PRACTICAL APPLICATIONS

An important part of the history curriculum in the upper elementary grades is the emphasis placed on settling the English colonies, where political values and institutions of the new nation were shaped. Life in New England formed the basis for self-government and the importance of freedom. Events leading up to the Revolutionary War present a dramatic story. As a result of the British imposing their will on the colonies, the strong reaction by the colonists, and a growing spirit of independence, Boston became a hotbed of strife over taxation and repression by the British Parliament.

This unit focuses on British taxation and the Boston Tea Party, events that had a far-reaching effect on efforts in the colonies toward freedom from Britain. However, it is important to link past to present. What do these events experienced in the 1700s have to do with life today? Students must be able to identify similarities and differences between the colonists' fight for freedom and actions taking place in today's world.

Unit Plan for Social Studies on the American Revolutionary War

This unit focuses on events leading up to the Revolutionary War and is designed to involve students in activities where they can research events such as the Stamp Act, Townshend Acts, and the Boston Tea Party through exploration of primary source materials, including newspapers, photos, interviews, diaries, autobiographies, and other resources. They will delve into the Coming of the American Revolution site on the Internet to view some primary sources that provide factual and visual representations of acts occurring in Boston during 1773, what the significance was, and how the

---

Lesson Clips

Sixth-graders at Lincoln Middle School in Santa Monica, California, have found a way to learn math and become teachers as well. At Mathtrain.com (http://mathtrain.com/), students post their own podcasts and vodcasts on MathTrain.TV to show others how to solve math problems on everything from proportions to multiplication, fractions, and algebraic equations. Started by their teacher to explain a math problem a student didn't understand, Eric Marcos created a two-minute video example showing the student how to solve the homework problem. Students jumped at the chance to create their own short tutorials using screen captures and podcasts (see Figure 4.7).

Figure 4.7. MathTrain.TV

Simple Interest our 2nd Video remix from 2007
This was our 2nd student-created video we aired. Billy Billy created it in 2007. We added some music to this release.
Rating ☆☆☆☆☆   Views: (1304)   Duration: (00:02:31)   Uploaded: 26-02-11
Tags: BillyBilly simple interest 2007 2nd mathtrain...

Percents with papatom
Watch papatom explain how to find percents.
Rating ★★★★★   Views: (2207)   Duration: (00:02:26)   Uploaded: 12-02-11
Tags: percent papatom Lincoln student mathcast math...

Binary with Drew
Lincoln Middle School student, Drew, shows us binary numbers
Rating ☆☆☆☆☆   Views: (1468)   Duration: (00:02:33)   Uploaded: 14-12-10
Tags: binary drew numbers base 10 2 powers convert ...

Inequalities with Vincent
Vincent makes her debut. She shows us how to work with an inequality problem.
Rating ☆☆☆☆☆   Views: (2002)   Duration: (00:01:24)   Uploaded: 30-11-10
Tags: inequality solve student Vincent Lincoln prea...

Source: Used by permission of Eric Marcos, Lincoln Middle School.

---

results affected actions of people in the United States and other countries today. Once students feel comfortable with the source material, they will begin to preplan their podcasts. The tasks in the unit can be adapted with varying degrees of sophistication for upper elementary, middle school, and high school levels.

Students begin with the broad study of events leading up to the Boston Tea Party in 1773. This will require research of primary source documents to learn what factors caused colonists to rebel, why they reacted as they did, and what effects their actions had on the mother country England. Students will study the events in historical context so they understand the economic, social, and political conditions of the times. As the culminating activity, students will create podcasts playing the roles of newspaper reporters interviewing citizens of Boston, leaders who initiated the Boston Tea Party, tea party participants, and loyalists.

This unit bases activities and tasks on national standards and state framework goals and objectives. It illustrates some of the resources that are available for projects on the Internet, offers suggestions on how to integrate them into the social studies curriculum, and requires that students become familiar with Web 2.0 technology. Finally, it provides a model for creative teachers to use as they review their own subject matter for other units and as they tailor the activities to meet the needs of their own students.

Step 1: Connect to the Standards—What Should Be Taught?

The Boston Tea Party in 1773, an important event in American history, represented one of the first significant rebellions against British rule of the American colonies. It was an act of courage and a demonstration against taxation without representation.

The study of American history can be traced through the K–12 curriculum. In fifth grade, as part of U.S. history and geography, students learn about events leading up to the Revolutionary War—the causes, effects, and why these changes occurred. In eleventh grade, students draw on their earlier studies of the rise of democratic ideas as the context in which this nation was founded, especially the ideological origins of the American Revolution and its grounding in the democratic political tradition. Thus, the curriculum provides for an integrated and sequential framework throughout students' school years.

Social studies and English/language arts standards are accommodated in this unit:

- Researches multiple perspectives to take a position on a public or historical issue.
- Understands that significant historical events in the United States have implications for current decisions and influence the future.
- Gathers and uses information for research purposes.
- Connects learning of the past with the present.
- Supports a variety of content-appropriate teaching methods that engage students actively in the learning process.
- Emphasizes critical thinking skills, as well as reading, writing, speaking, and listening.

Additionally, the *National Educational Technology Standards* (NETS; ISTE, 2007, 2008), so necessary to work and live in the twenty-first century, are also an integral part of this unit.

Step 2: Identify General Goals and Specific Objectives

As part of their growth and development throughout their school careers, students will work independently, competitively, and cooperatively on tasks and projects. During this unit, the primary focus will be students working cooperatively to perform research and create podcasts.

Goals

At the end of this unit, students will be able to:

- conduct research on issues and interests by generating ideas and questions, and by posing problems;
- share ideas in small and large groups; and
- use technology for research and presentation.

Content-Related Objectives

After performing activities in this unit, students will be able to:

- gather, evaluate, and synthesize data from a variety of sources (e.g., print and nonprint texts, artifacts, people) to communicate their discoveries in ways that suit their purpose and audience;
- investigate events leading to the Revolutionary War to explain the reasons for colonists' decisions to take matters into their own hands, and answer questions such as: Why do people want to be free? How can citizens be heard by their government? What were the causes of the American Revolution?;

- describe the Boston Tea Party, identify historical events leading up to the conflict, and discuss cause and effect relationships;
- form opinions based on critical examination of relevant information;
- write scripts for their podcasts; and
- present in podcasts what they have uncovered from inquiry and research relevant to past events and how they affect future ones.

Technology Objectives

Based on NETS, students will:

- work together to create podcasts;
- organize their podcasts to describe events leading up to the Boston Tea Party;
- record podcast segments on events leading to the Revolutionary War;
- determine how people can cause change today; and
- use technology to publish their podcast.

Note: Depending on the age of the students, the teacher may need to edit the podcast.

Step 3: Gather Materials

For this unit, educators will have students look at different resources to collect information for podcasts they will create. Some resources may be found on the Internet or in the school or public libraries. Students will:

- review primary source material including photos, audio, newspapers, and other historical documents (see Table 4.1 for appropriate URLs); and
- seek out secondary sources such as oral interviews with relatives, family members, and friends, as well as pictures, records, and other documents.

Step 4: Create Sample Activities

There are four basic aspects to the unit:

1. Learning about primary source materials
2. Understanding the problems and conditions existing in the United States prior to the Revolutionary War
3. Comparing and contrasting conditions in the 1770s regarding taxes and representation to those of today
4. Using podcasts to organize and present information they have collected for a specific purpose and audience

Activities to Introduce the Unit

At the beginning of the unit it is important to draw upon students' prior knowledge. Have them think back to what they remember about the American Revolution. Inform students that one of the items that Britain heavily taxed was tea, and because of this taxation without representation, the Boston Tea Party occurred. Using primary sources, students will then explore what happened at the "party."

The following tasks will review some of the acts, taxes, and events and increase students' knowledge of primary sources, as well as events leading to the Revolutionary War.

- For a preassessment, as a class students will answer the following questions:
  ◦ A Loyalist in Boston in the 1770s was a person who supported King George III and the British Parliament. What reasons would a Loyalist give for supporting the King and Parliament?
  ◦ A Patriot in Boston in the 1770s was a person who wanted American independence from Britain. What reasons would a Patriot give for wanting independence?

Table 4.1. URLs for Boston Tea Party Unit	
URL	**Description**
http://www.history.com/topics/boston-tea-party/	History of Boston Tea Party
http://www.eyewitnesstohistory.com/teaparty.htm	Historical information on Boston Tea Party
http://www.loc.gov/teachers/usingprimarysources/whyuse.html	Why use primary sources?
http://www.youtube.com/watch?v=GJ-FWHN3ljl	Video showing cartoon feature of Boston Tea Party
http://www.youtube.com/watch?v=m2szfaluHoM&feature=related	Boston Tea Party video
http://www.kidport.com/reflib/usahistory/american revolution/Video/BostonTeaParty.htm	Boston Tea Party read by kids
http://www.eyewitnesstohistory.com/teaparty.htm	George Hewes's eyewitness account of Boston Tea Party
http://teachhistory.com/2009/12/16/primary-source-audio-podcast-the-boston-tea-party/	Podcasts about Boston Tea Party
http://www.ehow.com/about_5056994_were-causes-boston-tea-party.html	Causes of Boston Tea Party
http://www.ehow.com/about_4572094_did-boston-tea-party-lead.html	Effects of Boston Tea Party
http://www.ehow.com/list_5977989_ideas-boston-tea-party-diorama.html	Information for reenactment of Boston Tea Party
http://www.youtube.com/watch?v=GJ-FWHN3ljl http://www.youtube.com/watch?v=GkNObgK43Z4&feature=related	Liberty Kids on the Boston Tea Party (videos)
http://www.youtube.com/watch?v=slx8CCjoL4E&feature=related	Sons of Liberty (video)
http://www.youtube.com/watch?v=fALa2zjlSN0&feature=related http://www.youtube.com/watch?v=zs86WYACbr8&feature=related	Intolerable Acts (videos)

- Watch several videos on events during this time period (see Table 4.1).
- Brainstorm issues and conflicts students identified after watching the videos. Map out the economic, political, and personal reasons for colonists' dissatisfaction with British rule. (Students will most likely include the ideas of "taxation without representation," higher prices paid by the colonists for goods because of British trading policies, and restrictions on manufacturing and selling colonial products.)
- Create a cluster diagram. Map out all reasons for the issues between the colonists, the British government, and the Loyalists (see Figure 4.8).

Activities to Use during the Unit
Activities to be completed during the unit will be based on both the content and technology objectives. In teams of four, students will select from the following:

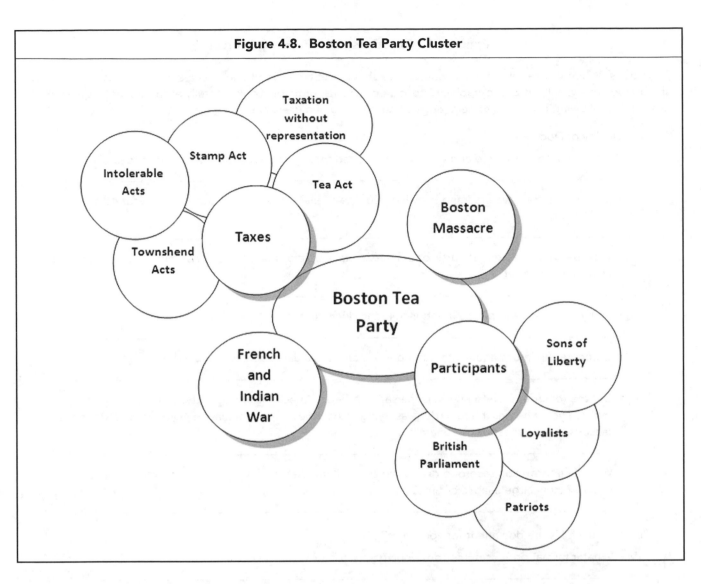

Figure 4.8. Boston Tea Party Cluster

- Review primary sources on events leading to the Boston Tea Party (e.g., published documents, unpublished documents, photographs, and interviews) (http://www.masshist.org/revolution/). Use questions (see Figure 4.9) to analyze the sources they reviewed.
- Read a document and in groups draw up a list of what political tactics (economic protest, public protest, written protest) the colonists used to defeat British taxation.
- Examine important dates of a variety of events including: Stamp Act, Townshend Acts, Boston Massacre, East India Company monopoly, Boston Tea Party, Intolerable Acts, Paul Revere's ride, and the Lexington and Concord battles. Create a rough draft of a timeline with at least one sentence for each event. This will help students understand the context for the Boston Tea Party. As a class, decide how many events will be placed on the timeline. Use Google Docs to create the timeline (see Chapter 7).
- Draw a political cartoon for a newspaper representing the Boston Tea Party. This activity enables students to adopt a particular point of view, such as a Boston colonist, King George III, or a Loyalist.
- In groups, express British, Patriot, and Loyalist points of view in a discussion/debate of British-American relations in the late 1760s and early 1770s. Each group will select one of the issues identified in the cluster diagram and give three supporting arguments for each position.

Figure 4.9. Questions about Primary Sources

Directions: When you review primary sources, you should not take everything you see or hear at face value. You should look analytically at photographs, historical documents, or maps. Look carefully at the document and try to answer the following questions to help judge its authenticity and usefulness.

A. Quality of Document

- Who created the source and why? Was it created through a thoughtful, deliberate process?

  _____

- Did the creator have firsthand knowledge of the event? Or, did the creator report what others saw and heard?

  _____

- Was the creator a neutral party, or did he/she have opinions or interests that might have influenced what was recorded?

  _____

- Verify the dates and places mentioned in the document.

  _____

- Compare the information with other primary and secondary sources. Is it valid?

  _____

- Did the recorder wish to inform or persuade others? (Check the words in the source. The words may tell you whether the recorder was trying to be objective or persuasive.) Did the recorder have reasons to be honest or dishonest?

  _____

- Was the information recorded during the event, immediately after the event, or after some lapse of time? How large a lapse of time?

  _____

B. How useful is the document for your topic?

- What information is useful for developing your topic?

  _____

- How will you use the information in your research?

  _____

- Is any information biased or incorrect?

  _____

- Write a newspaper editorial about the Tea Act.
- Create a Glogster poster that represents visual and factual representations of highlights leading up to the Revolutionary War for their class wiki page (see Chapter 3 for more on wikis).

Culminating Project. Plan and create a podcast as the final project. With research completed, the focus is now on preplanning for the podcasts. The goal is to get all students to participate, whether in writing the script, presenting the material, post-processing, or publishing. During these activities students will work together in pairs:

- Create the content for the podcast segment on a storyboard. Make sure to include parts for the broadcaster/host at the beginning of the segment and introductions for each participant.

- Write interview questions and answers. In pairs, assume the roles of interviewer and Boston Tea Party character and prepare a script of questions for the interviewer and answers for the interviewee (e.g., native Indian). Both questions and answers will be used during the podcast. See sample interview questions at http://teachers.ewrsd.k12.nj.us/savedoff/journalism/ miscellaneous/interviewing/ good_interview_questions.htm.
- Create an introduction for the podcast that provides some background and specific details about the topic.
- Practice once the script is finalized.
- Create podcasts to place on the class wiki with other information they have assembled during the unit.
- Work together in pairs on the technical aspects of the podcast:
  - *Assume a role in the podcast.* Host the podcast, name the podcast, write the teaser that introduces the podcast, deliver a segment, or assume other possible roles (e.g., compiling visuals).
  - *Select music for the podcast* and determine where it will be placed (e.g., beginning, between segments, end).
  - *Assemble equipment,* including the room in which to broadcast, download software, if necessary, decide where to locate the podcast, create an account with iTunes.
  - *Prepare the site* to host the podcast. Assemble the graphics (e.g., Glogster poster, cartoons) already created. These will be used as part of the wiki page where podcasts are placed.

> ➤ *Activities in social studies and language arts are available at Bev's website at http://www.neal-schuman.com/webclassroom.*

Activities to Be Used as Follow-Up

As extension activities, have students try one of the following:

- Dramatize a reenactment of the Boston Tea Party. Have students select roles (e.g., Indian, Samuel Adams, member of the crowd, Loyalist, British citizen).
- Create additional podcasts for the class wiki as they explore other information about the Revolutionary War.
- Based on what students learned from their research into events faced by the colonists in the eighteenth century, compare/contrast people's taxation problems past and present. Research information about other tea partiers through modern history, including the latest tea party movement and tea party protests. Answer questions such as: What does this movement have in common with the Boston Tea Party? Why do some people feel it necessary to identify with the colonists in the eighteenth century? Select three resources illustrating pro and con arguments involving the current tea party movement. In pairs, choose one issue, select one side (pro or con), and provide information to support the position. Create a podcast explaining your position. Check the following URLs for help:
  - http://en.wikipedia.org/wiki/Boston_Tea_Party
  - http://en.wikipedia.org/wiki/Tea_Party_protests

Step 5: Evaluate What Was Learned

Educators who are currently using podcasts in their classrooms have found that students like this activity. Because there are several different types of activities, evaluation needs to take place as students are performing these various tasks. You will be assessing the content they learned about the Boston Tea Party and other events prior to the Revolutionary War, their interaction in groups, and their ability to use both web resources and podcasting. It is also important for students to participate in the evaluation process. Some possible evaluation strategies for each task in this unit include:

1. *Primary sources.*
   - Have students write blog posts about a primary source (speech, news article, photo), taking the position of someone who lived at the time the source was created. Explain how the source supports or challenges a commonly accepted conclusion about a time or event in history.
   - Select primary source documents to create a museum display about a historical topic. Write captions for the items and justify the documents that were selected.
   - Prepare a visual display (poster, magazine cover, illustrated timeline) that highlights the most important points to be gained from the primary sources under study.
2. *Podcast.* Use the Podcast rubric to assess the four parts of the podcast (see Figure 4.10):
   - Content and organization, writing quality of the interview, including the introduction, questions and answers, and conclusion.
   - Visuals and music.
   - Technical side of the podcast, including recording, podcast webpage and delivery.
   - Group work, including working well with teammates, contributing to team effort, and equally to the workload.

Figure 4.10. Podcast Rubric

A podcast has four main sections that need to be evaluated—the content (i.e., the script), the total presentation (e.g., visuals, music, editing), the delivery, and teamwork. This rubric identifies different parts of each section listed. Separate rubrics could also be created for each section.

Category	Exemplary 9 points	Proficient 6 points	Partially Proficient 3 points	Incomplete 0 points
Interview content and organization	Catchy and clever introduction. Provides relevant information and establishes a clear purpose engaging the listener immediately.	Describes the topic and engages the audience as the introduction proceeds.	Somewhat engaging (covers well-known topic), and provides a vague purpose.	Irrelevant or inappropriate topic that minimally engages listener. Does not include an introduction or the purpose is vague and unclear.
	Tells who is speaking, date the podcast was produced, and where the speaker is located.	Tells most of the following: who is speaking, date of the podcast, and location of speaker.	Alludes to who is speaking, date of the podcast, and location of speaker.	Speaker is not identified. No production date or location of the speaker is provided.
	Creativity and original content enhance the purpose of the podcast in an innovative way. Accurate information and succinct concepts are presented.	Accurate information is provided succinctly.	Some information is inaccurate or long-winded.	Information is inaccurate.
	Keeps focus on the topic.	Stays on the topic.	Occasionally strays from the topic.	Does not stay on the topic.
	Conclusion clearly summarizes key information.	Conclusion summarizes information.	Conclusion vaguely summarizes key information.	No conclusion is provided.

(Continued)

	Figure 4.10. Podcast Rubric (Continued)			
Category	**Exemplary 9 points**	**Proficient 6 points**	**Partially Proficient 3 points**	**Incomplete 0 points**
Delivery	Well rehearsed, smooth delivery in a conversational style.	Rehearsed, smooth delivery.	Appears unrehearsed with uneven delivery.	Delivery is hesitant and choppy and sounds like the presenter is reading.
	Uses a clear voice and correct, precise pronunciation of terms.	Voice is clear; pronounces most words correctly.	Voice is low; incorrectly pronounces terms.	Mumbles, incorrectly pronounces terms, and speaks too quietly to be heard.
Visuals and music	Creates a unique and effective presentation that enhances what is being said in the podcast and follows the rules for quality graphic design.	Relates to the audio, reinforces content, and demonstrates functionality.	Sometimes enhances the quality and understanding of the presentation.	Unrelated to the podcast. Artwork is inappropriate to podcast.
	Music enhances the mood, quality, and understanding of the presentation.	Music provides supportive background to the podcast.	Music provides somewhat distracting background to the podcast.	Music is distracting to the presentation.
Presentation	Recorded in a quiet environment without background noise and distractions.	Recorded in a quiet environment with minimal background noise and distractions.	Recorded in a semi-quiet environment with some background noise and distractions.	Recorded in a noisy environment with constant background noise and distractions.
	Volume of voice, music and effects enhance the presentation.	Volume is acceptable.	Volume is occasionally inconsistent.	Volume changes are highly distracting.
	Podcast length keeps the audience interested and engaged.	Podcast length keeps audience listening.	Podcast length is somewhat long or somewhat short to keep audience engaged.	Podcast is either two long or too short to keep the audience engaged.
Teamwork	Performs all duties of assigned team role and contributes knowledge, opinions, and skills to share with the team. Always does the work.	Performs nearly all duties or assigned team role and contributes knowledge, opinions, and skills to share with the team. Completes most of the assigned work.	Performs a few duties of assigned team role and contributes a small amount of knowledge, opinions, and skills to share with the team. Completes some of the assigned work.	Does not perform any duties of assigned team role and does not contribute knowledge, opinions or skills to share with the team. Relies on others to do the work.

3. *Self-Reflection.* Have students complete the Self-Reflection Checklist so they identify how well they accomplished various tasks in the unit (see Figure 4.11).

Summary

This chapter combines not only podcasting technology but also the Web 2.0 tools we learned about in Chapters 2 and 3—blogs, RSS feeds, and wikis. Podcasts can be set up on blogs or wikis. When a listener subscribes to a podcast via an RSS feed, any new podcast episode will automatically be downloaded to the subscriber's computer. All four tools work together to make communication among educators and their students an easy process.

Figure 4.11. Self-Reflection Checklist

Reflect on the work you did to create the podcast, including writing the script, delivering the podcast, working on the technical end of creating the presentation, and working with your teammates. Then, answer the questions below.

1. About the Podcast:

   • What I heard that surprised me was

   _____

   _____

   • Something I learned from the podcast was

   _____

   _____

   • One thing I thought was important from the interviews was

   _____

   _____

   • From what I heard and read, I have a question or would like to know more about

   _____

   _____

2. As a group, assess whether you worked well with your teammates, contributed to the team effort, and shouldered work equally. Answer the following questions:

   • Did you do your best?

   _____

   _____

   • Did you work hard, enjoy the project, and feel good about what you completed?

   _____

   _____

   • How much did you contribute to the group's project?

   _____

   _____

   • Did you finish your work on time?

   _____

   _____

   • If you had to do it again, would you do anything differently?

   _____

   _____

Teacher Exercises: Now You Try It . . .

Now that you've reviewed in detail a unit plan that incorporates podcasts, try the following exercises. Be sure to focus your attention on how the technology can enhance student learning.

1. Review several more podcasts in your subject area and grade level to get ideas on how other educators are using podcasts in their classrooms. Check the General URLs in Table 4.2.

Table 4.2. General URLs for Podcasting	
URL	Description
http://learninginhand.com/podcasting-booklet/	Podcasting for Teachers and Students, updated in 2009
http://mrcoley.com/coleycast/podcastingresources.htm	Podcasting resources
http://epnweb.org/	Education Podcasting Network-directory of school-produced and educationally relevant podcasts
http://www.poducateme.com/guide/	Guide to podcasting in education
http://www.det.wa.edu.au/education/cmis/eval/curriculum/ict/podcasts/	Podcasts in the classroom from the Washington Department of Education
http://theedublogger.com/2009/05/29/what-everybody-ought-to-know-about-podcasting-part-ii/	Basics of podcasting, including setting up an RSS feed and hosting a podcast
http://www.how-to-podcast-tutorial.com/00-podcast-tutorial-four-ps.htm	Four steps to podcasting

2. Sign up for a podcast service.
3. Create a simple lesson plan that focuses on either language arts, history objectives, or both. This should be one you think you can implement in your classroom at your grade level.

> ➤ *Review additional exercises at Bev's website at http://www.neal-schuman.com/webclassroom.*

CONCLUSION

To make podcasting a success at a school, educators must incorporate it into the classroom routine and motivate their students to produce podcasts regularly. The goal is to make students look forward to creating them. Thus, podcasts need to be included as part of lesson development. Podcasts are a great way to expand the learning environment of your class, and a surefire way to make the learning experience authentic and personally meaningful for your students.

REFERENCES AND FURTHER READING

Bernard, Sara. 2011. "Move Over Sal Khan: Sixth Graders Create Their Own Math Videos!" *Mind/Shift*. KQED. August 11. http://mindshift.kqed.org/2011/08/move-over-sal-khan-sixth-graders-create-their-own-math-videos/.

California State Department of Education. 2009. *English—Language Arts Framework for California Public Schools: Kindergarten Through Grade Twelve*. Sacramento: California State Department of Education.

ISTE (The International Society for Technology in Education). 2007. *National Educational Technology Standards for Students*. Eugene, OR: The International Society for Technology in Education. http://www .iste.org/standards/nets-for-students/nets-student-standards-2007.aspx.

ISTE (The International Society for Technology in Education). 2008. *National Educational Technology Standards for Teachers*. Eugene, OR: The International Society for Technology in Education. http://www .iste.org/standards/nets-for-teachers/nets-for-teachers-2008.aspx.

National Council for the Social Studies. 2010. *Curriculum Standards for Social Studies: A Framework for Teaching, Learning, and Assessment*. Silver Spring, MD: National Council for the Social Studies.

Wikipedia. 2011. "Podcast." Wikimedia Foundation. Last modified October 31. http://en.wikipedia.org/ wiki/Podcast.

CHAPTER 5

Opening Your Classrooms to the World via Skype

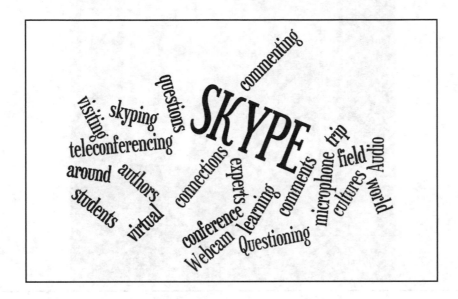

PART 1: IDEAS AND INSIGHTS

Looking for ways to get students excited about learning a language, about reading, writing, and books about a science innovation? Connect your class with authors, experts in subjects you are teaching, native language speakers, and more. With videoconferencing, students can learn from other students, connect with other cultures, and expand their knowledge in amazing ways. The most well-known is Skype, a free Internet telephone service allowing you to chat, share files and hyperlinks, and make conference calls, as well as see each other on video if both parties have a Skype account. It is available via a PC or Mac.

Skype has dramatically increased its numbers of users since its inception in 2003 and allowed educators to open their classrooms to the world (see Figure 5.1). For example, in mid-2010, an average of 124 million users connected per month, and at peak times approximately 23 million were using Skype simultaneously. Apple's iChat and Google Talk also offer free videoconferencing capabilities.

Why has videoconferencing become an integral tool for K–12 educators? Educators and students alike offer their opinions:

"Skyping, skyping: it's to my liking." (Author Marsha Diane Arnold)

"I like skyping. My favorite part is when the author reads from the book." (Elementary student)

"My students absolutely loved it!" (Second language teacher)

"It's so amazing how we do this." (Third-grader from Brewer, Maine)

Figure 5.1. Opening Classrooms to the World

Objectives of This Chapter

This chapter is designed for K–12 students for use in most subject areas. Although the unit plan focuses on elementary grades, it can be adapted for other levels. After reading Chapter 5 and working through the exercises, teachers and librarians will be able to:

- state uses for implementing a videoconference call;
- find skyping partners;
- explain and implement tasks before, during, and following a Skype call;
- create a lesson plan to use with a videoconference; and
- guide students through activities to learn questioning and commenting techniques.

Glossary

Review the following terms before starting the chapter to fully understand the concepts discussed.

broadband Internet access: A high data rate connection to the Internet.
KWL: A graphic organizer, which tracks what a student knows (K), wants to know (W), and has learned (L) about a topic, and can be used before, during, and after research.
Skype: A software application that allows users to make voice calls and videoconferences over the Internet.
skyping: Making a voice or videoconference over the Internet using Skype.
videoconference: a set of interactive telecommunication technologies that allows two or more locations to interact via two-way video and audio transmissions simultaneously.
webcam: A video camera that feeds its images in real time to a computer or computer network.

Implications for Education

Skype is used in education across the globe every day, from virtual global classroom visits to a boy who goes to school every day via Skype to conversations taking your class on a virtual field trip every week or visiting 80 schools in the Around the World with 80 Schools project (Tolisano, 2009a). The number of schools using Skype increases daily. Educators teach students at the early primary level to collaborate with each other while learning how to communicate and appreciate differences in appearance, culture, traditions, language, dialects, and countries. Students work on cooperative projects, show-and-tell, chat informally about their school, build communication skills among language learners, and report the news, to name some activities. Classes interview guest experts or visitors. Via Skype, students at home with extended illness connect with their class, others go on virtual field trips, and some participate in competitions (spelling bees, etc.). The learning opportunities are endless!

> ➤ *Review Bev's website at http://www.neal-schuman .com/webclassroom to learn more about Skype.*

Why Use Videoconferencing in the Classroom?

Many teachers complain about their isolation in their classrooms. Skype provides an alternative. K–12 educators currently skyping offer some reasons:

- Students from different countries connect to raise global awareness. Different cultures, time zones, holidays, traditions, opposite seasons, and language all enable students to learn more about our increasingly smaller world.
- Students expand their knowledge and address different learning styles by receiving or sharing information about content they have been studying, by viewing scientific demonstrations, and by reading student poetry or stories with other student classes or experts.
- By connecting live with a tourist in another country, students can see volcanoes, llamas in Peru, or native villagers and ask questions about what they are viewing.
- Students can practice public speaking and/or language skills.
- Talking to eyewitnesses, such as at natural disasters (Katrina hurricane on the U.S. Gulf coast, a rumbling earthquake in New Zealand, or a disastrous tsunami in Japan) provides a live experience.
- Students are able to participate in debates, discussions, or literature circles with other classes locally and around the world.

Learning with Skype Videoconferencing

The opportunity not only to talk to students from distant places but to visit with them visually makes for exciting educating. However, to justify dedicating class time to videoconferences, skyping experiences must target specific educational goals.

The number of Skype visits has increased in K–12 classrooms and libraries, and the purposes for a call have diversified from just saying hello to conferences with NASA scientists, authors and illustrators, and classrooms worldwide, to language instruction. Some examples illustrate these uses.

Example 1: Connecting with Classrooms Globally and Teaching One Another

Learning from others and teaching one another can happen when you connect classrooms globally or in different states. For example, a seventh-grade class in Florida composed of Jewish students connected via Skype through the Around the World with 80 Schools network to the Khartoum American School in Sudan with mostly Muslim students (see Figure 5.2). The goal of a series of calls was to learn from one another about different religions. Interactive questioning among the students brought out similarities and differences between Jewish and Muslim religions. They discussed basic beliefs among the two: common beliefs, ceremonies, prayer shawls, the story of Abraham, and more. Following the Skype call, the seventh-graders wrote blog posts about the experience. Here's one: "Hopefully, technology can bring us together so we can see the good and the similarities in each other, instead of the differences." See more about this call at http://langwitches.org/blog/2010/05/19/learning-with-from-and-about-each-other/.

Example 2: Skyping an Author

Developed by two librarians, Skype an Author Network (http://skypeanauthor.wetpaint.com/) is designed to provide K–12 teachers and librarians with a way to connect authors, books, and young readers through virtual visits. A typical call of 10 to 20 minutes is usually free and includes a bit about the author, student questions about the book they are reading, and perhaps a short reading from the book. There is usually a charge for more in-depth meetings, depending on the author.

In a university children's literature class, the professor introduced the idea of using Skype to her students. Two students, who were teaching first and fourth grades, agreed to incorporate a Skype event into their literature study. The first-grade teacher communicated with a children's book illustrator, LeUyen Pham, who sent the class some of her illustrated books so students could study her medium, color, style, and content. Prior to the call, the first-graders discussed the illustrations in terms of warm and cool colors and full bleed versus framed—quite a mouthful for these youngsters. The teacher also communicated with Pham and together they set the content for the call (see Figure 5.3).

During the call, using a Japanese brush pen, the guest demonstrated creating characters based on the students. She turned one student into a cat, another into a spider, and another into a lion. Students then asked questions they had created in advance. Pham also referred to some illustrations created by the first-graders the teacher had scanned and sent to her. Students couldn't believe that she was holding their very own artwork!

Example 3: Meeting an Expert

Learning from an expert drives home the importance of events in science, geology, space, and more. During a trip to Antarctica to test a new drill for use on a possible future mission to Mars, Arwen Davé, a NASA engineer on the IceBite project, connected with Mr. Palassou's class of fifth-

---

Figure 5.2. Around the World with 80 Schools

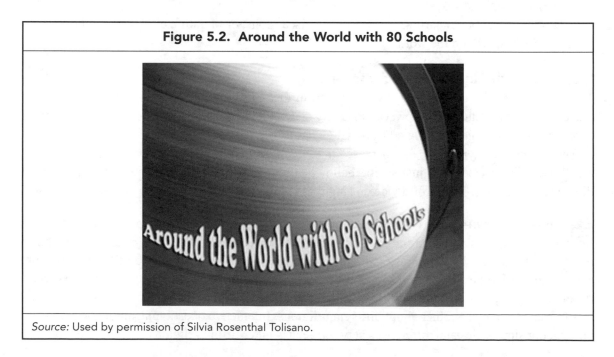

Source: Used by permission of Silvia Rosenthal Tolisano.

Figure 5.3. Skype Illustrator Call

graders from Valley View School in Pleasanton, California (http://www.astrobio.net/index.php?
option=com_expedition&task=detail&id=3692). The exciting event via a Skype connection enabled
the team to talk to the students and the students to watch and listen to activity in Antarctica as it
happened. At least a dozen students actually took turns issuing commands to the IceBreaker drill in
Antarctica, and at the same time IceBite team members in Antarctica talked to the students, filling in
details about what was taking place on their end of the operation. The result was the drill collected
several samples that were sent back to California for analysis, some to the NASA Ames Research
Center, and some to the students (see Figure 5.4).

From the fifth-graders' perspective, the whole experience was "off the charts" exciting. One
student was inspired to think about the possibility of being someone who works for NASA because
she never knew that being a scientist could be so much fun. Another student who operated the drill
commented: "It was really cool how when you pressed the button and you did 'Send Command' it
actually worked in a place really far away." Palassou encourages bringing scientists and K–12
teachers together in the field to develop hands-on science education (see Figure 5.5).

Figure 5.4. Antarctica

Figure 5.5. Fifth-Graders Meeting Experts

Example 4: Learning through Virtual Field Trips

With school budgets being slashed and gasoline prices rising, class field trips are at a minimum. Skype provides an opportunity for virtual field trips. A broadcast journalism high school class in Howe, Oklahoma, created one such experience that they then shared via Skype with a sixth-grade class in Michigan. The field trip took students on a treasure hunt to Indian mounds in Oklahoma. Students at Howe explored the Spiro Mounds in eastern Oklahoma, considered by archaeologists to be one of the most important pre-Columbian sites in the United States, spanning from 1200 AD to the early twentieth century. This virtual learning partnership expanded tenth-graders' interest in the pre-Columbian history of their own communities and state. By simulating an excavation on a gelatin mold, students learned how archeologists excavate sites (see Figure 5.6).

Prior to the Skype call the sixth-grade class read about the "Mounds." Journalism students presented their virtual field trip with each student taking a role, including having the Jello Mold Excavation explained by "Dr. Dirt" and his assistant "Lucy Looter." After the presentation, sixth-graders worked on follow-up activities to reinforce what they had heard and seen, including creating a model of an Indian village, making a three-dimensional map, and writing a story describing life as a farmer living near the mounds. See the entire project at http://web.mac.com/tammygparks/VFT_Creations/About_VFT.html, and view the video they created at http://www.vimeo.com/6705027. Both tenth- and sixth-grade students enjoyed the virtual field trip:

> "There was nothing boring about the video conference. I learned that the mounds were buried with 'Spiroan Chiefs,' when they died the mound just kept getting higher and higher." (Sixth-grader Amanda)

> "I had a lot of fun producing this as being a teacher. It's a hard job, and I have come to understand why teachers can get frustrated sometimes with students." (Eleventh-grader Samantha)

Figure 5.6. Tenth-Graders–Sixth-Graders Virtual Field Trip

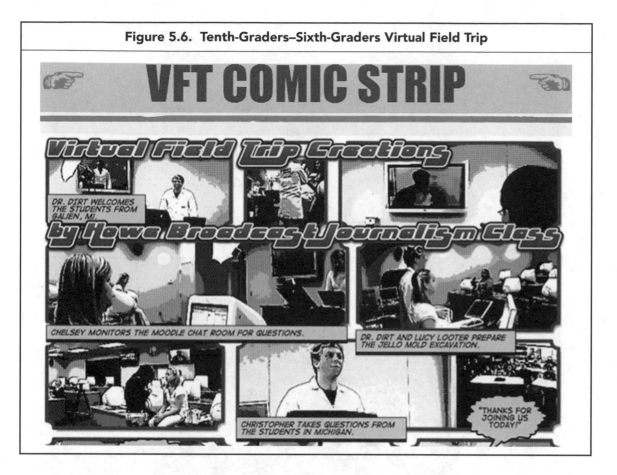

Example 5: Understanding Each Other's Culture

Introduce your students to new ways of seeing the world with a cultural exchange between your class and another classroom anywhere in the world. According to the Partnership for 21st Century Skills (2011), raising global awareness and making global connections for teachers and students requires:

- Using 21st century skills to understand and address global issues
- Learning from and working collaboratively with individuals representing diverse cultures, religions, and lifestyles with mutual respect and open dialogue in personal, work, and community contexts
- Understanding other nations and cultures, including the use of non-English languages (see Figure 5.7)

What better way to learn about animals than for a class in the United States to connect with a class in Australia. Mrs. Yollis' third-graders did just that through a Skype videoconference (http://yollisclassblog.blogspot.com/). U.S. children asked questions about kangaroos and koalas, and Australian students shared photos of the animals, which were then captured by the student photographer in Mrs. Yollis' class. Looking at similarities such as clothing and food and differences such as time zones, seasons, animals, and sports offered many learning experiences for follow-up (see Figure 5.8).

Not only did students ask and respond to questions but they also had tasks. For example, several students listened carefully and took notes on the computer for the class blog, and another student photographed the event. As a result of the call, students from both classes wrote entries on their class blogs and created video and photo albums based on what they learned. Follow-up on the blog

Figure 5.7. Eliminating Time Zone Differences

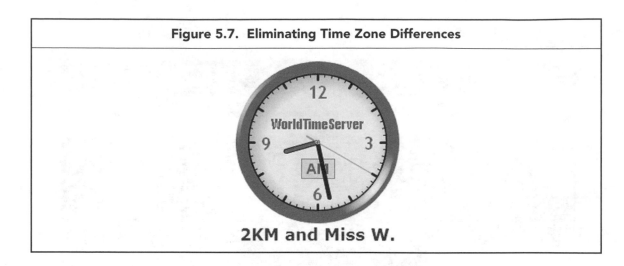

Figure 5.8. U.S. Third-Graders Visiting Australia

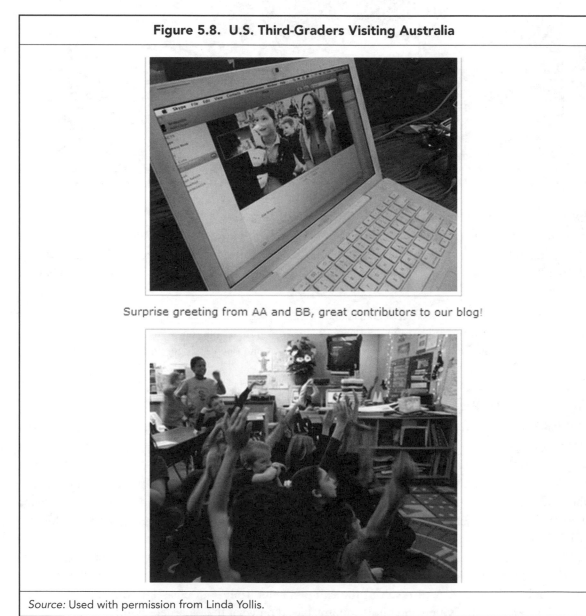

Surprise greeting from AA and BB, great contributors to our blog!

Source: Used with permission from Linda Yollis.

included comments from students, as well as from parents and other teachers. In addition, a lesson on how to write comments to questions evolved from the call.

Making students aware of a bigger world than their own backyard is a first step toward global education. Hearing students use names of distant countries and talk about different languages and cultures identifies the learning that took place (http://www.youtube.com/watch?v=LXlvOFuCs7o& feature=related).

Example 6: Teaching and Learning Languages

When learning a foreign language, it's essential that pupils have the opportunity to communicate with native speakers. Skype takes advantage of the power of the Internet to bring native speakers right into classrooms, allowing language learners to speak with each other in real time anywhere in the world. Now interactive language, learning back and forth, makes learning easier and more fun. Students can improve their language abilities in the following ways:

- Gain fluency
- Improve pronunciation, grammar, and vocabulary
- Increase comprehension
- Repeat sequential events
- Tell stories and add descriptive details
- Practice improvisational and creative speech
- Expand critical thinking

Often visuals are necessary in teaching a language and with Skype you can send videos, pictures, and text messages. You can record the audio and then repeat the material later for follow-up, and you can see the person with whom you are communicating.

Colleen Blaurock (http://record-eagle.com/business/x998539803/Teachers-find-learning-tool-in-Skype), a Spanish teacher at Perry High School in Perry, Ohio, connected her students with a large population of native Spanish-speaking students in nearby Painesville for regular Skype conferences. Students conversed in both English and Spanish. Blaurock comments, "The kids saw a reason in a traditional classroom to learn. And, Skype helped make that happen."

Example 7: Students Helping Students

Combating logistical hurdles, Mr. Crosby's fourth-graders at Agnes Risley School skyped a classmate ill with leukemia. The class was studying the theme "inclusion" and what people could do for others to make them feel better about themselves if they had to be isolated because of an illness. Mr. Crosby was told he had a student ill with leukemia who could not attend school because of radiation and chemo treatments. Voilà, Skype provided the answer. The class connected to the homebound student through a wireless laptop computer with a webcam, and the first meeting took place (see Figure 5.9). As a follow-up to their Skype meeting, the fourth-graders produced a five-minute video telling the story of this meeting with comments from the ill student and others in the class. Learn more at http://learningismessy.com/blog/?p=196.

In middle and high schools, Skype can also prove critical to help students keep pace when they are absent because of illness, college visits, or school suspensions. Educators can keep parents updated about classroom activities and their own child.

Example 8: Providing Authentic Audiences

In Virginia's Albemarle County district, teachers use Skype and other collaboration tools because it gives students an authentic audience for their work. That's true for writing and for oral presentations as part of a videoconference. For example, a third-grader at Washington Street Elementary School

Figure 5.9. Fourth-Graders Helping an Ill Classmate

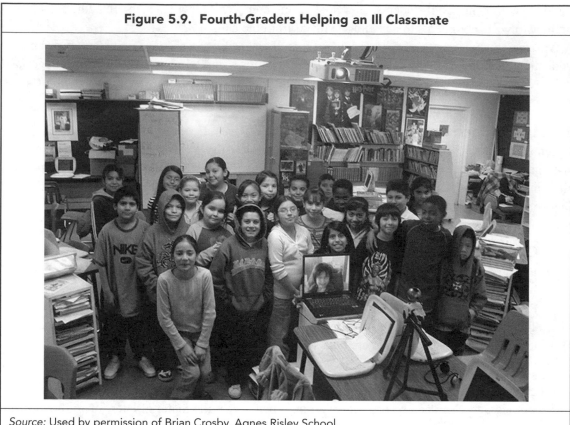

Source: Used by permission of Brian Crosby, Agnes Risley School.

in Brewer, Maine, shares facts about her state via Skype with students in South Dakota (http://www .edweek.org/dd/articles/2011/02/09/02skype.h04.html).

While skyping offers many unique opportunities, it's important that it have a pedagogical basis. Review the presentation "Around the World with Skype" (http://k12onlineconference.org/?p=481) for some great tips.

Finding Like-Minded Educators

Finding educators who want to use Skype in their classrooms and libraries is an important step in the skyping process. For example, you will get a much better response if you have a very specific idea of what you want to accomplish and when. Suggest a date and time you can negotiate, if necessary. Several resources will help you find skyping partners:

- Skype sponsors a free directory of educators interested in skyping and offers tips on using Skype to enrich students' educational experience (http://blogs.skype.com/classroom-pre-register).
- Skype an Author Network (http://skypeanauthor.wetpaint.com/) facilitates connections between educators and authors for virtual author tours. Almost all authors have an online presence with websites and e-mail links, so it's often possible to send a quick note to inquire about their interest in a virtual author meeting.
- Around the World with 80 Schools (http://www.aroundtheworldwith80schools.net/) provides a wealth of information about videoconferencing especially with Skype. It includes blogs by educators who are skyping and much more.
- Skype in the Classroom—The EduSkypers Phonebook gives comments from educators interested in skyping (http://skypeintheclassroom.wordpress.com/).

Teacher Exercises: Now You Try It . . .

Get your feet wet with Skype by trying the following:

> ➤ *Review Bev's website at http://www*
> *.neal-schuman.com/webclassroom for more*
> *exercises about Skype.*

1. Review some of the URLs in this chapter, especially those providing examples at your grade level or subject.
2. Set up a Skype account at home and test it out with family or friends. Evaluate what worked well and what you would change. If you had done this with your students, where do you think you would see successes? Problems?

PART 2: GETTING STARTED WITH SKYPE

When contemplating a Skype call, educators must consider several factors, including what service they plan to use, whether that service is blocked by school administration, and what equipment is necessary. First, check with school authorities on whether they have any objections to students using Skype as a social media tool in the classroom. Because Skype use in K–12 is becoming more widespread, this is often not a problem. Of course, a computer or mobile phone connected to broadband Internet is necessary. You also need a microphone and speakers, built in or separate, and a webcam to make video calls. Often for videoconferencing a large screen is desirable to enable a whole class or school auditorium to participate in the call.

Making Videoconferencing a Learning Activity

An important part of learning is connecting prior knowledge to new experiences. Thus, although the excitement of connecting students via Skype is exhilarating, a Skype call is more than just a visual phone call. It takes preparation through pre-activities enabling students to activate their prior knowledge and post-activities to assess knowledge gained and provide students with opportunities to reflect on and connect these new experiences. The call should also be connected to learning standards and curriculum content. This is what makes a videoconferencing call a learning experience (see Figure 5.10). A few suggestions will help you get started.

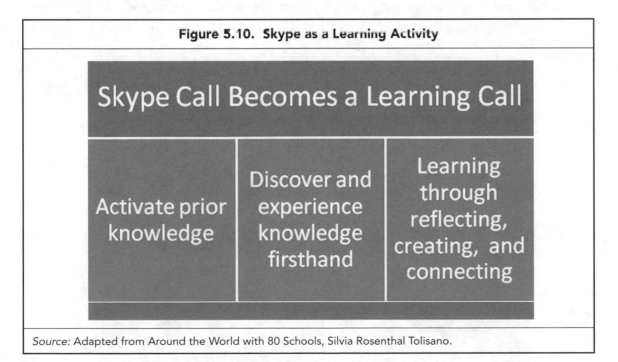

Figure 5.10. Skype as a Learning Activity

Skype Call Becomes a Learning Call

| Activate prior knowledge | Discover and experience knowledge firsthand | Learning through reflecting, creating, and connecting |

Source: Adapted from Around the World with 80 Schools, Silvia Rosenthal Tolisano.

Prior to the Call

Completing a number of tasks before initiating the actual call will make the call go more smoothly.

Identifying Technical Responsibilities

Prior to the videoconference call, educators must make sure the technical aspects of the call are ready and that their guest and students are prepared to make the call interactive.

1. Contact your technology coordinator to make sure you can use the videoconferencing software. Some districts block programs such as Skype, and if that's the case, you'll want to see if it's possible to unblock it for your call.
2. Make sure you have all the necessary equipment—computer, broadband Internet connection, webcam, and microphone—and that it is working properly (see Figure 5.11).
3. Check that your school and the connecting school or guest have the same videoconference program.
4. Download Skype or other videoconferencing software at home first, if possible, and try it with someone you know—a friend or family member.
5. Perform a test run in school. Educators should familiarize themselves with the videoconferencing technology, try it, and even perform a practice call with another educator or perhaps a class in the same building.

Working with Your Guest(s)

Meeting with your guest or the educator of another class via Skype or e-mail should precede any audio- or videoconference.

1. Contact the guest or educator to arrange your virtual visit. Set a date and time and decide which videoconferencing program you'll use and who will initiate the call.
2. Plan your meeting, including how long it will last.
3. Describe to your guest what you plan to have students do during the call. For example, with an author, students might share their favorite parts of the author's book, ask questions about the research behind it, and at the end discuss other books they've read and enjoyed. Students could also share short pieces of their own writing or show their artwork inspired by the book.

Figure 5.11. Skype Equipment

Preparing Students

Students should engage in learning activities before the call that include speaking up, writing, and practicing their parts.

1. Discuss the topic for the visit—what students want to learn, how they will follow up after the call, and questions they want to ask. (See the sample lesson plan in Part 3 for more information about questioning and commenting techniques.)
2. Require students to prepare for the call. For example, if it's an author visit, they should read the book, either individually or in a read-around, as well as write questions to ask the author, read articles about the author, visit websites, and share information about the guest. If the visit is with a partner class, identify the time zone and geographic location as well. Use Google Earth and Google Maps to find both locations of the call on the map and compare them. (See more on Google Earth in Chapter 7.)
3. Create a timeline including what will happen by whom in sequential order.
4. Discuss etiquette for a virtual visit. Emphasize the rules of courteous behavior. Remind students about background noise.
5. Discuss the logistics of the call: Will students stand or sit so they can be seen and heard? How will students ask their questions?
6. Determine what students will do during the call and set up a dress rehearsal where they practice their parts, speaking into the microphone.
7. Make sure students understand that the connection could be lost temporarily during the chat and discuss Plan B in case of technical problems. For example, if visiting with an author, have students bring their novels with the understanding that a lost connection is their signal to start reading while the teacher works with the technology.
8. Only allow student-supervised access to Skype.

During the Call

Small groups are a plus, allowing all students to be involved and decreasing chances that non-participating students will become bored and act out. Giving students roles to perform also keeps them involved. Remember that kids can learn from and teach one another.

1. Assign students' roles so they are occupied during the call and feel a part of it. Some tasks include producer, camera person, host, interviewer, interviewee, photographer, note taker, videographer, and blogger. See http://educational-blogging.wikispaces.com/Using+Skype for roles assigned to students in Mrs. Yollis' third-grade class during their Skype calls.
2. Depending on the age of the students, let them make the call, orchestrate student speakers, and document the call via photos, screen captures, and a blog.
3. If possible, give each student a chance in front of the camera to ask or comment on a question.

Following the Call

1. Have students reflect on what they learned. Keep a blog so they remember what happened during the call, and share conversations about the call with other students.
2. Create a poster with Glogster, a poster-building website, to include images of the area visited, quotes from and summary of the call, and photos of students and the guest talking, to name just a few.
3. Review technical aspects—what went well, what you would do differently.
4. Determine if a follow-up call is needed; write thank-you messages to your guest(s).

Combining the activities in this section with the lesson plan that follows will provide a comprehensive unit plan to use for videoconferencing. See Table 5.1 for more ideas.

Table 5.1. General URLs for Skype	
URL	Description
http://www.mrmayo.org/?p=272	Skype visit with Harvard Law Professor Lawrence Lessig, an expert on copyright
https://docs.google.com/View?docID=0AcbcPV7RaR NuZGM0Z2NiZnRfMjRkd2h2djZnOQ&revision=_latest	Questions from seventh graders on copyright, laws, downloading illegally, and more
http://www.teachingdegree.org/2009/06/30/50-awesome-ways-to-use-skype-in-the-classroom/	*50 Awesome Ways to Use Skype in the Classroom*
http://www.iste.org/connect/iste-connects/blog-detail/09-02-15/The_Many_Roles_of_Skype_in_the_Classroom.aspx	Canadian seventh grade history project using Skype to connect with a curator at the National Museum
http://livebinders.com/play/play_or_edit/8641	Skype in Schools Live Binders
http://www.skypeforeducators.com/	Skype for Educators
http://educational-blogging.wikispaces.com/Using+Skype	Projects incorporating Skype with elementary school students
http://vimeo.com/25284448	The Mystery Skype Call

PART 3: PRACTICAL APPLICATIONS

A Skype call offers students the opportunity to improve their communication skills: reading books or information about another location, writing questions for the call, speaking to the guest(s), and listening to new information. An interactive call—one where students ask questions and respond to questions from their guests, as well as adding follow-up questions and comments—offers the most learning potential. Educators can use this sample lesson plan in preparation for a Skype call.

Sample Lesson Plan: Writing Responsive Questions and Comments for an Authentic Audience

Questioning informs a large part of how students learn in the classroom and is important to any videoconference call. When students generate questions and comments, they promote inquiry, thinking, and ultimately learning.

The following lesson designed for elementary-age students focuses on preparing good questions and comments for a Skype call. Although this lesson was created to help students take part in a Skype videoconference, the tasks are also useful for writing essential questions, interviews, blog posts, and more, and could be used with other grade levels and subject areas.

Step 1: Connect to the Standards, Set Goals, and Identify Objectives

In this lesson, students present multiple points of view, respond to the ideas of others, and reflect on their own ideas in an effort to build their knowledge, understanding, or interpretation of what they are studying. Teachers and school librarians work together daily to build a flexible learning environment with the goal of producing successful learners skilled in multiple literacies. The American Association of School Librarians recently updated *Standards for the 21st-Century Learner* (AASL, 2009) to emphasize opportunities to share and learn with others, and the International Society for Technology in Education incorporates working collaboratively and communicating with learners of other cultures to develop cultural understanding in their *National Educational Technology Standards for Students* (NETS; ISTE, 2007). By developing innovative products using technology, demonstrating critical thinking, processing data, and reporting results, this lesson emphasizes these new AASL literacy standards and NETS, as well as content goals and objectives such as analysis, evaluation, and critical thinking skills. Practicing questioning and commenting fosters skills needed for a Skype call. As a result of the videoconference, students will enhance their reading and writing skills and improve their ability to write for and communicate verbally with an authentic audience.

Objectives

After performing activities in this unit, students will be able to:

- research on the Internet and in the library about people and geographic areas;
- write pertinent questions that solicit more than yes/no responses;
- expand answers to questions that add new ideas or request additional information;
- work together in groups on a project, each student participating equally;
- evaluate questions and responses; and
- use a microphone and webcam.

Step 2: Outline the Task and Gather Materials

As preparation for the Skype call, the teacher or librarian determines how the Skype call fits into the curriculum. Whether the call is with an expert or another class, students need to learn more about the visitor by reading articles, exploring books from the library, and researching on the Internet. This step adds to their prior knowledge before the call and enables them to ask pertinent questions and respond with interesting, relevant comments. For example, if the visitor is an author, students may read one of her books, or if visiting with a partner class, identify the school's location and map it out with Google Earth.

Step 3: Plan the Instruction

Included are activities to introduce the lesson, use during the lesson, and follow the lesson.

Introduce the Lesson

Emphasize the importance of creating questions that elicit more than a yes or no answer so students' questions and comments will create a "conversation" with their guest(s).

- Review question words: Why? What? How? In what ways? Responses might give rise to subsequent questions and comments.
- Depending on student level, as a class or individually, have them create a KWL chart (abbreviated from Know-Want-Learn) on the class wiki or on large sheets of paper. The chart requires students to think about what they already know about the person or class that is the object of the upcoming call and facilitates their ability to frame questions about what they wonder about or want to know (see Figure 5.12). To create the KWL chart, have students:
  - Write what they know in column 1.
  - In column 2, brainstorm a list of questions. Identify questions that are designed to solicit information of interest and in-depth answers. For example, sample questions written by a seventh-grade class prior to a videoconference with an author illustrate some question types:
- What do you like to write about?
- Where do you get your ideas to write your books?
- When you write your books, what inspires you and why?
- What was your favorite book as a child and why?

Figure 5.12. KWL Chart		
K—What I Know	**W—What I Want to Know**	**L—What I Learned**

- Have students or the teacher place the questions into a few categories, for example, those about an author's book, others concerning the author, etc.

During the Lesson

Select some of the following activities so students can practice questioning and commenting.

- Give examples of poor/high quality comments and questions (see Figure 5.13).
- Divide students into groups of three and have each group complete its own KWL chart to include at least three questions, answers, and comments as they did in the class activity.
- Provide some commenting examples:
  - Compliment the visitor in a specific way.
  - Add new information to the discussion. Perhaps the remark reminds you of an experience you've had and you can share that connection.
  - Try to end your comment with a relevant question so that an interesting conversation can develop (see Figure 5.14).

Figure 5.13. Commenting Video

Source: Used with permission from Linda Yollis.

Figure 5.14. Comment Starters

Some good commenting starters might include:

- This made me think about...
- I wonder why...
- Your writing made me form an opinion about...
- This post is relevant because...
- Your writing made me think that we should...
- I wish I understood why...
- This is important because...

- Another thing to consider is...
- I can relate to this...
- I discovered...
- I don't understand...
- I was reminded that...
- I found myself wondering...

Source: Adapted from Excellence and Imagination, http://mr-fisher.edublogs.org/2006/04/11/comment-starters/.

- Have each group role-play the call using the questions/comments they created. One student asks a question, another comments, and a third asks a follow-up question.
- Have students in other groups vote to accept or reject the comments and questions. They should justify their votes by explaining why some are good and why others will not promote the conversation (see Figure 5.15).

Figure 5.15. Examples of Relevant Comments

Submitted on 2011/01/17 at 9:21 am

What did I learn? I learned that you don't have to be a reader to be a good writer. What did I like best? I liked the part when Mrs. O' Connor answered our questions. I didn't know that before you published a book that you have to put all the parts of that story into 1 or maybe, 2 boxes! Skyping with her was exciting.

go beyond words, such as "fun", "exciting", "amazing", etc

Submitted on 2011/01/13 at 5:13 pm

I learned that if you want to be a good writer you need to read, but you don't have to be a great reader. You should read though because it will make you a better writer. My favorite part of the skype call was when Mrs. O' Connor answered my question. My question was " How long does it take to write a book and why does the process take that long?". That was my favorite part, because she showed me almost all the things she did to write How To Steal A Dog. Mrs. O' Connor also showed me notebooks and boxes. She even showed me a giant stuffed frog. At another point during the skype call she said stuff about her inspiration for How To Steal A Dog. It was a lot of fun!

Submitted on 2011/01/12 at 6:42 pm

I was not there when we made the skype call but my favorite part practicing was making up all of the questions. I learned that you can practice before you skype on photo both. I wish that we can skype again. I think it was very nice that she let us skype with her.

elaborate...what was the question? What was the answer?

Submitted on 2011/01/11 at 8:32 pm

I learned from skyping with Barbra O'Connor that it takes a very long time to make just one book. My favorite part about skyping with her is when I asked her my question because it was my question and I got a very good answer, and I will never forget it. I had a wonderful time skyping with Barbra O' Connor. It was an amazing experience!

more info needed

Submitted on 2011/01/11 at 7:15 pm

I learned from the skype call that it helps be a good reader in order to be a better writer. Also I learned to try to keep the video camera still when filming. My favorite part was when we asked Mrs. O' Connor what book she would make into a movie because I would like to read that book to see if it would make a good movie. Skyping with Mrs. O' Conner was very fun!

Submitted on 2011/01/11 at 6:00 pm

What I learned from our skype call is that it is hard to make a book and that it takes a long time to make a book. The part of the skype session I liked best was when we skyped with Mrs. O'Connor I learnd a lot and that it is special and hard to become an author.

Source: From Silvia Tolisano's Elementary Blogging Unit, Creative Commons license, http://langwitches.org/blog/wp-content/uploads/2008/12/blogging-unit.pdf.

Following the Lesson

After the lesson but before the call, have students reflect on what they learned about maintaining an interactive conversation using questions and comments.

- Have groups discuss the new questions and comments, prioritizing and indicating why they wanted to add them to the W column on the KWL chart.
- After all groups complete the role-play, ask if there are additional questions the class wants to add to the group chart.
- Write what they learned in the L column of the KWL chart.

Evaluate What Was Learned

Assessment on the lesson content can take place before the Skype call or at its end.

- After the Skype call, have students complete the L column in the class KWL chart so they can see what they learned. Educators can evaluate what they learned using the rubric shown in Figure 5.16.

Figure 5.16. Rubric for Skype Questioning/Commenting Lesson			
Category	**3 points**	**2 points**	**1 point**
Content	Added question and detail to the response.	Added question or comment but not both.	No new information added.
Teamwork	The workload is divided and shared equally by all team members.	The workload is divided and shared fairly by all team members, though workloads may vary from person to person.	The workload was divided, but one person in the group is viewed as not doing his/her fair share of the work.
Delivery	Student uses a clear voice and correct, precise pronunciation of terms.	Student's voice is clear and pronounces most works correctly.	Student's voice is low and incorrectly pronounces terms.

- Have students complete a self-evaluation of their ability to write good questions and comments, why this skill is important for videoconferences, and where else they could use this skill (see Figure 5.17).

Summary

This lesson teaches important skills students will find useful in their course work throughout their school life and beyond. As students move to middle and high school, reinforcing in-depth questioning and commenting will continue to be important to promote critical thinking.

> ➤ *Review Bev's website at http://www.neal-schuman.com/webclassroom for new lessons using Skype.*

Teacher Exercises: Now You Try It . . .

Now that you've reviewed a lesson plan that incorporates Skype, try the following exercises. Be sure to focus your attention on how the technology can enhance student learning.

Figure 5.17. Student Self-Reflection Checklist

Reflect on the work that you did during the Skype videoconference, including writing the questions and comments and delivering the information on the call.

- What I heard that surprised me was

  _____

  _____

- Something I learned from the Skype call was

  _____

  _____

- One thing I thought was important from the interviews was

  _____

  _____

- From what I heard and read, I have a question or would like to know more about

  _____

  _____

Assess group participation, determining whether the student worked well with teammates, contributed to the team effort, and shouldered work equally. Students will answer the following questions:

- Did you do your best?

  _____

  _____

- Did you work hard, enjoy the project, and feel good about what you completed?

  _____

  _____

- How much did you contribute to the group's project?

  _____

  _____

- If you had to do it again, would you do anything differently?

  _____

  _____

---

1. Select a topic you plan to teach that would benefit from a Skype call and decide what type of Skype call fits your curriculum:
   a. Language arts = author
   b. Social studies = virtual field trip
   c. Science = interview expert
   d. Cooperative project = another class

2 Create a lesson plan. Review the uses of Skype to inform your selection. Address the following:
   a. What are student objectives?
   b. What tasks will students accomplish?
   c. What format will learning take—individual, groups, whole class?
   d. How will you evaluate student progress, knowledge, work in groups, in class, individually?

1. Critique the lesson afterward in the following categories:
   a. Technical
   b. Learning achieved: pre-call, during the call, post-call
   c. Students, including motivation, participation, enthusiasm

Note: If you cannot create a Skype call, try this procedure with another class at your own school.

CONCLUSION

As with any learning activity, challenges exist from connecting with different time zones, technical problems, or Skype being blocked at your school site to trying to keep all students engaged. Despite these issues, connecting, communicating, and collaborating is getting easier, and classroom doors are opening wider. The role of the twenty-first century educator is to help administrators, school boards, and parents understand the benefits of videoconferencing. With most schools having Internet access and school budgets tightening, now is the time to get started with new free technologies. Your students are already using social media, so make the classroom a place that is motivating, interesting, and engages them with visual, real-time discussion and learning.

REFERENCES AND FURTHER READING

AASL (American Association of School Librarians). 2009. *Standards for the 21st-Century Learner*. American Library Association. http://www.ala.org/ala/mgrps/divs/aasl/guidelinesandstandards/learningstandards/standards.cfm.

Bortman, Harry. 2010. "Drilling for the Future of Science." *Astrobiology Magazine* (blog), December 6. http://www.astrobio.net/index.php?option=com_expedition&task=detail&id=3703.

ISTE (International Society for Technology in Education). 2007. *National Educational Technology Standards for Students*. Eugene, OR: International Society for Technology in Education. http://www.iste.org/standards/nets-for-students/nets-student-standards-2007.aspx.

Partnership for 21st Century Skills. 2011. "Global Awareness." Partnership for 21st Century Skills. Accessed December 6. http://p21.org/component/content/article/256.

Quillen, Ian. 2011. "Educators Move Beyond the Hype Over Skype." *Education Week Digital Directions*. February 4. http://www.edweek.org/dd/articles/2011/02/09/02skype.h04.html.

Tolisano, Silvia Rosenthal. 2009a. "Around the World with 80 Schools." *Langwitches* (blog), January 3. http://langwitches.org/blog/2009/01/03/around-the-world-with-80-schools/.

Tolisano, Silvia Rosenthal. 2009b. "Around the World with Skype." *Langwitches* (blog), December 16. http://langwitches.org/blog/2009/12/16/k12online09/.

Tolisano, Silvia Rosenthal. 2009c. "Reasons for Skyping in the Classroom." *Langwitches* (blog), January 2. http://langwitches.org/blog/2009/01/02/reasons-for-skyping-in-the-classroom/.

Tolisano, Silvia Rosenthal. 2010. "A Skype Odyssey." *Langwitches* (blog), March 5. http://langwitches.org/blog/2010/03/05/a-skype-odyssey/.

Tolisano, Silvia Rosenthal. 2011a. "Quality Commenting Video by Third Graders." *Langwitches* (blog), February 6. http://langwitches.org/blog/2011/02/06/quality-commenting-video-by-third-graders/.

Tolisano, Silvia Rosenthal. 2011b. "Skype Call—Learning Call." *Langwitches* (blog), http://langwitches.org/blog/wp-content/uploads/2010/11/Skype-call-learning-call.pdf.

CHAPTER 6

Bringing the Social Networking Revolution to K–12 Classrooms

PART 1: IDEAS AND INSIGHTS

Statistics from a Pew Research Center (2010) report emphasize the importance of social media and its tremendous growth in the last few years:

- Facebook added over 200 million users in less than one year.
- There are more than 2 million blogs; 54 percent of these bloggers post or tweet daily.
- Facebook has over 350 million active users on a global basis, a 40 percent increase in six months.
- Two to three new Twitter accounts are activated every second.
- If Facebook were a country, it would be the world's third largest.
- There are 50 million tweets per day.
- More than 1.5 million pieces of content (e.g., web links, news stories, blog posts, photos, notes) are shared on Facebook daily.
- YouTube is the second largest search engine in the world.

Social media is everywhere and it's not going away anytime soon. It is not a fad but rather a fundamental shift in the way people communicate. It is more than pictures of babies, what you ate for breakfast, and what movie you plan to see. If "96 percent of Millennials [American teens and twentysomethings] have joined a social network" (YouTube, 2010), it must mean more. Where are the schools in this new revolution?

Objectives of This Chapter

Many educators agree that social networking and social media has a place in K–12. This chapter and previous ones on blogging, wikis, podcasts, and Skype demonstrate how Web 2.0 social networking tools support the five Cs—communication, collaboration, critical thinking, creativity, and content—important for twenty-first-century learning.

After reading Chapter 6 and completing the exercises, teachers and librarians at the middle and high school levels will be able to:

- understand the basics of social networking and why to use it;
- explain the basics of social bookmarking;
- create social bookmarks for their own and their students' use;
- use social networks and information tools to gather and share information;
- use examples to demonstrate to students how to use social networking in different subject areas;
- teach safe use of several social media; and
- create their own social networking lessons.

As the previous statistics show, many students as young as elementary school are familiar with and actually use social networking tools from computers, iPads, and mobile devices. Yet there are diverse opinions about whether these tools should be incorporated into the K–12 curriculum.

Glossary

Review the following terms before starting the chapter to fully understand the concepts discussed.

Delicious: A social bookmarking web service for storing, sharing, and discovering web bookmarks.

Diigo: A social bookmarking website that allows signed users to bookmark and tag webpages.

Edmodo: A network specifically built for teachers and students, connecting them at a class, school, or even district level.

Facebook: A popular free social networking website that allows registered users to create profiles, upload photos and video, and send messages.

Flickr: A photo-sharing website.

following: Subscribing to someone's Tweets as a follower.

hashtag: The # symbol, called a hashtag, used to mark keywords or topics in a Tweet.

SchoolTube: Place for students and teachers to share videos online.

social bookmarking: A method used to store, organize, search, and manage bookmarks of webpages on the Internet.

social media: Media for social interaction, using highly accessible communication techniques. The term refers to the use of web-based and mobile technologies to turn communication into interactive dialogue.

social network: A social structure made up of individuals (or organizations) called "nodes," which are connected by one or more specific types of interdependency, such as friendship, kinship, common interest, financial exchange, dislike, or relationships of beliefs or knowledge.

tag: A keyword or term associated with or assigned to a piece of information (e.g., a picture, article, or video clip), thus describing the item and enabling keyword-based classification of information.

tag cloud: A visual depiction of user-generated tags.

tweet: Text-based posts of up to 140 characters in length.

TweetDeck: Your personal browser for staying in touch with your contacts that allows you to monitor, manage, and engage in your social world by bringing together your Twitter, Facebook, LinkedIn, and MySpace feeds all at once, saving time and resources.

Twitter: An online service that enables you to broadcast short messages to your "followers."

YouTube: A video-sharing website on which users can upload, share, and view videos.

Introduction

There has been explosive growth in creative and authoring activities by students on social networking sites in recent years. As far back as 2007, the National School Boards Association (2007) reported that 9- to 17-year-olds spend almost as much time using social networking services and websites as they spend watching television, and almost 60 percent of students who use social networking talk about education topics online. Surprisingly, more than 50 percent specifically discuss schoolwork. Then why is social networking blocked from so many schools?

Part 1 of this chapter provides an introduction to social networking and social media tools, as well as examples of their use in the curriculum. Part 2 suggests how to get started, including specific social networking tools. In Part 3, a sample unit plan illustrates how social networking tools were used in a real-life example, that of the uprisings in the Middle East. The unit encompasses history, civics, and English at the secondary level.

What Is Social Networking?

A social network is a website on the Internet that brings people together in a central location to talk, gossip, share ideas, activities, and interests, make new friends, and more. Within their individual networks, people discuss interests and activities across political, economic, and geographic borders; however, often different countries have their own versions of social networking sites, with Facebook being used worldwide. Social networks include sites such as blogs (see Chapter 2), Twitter, Facebook, Edmodo, My Space, and SchoolTube, to name some (see Figure 6.1).

Social networks are also being used by teachers and students as communication tools. Social networks, focused on supporting relationships between teachers and their students, are now part of learning, educator professional development, and content-sharing. Ning for teachers, We Collaborate!, and other sites foster relationships that include educational blogs and e-portfolios, as well

Figure 6.1. Diagram of a Social Network

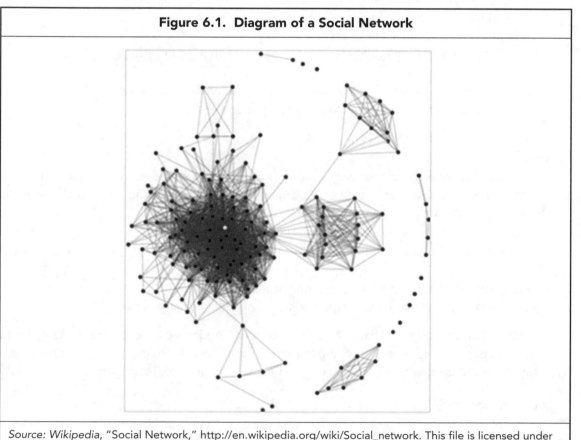

as communication such as chats, discussion threads, and synchronous forums. These sites also share content and rate features. Review Chapter 11 for more information.

Why Use Social Networking in the Classroom?

Statistics from the National School Boards Association (2007) indicate that schools and parents have strong expectations about the positive roles social networking can play in students' lives. District leaders expect social networking to introduce students to "new and different kinds of students," and more than four in 10 (43 percent) hope social networking will help students "learn to express themselves better creatively" and "develop global relationships." More than three in four parents (76 percent) expect social networking to help their children improve their reading and writing skills or express themselves more clearly; three out of four (75 percent) also expect social networking to improve children's ability to resolve conflicts. Almost as many (72 percent) expect social networking to improve their children's social skills.

Many uses are suggested for social networking. Here are some of them. Social networking can help teachers by:

- acting as a communication tool—creating chat-room forums and groups to extend classroom discussion, posting assignments, tests and quizzes, and assisting with homework outside the classroom setting;
- fostering teacher-parent communication— parents can ask questions and voice concerns without having to meet face-to-face;
- supporting relationships between teachers and their students;
- enhancing educator professional development;
- sharing content among colleagues;
- asking questions of an author or expert;
- engaging students in exploring real-world issues and solving authentic problems using digital tools and resources; and
- customizing and personalizing learning activities to address students' diverse learning styles, working strategies, and abilities using digital tools and resources.

Social networking can help students:

- gather and share information;
- maintain openness to new ideas by considering divergent opinions, changing opinions, or conclusions when evidence supports change, and seeking information about new ideas encountered through academic or personal experiences;
- collaborate with others to exchange ideas, develop new understandings, and make decisions;
- engage in exploring real-world issues and solving authentic problems using digital tools and resources;
- practice the skill of summarizing and condensing; and
- share work in a variety of media both inside and outside the classroom 24/7.

Social networking encourages collaborating in "real time." Students can contribute content, which is then broadcast as it is being uploaded. No longer is access "location based." They can now access from any device connected to the Internet (e.g., computer, iPhone, iPad) at any time.

Safety on Social Sites

One of the major reasons school administrators hesitate to allow social networking in the classroom is the potential risk to students. Risks may take the form of online predators, hackers, viewing inappropriate content, cyberbullying, and privacy issues. Therefore, it is vital that educators who use social media teach students about and emphasize ways to be safe on social sites.

Many schools initially banned or restricted Internet use, only to ease up when the educational value of the Internet became clear. The same is likely to be the case with social networking. Safety policies remain important, as does teaching students about online safety and responsible online expression, but students may learn these lessons better while they're actually using social networking tools in a guided environment.

Examples of Social Networking Projects in the Curriculum

Many students are already using social networking, specifically Facebook, blogs, Twitter, and YouTube. With its rising popularity, educators need to use this tool to their advantage, as well as exemplify its use in a controlled environment for specific curricular purposes. Several specific examples illustrate the use of Edmodo, Facebook, and Twitter in both elementary and secondary classrooms.

> **Tips for Safety on Social Sites**
> - Be as anonymous as possible.
> - Use privacy settings.
> - Think before posting.
> - Avoid in-person meetings.
> - Be honest about your age.
> - Remember social networking sites are public spaces.
> - Avoid posting anything that could embarrass you later or expose you to danger.
> - Remember people aren't always who they say they are.
> - Check comments regularly.
> - Avoid inappropriate content and behavior, and, if encountered, report it to an adult.

Example 1: Connecting Beyond the Four Walls

One of the most powerful ways to help students prepare for their future is to connect with others outside the classroom. One teacher in Hawaii used Edmodo to make this a reality. Relying on educator contacts she had met at conferences, she formed a group with three other science teachers from Michigan, Pennsylvania, and North Carolina. The goal of the Our Footprints project was to have students from each region look at the unique features of their environment and the negative impact humans have made on these environments and, as a result, to value the environments they live in. They then were to compare the similarities and differences with the other students and schools. The desired outcome was that the students would realize that, despite their differences, they all shared similar challenges and had the same responsibility to care about the global environment.

Edmodo was the tool used to connect students with one another because they easily adapted to the Edmodo interface. Students involved were between sixth and twelfth grades, and the technology access ranged from 1:1 to limited use of a computer lab (see Figure 6.2; http://blog.edmodo.com/2011/06/16/connecting-beyond-our-four-walls%e2%80%a8/).

Figure 6.2. The Footprint Project

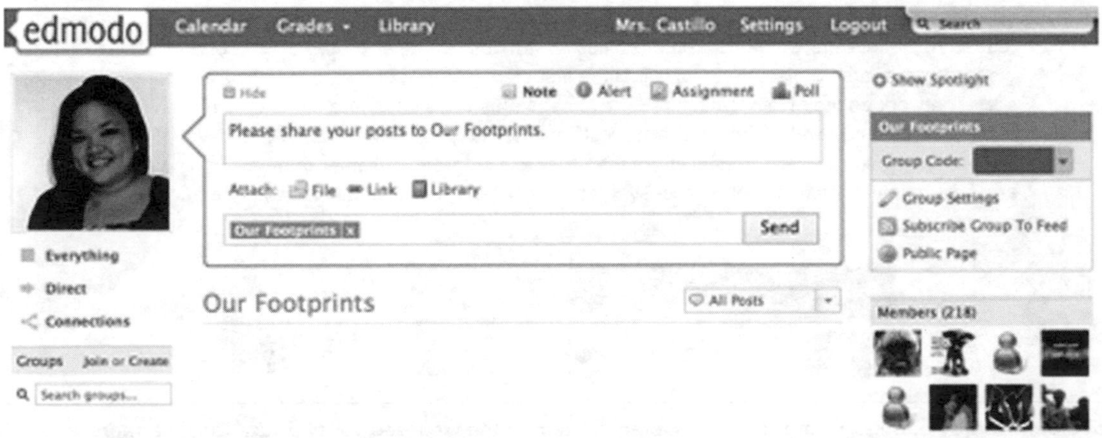

Students immediately started posting their projects and making comments to one another. After completing their research, they used a variety of tools ranging from videos and glogs to PowerPoint presentations to explain their research.

Participants benefited from the experience of connecting virtually with others. Because they were sharing with students outside of Hawaii, they took extra time in making sure they produced their highest quality work, double-checked their facts, and presented their ideas in a clear and concise manner. They also had to think about how to communicate with others whose perspectives, backgrounds, values, cultures, and knowledge might be different. In their project reflections, many of the students said the experience was one of the highlights of the year. For more about the project, visit http://blog.edmodo.com/2011/06/16/connecting-beyond-our-four-walls%e2%80%a8/.

Example 2: Biographical Research Using Social Networking

A librarian at John Kennedy Elementary School in Batavia, New York, wanted her fifth-graders to become more engaged in the inquiry process surrounding biographical research by having them create profiles of famous figures in a Facebook-like environment. Wondering what interface to use, the School Library System of the Genesee Valley Educational Partnership came to the rescue and created FameCity.org, an educational social network where students bring biographies to life.

Students select famous historical figures and create profiles as part of a biography research project. Next, they interact within a social network as if they were the historical figures they represent. They post status updates, share pictures, comment on other profiles, and even "friend" other historical figures. This requires a much higher level of understanding about the historical figure than a simple biography. Rather than just finding facts, students must synthesize information and empathize with their figure (see Figure 6.3).

A fifth-grade history teacher at Port Orange Elementary School in Florida provided another twist on this project. He had his students chat with historical figures. They gave Thomas Jefferson advice

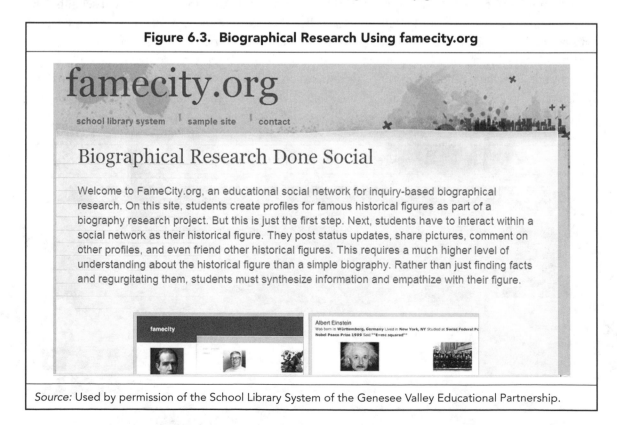

Figure 6.3. Biographical Research Using famecity.org

Source: Used by permission of the School Library System of the Genesee Valley Educational Partnership.

on how to write the Declaration of Independence and talked to Benjamin Franklin. They had conversations with explorers Meriwether Lewis and William Clark as they made their way west. The explorers sent back detailed descriptions of prairie dogs and the sights they saw on their travels. After reading the comments, students recognized the language used at the time. They then wrote comments to the figures using the same language and style.

Example 3: U.S. History with Facebook

At Bullis School in Maryland, a history teacher talks about using Facebook as a teaching tool in her Advanced Placement junior class (Romeyn, 2011). The class does a chronological study of American history. Previously, students had created PowerPoint presentations and oral reports as in a traditional biography project. For a project studying the early nineteenth century, students were to create Facebook Fan Pages. The idea was to make the project more realistic and have students use a tool they were already using outside of school on their own.

For Part 1, each student took on the identity of a person, such as a reformer, political or religious leader, or inventor; collected biographical information, pictures of the person, the family, and the hometown; and posted them on their Facebook page. In Part 2 they wrote status updates on their character. For example, a student who assumed the identity of DeWitt Clinton (http://www.facebook.com/pages/DeWitt-APUSH-Clinton/191556088827) posted about the opening of the Erie Canal as if it were taking place at that moment (see Figure 6.4). Students became so involved that they were posting information at 11 p.m. on a Saturday night! They also became quite creative; for example, one student posted his status updates about Samuel Morse using Morse code. See the teacher describing this project on a video at http://www.youtube.com/watch?v=Vj-XCUIbbcE.

On the last day of the project, using the computers in the school library, all students posted simultaneously on each other's pages. A great amount of discussion was going on in the class, but it was all happening online.

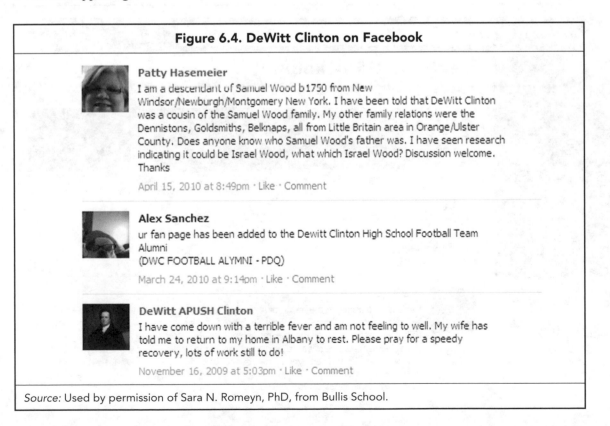

Figure 6.4. DeWitt Clinton on Facebook

Patty Hasemeier
I am a descendant of Samuel Wood b 1750 from New Windsor/Newburgh/Montgomery New York. I have been told that DeWitt Clinton was a cousin of the Samuel Wood family. My other family relations were the Dennistons, Goldsmiths, Belknaps, all from Little Britain area in Orange/Ulster County. Does anyone know who Samuel Wood's father was. I have seen research indicating it could be Israel Wood, what which Israel Wood? Discussion welcome. Thanks
April 15, 2010 at 8:49pm · Like · Comment

Alex Sanchez
ur fan page has been added to the Dewitt Clinton High School Football Team Alumni
(DWC FOOTBALL ALYMNI - PDQ)
March 24, 2010 at 9:14pm · Like · Comment

DeWitt APUSH Clinton
I have come down with a terrible fever and am not feeling to well. My wife has told me to return to my home in Albany to rest. Please pray for a speedy recovery, lots of work still to do!
November 16, 2009 at 5:03pm · Like · Comment

Source: Used by permission of Sara N. Romeyn, PhD, from Bullis School.

Example 4: Creating Fake Social Networking Projects

Several educators at the K–12 level who do not have access to social networking sites from their classrooms have created "fake" walls that imitate those on Facebook or Twitter without having to go online. Here are some of their ideas, such as creating a fake Facebook page about a literary or historical character, including people the character would have had as friends, geographical information, educational background, groups they would have joined, and family members (see Figure 6.5; http://www.facebook.com/pages/DeWitt-APUSH-Clinton/191556088827?sk=wall).

Another example illustrates using Twitter to teach point of view and character. As part of reading a novel or short story, an English teacher had students become a character and create a Twitter account (e.g., @huckfinn, @tomsawyer). They used their study of that character to create conversations around key events in the plot, focus on situations omitted from the text but referred to, and write their own fiction based on their knowledge of the writer, the time period, and the characters.

> ➤ Review Bev's website at http://www.neal-schuman.com/webclassroom to see more examples about social networking tools.

PART 2: GETTING STARTED WITH SOCIAL NETWORKING

More and more educators are using social networking in the classroom that is integral to the curriculum, as well as to communicate with students, parents, and other educators. Several social networking tools—Edmodo, Facebook, Twitter, and SchoolTube—illustrate how. In addition, teachers and school librarians have been using social bookmarking for their own purposes and classroom

Figure 6.5. Dewitt APUSH Clinton on My Fake Wall

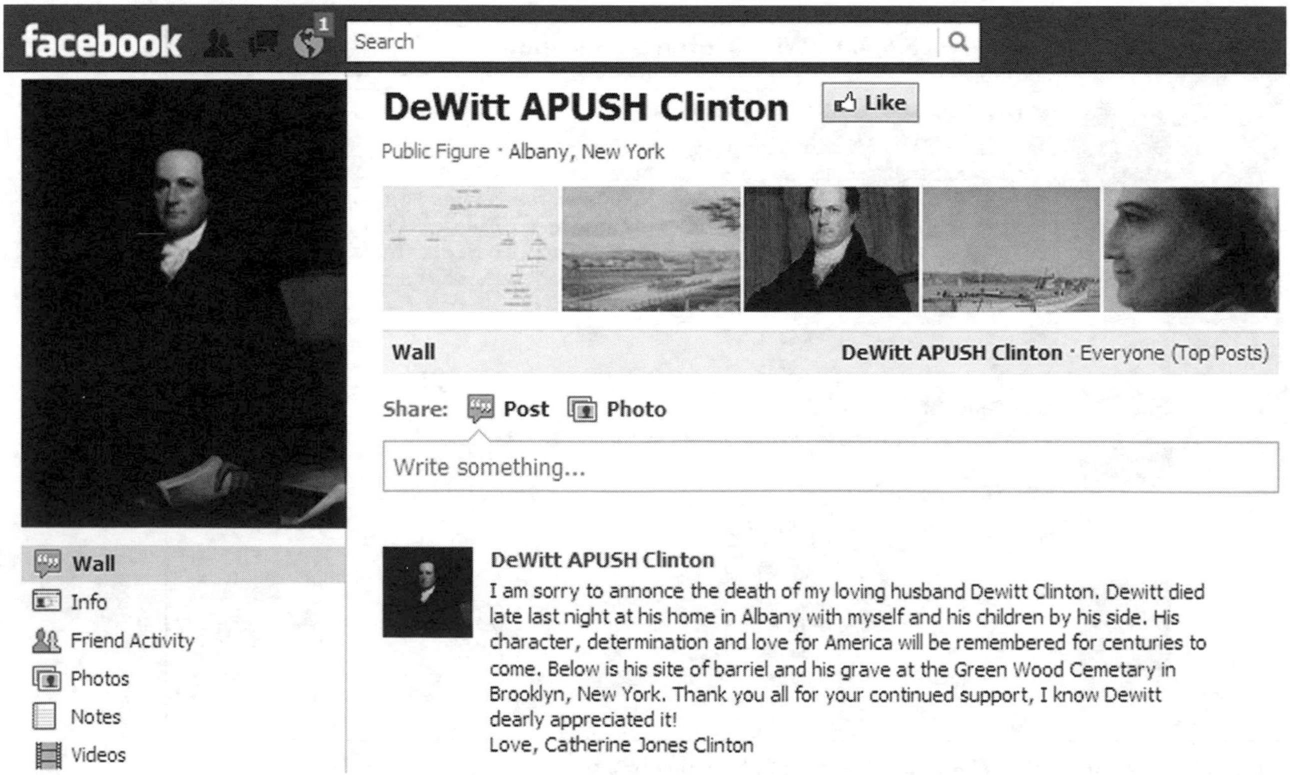

activities for a number of years. Two popular sites are Delicious and Diigo. Each has features that are important to education.

Social Bookmarking

According to *Wikipedia* (2011), social bookmarking lets you store, organize, annotate, and share saved bookmarks. Bookmarks are usually public, but can be saved privately, or shared only with specified people or groups. Most educators organize their bookmarks using tags that allow them to categorize bookmarks by grade level, subject, or lesson topic. School librarians have found social bookmarking to be an easy way to provide lists of informative links to teachers and students. One disadvantage, however, is that there is no uniform way to tag the bookmarks. Social bookmarking complements blogs, social networks, and RSS news aggregators. Look at links other people have saved, or browse to see what has been bookmarked on a subject. Find more about social bookmarking at http://digitallyspeaking.pbworks.com/w/page/17791579/Social-Bookmarking-and-Annotating.

Delicious

Delicious (http://www.delicious.com/), one of the first social bookmarking sites, is still very popular. For example, you can create an annotated resource list to use in a project about whales for science or battles of the Civil War in American History. Users usually add descriptive one-word tags to each bookmark to help them remember and organize them, for instance, whale or migration for a whale page. By tagging pages, users can classify and organize them into groups, making it easier to navigate the list of links. Delicious also lets users search their list by keywords and organize them chronologically by the date when links were added. The social part is that Delicious lets users see others' collections of links so they can subscribe to them using RSS feeds (see Chapter 2) and be notified when new links appear. In addition, each link contains a list of

> ➤ Review Bev's website at http://www.neal-schuman.com/webclassroom to see more examples of social bookmarking tools.

every user who has bookmarked it so users on Delicious now become an online community, joined by their desire to share links to webpages they like and find useful (see Figure 6.6).

Diigo

Diigo (http://www.diigo.com/) calls itself a personal research tool, a collaborative research platform, a social content site, and a knowledge-sharing community. One interesting feature is the ability to

Figure 6.6. Bev's Delicious Bookmarks

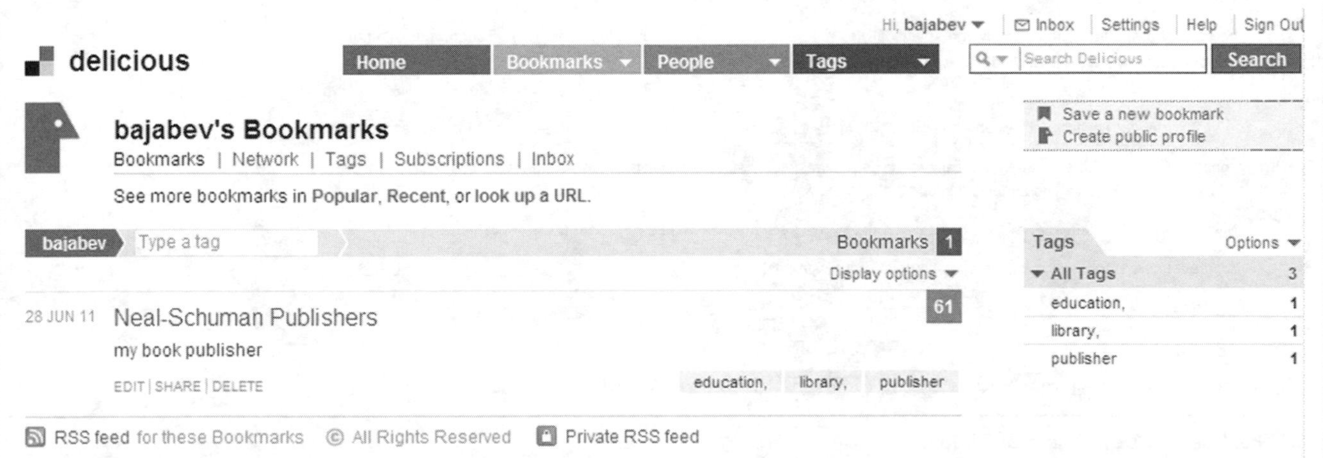

highlight ways to share your bookmarks: post them to your blog, send multiple annotated pages by e-mail, or save them to other websites such as Facebook or Diigo simultaneously. You can also set up groups, ideal for collaborative learning in the classroom. Groups can be public, private, or semiprivate. You can find bookmarks by popularity and the most recent bookmarks by site, user, or tags.

Diigo also has a site specifically for educators. Diigo for educators accounts' privacy settings, by default, limit communication to that of classmates and teachers only (see Figure 6.7). Students in the same class are automatically set up as a group, so all saved bookmarks can instantly be shared with peers. For more information, visit http://www.diigo.com/learn_more.

Social bookmarking is easy to use whether you are using Delicious or Diigo. Just go to the website, complete the registration form, and click Register. A button will be installed on your browser. Log in to your account and bookmark sites by clicking the Tag button on your toolbar. Enter tags in the keyword box. For example, an English teacher who found a site on Macbeth might enter keywords: Macbeth, Shakespeare, teaching, and English12. When you have enough sites bookmarked, you can easily organize them. With Diigo you can view your bookmarks as a cloud; this enables you to arrange your sites by the tags themselves. Try creating social bookmarks for research or science fair projects, so the information students find can be shared collectively. Find more at https://sites.google.com/site/team8project9440/introduction-to-diigo.

Social Networking

Collaboration and networking enable dynamic interaction among students when they work together on common goals. What makes Twitter and Facebook work are the connections they enable and the stories they allow to unfold. Social networks provide a variety of ways for users to interact. To get over the stigma attached to social networking, more and more educators are calling for educational or academic networking. One social networking site—Edmodo—meets the qualifications for safety and privacy, yet mirrors public sites such as Facebook and Twitter.

Figure 6.7. Diigo for Educators

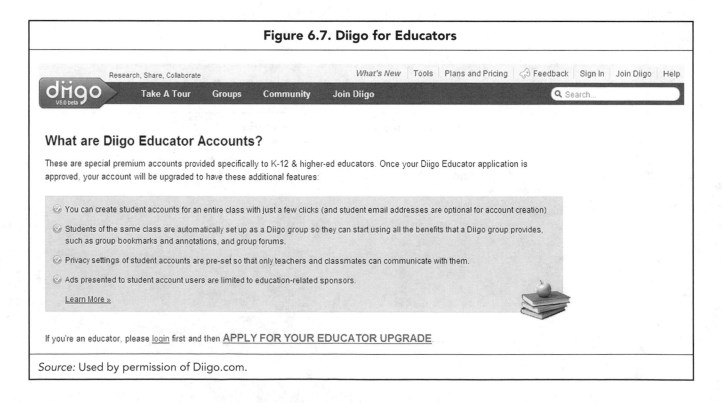

Source: Used by permission of Diigo.com.

What Is Edmodo?

Teachers and students say:

> "I can't stop using it; it has become a "must-have" tool for all my lessons. And kids love it." (Edmodo creator)

> "I use Edmodo CONSTANTLY." (Edmodo creator)

> "Our goal when we created Edmodo was to develop a space that easily enabled teachers to connect and communicate not only with their students, but also with each other through an online global network." (Edmodo creator)

Edmodo (http://www.edmodo.com/) is a free and secure social learning network for schools. With 1.5 million users and growing, Edmodo provides a safe and easy way for teachers and students to connect, share content, and access homework, grades, and school notices (see Figure 6.8).

Edmodo enables teacher-to-teacher resource sharing, global professional development, and networking opportunities (see Chapter 11), and is accessible from any Internet-enabled device, including smartphones. Edmodo's goal is to use safe social media to connect and engage students and teachers in the classroom via technology, closing the gap between how students live and how they learn. Edmodo is also good for young children wanting to use Facebook.

Edmodo lets the teacher create a social networking site that is totally closed and ad-free. Students join with a teacher-provided access code, and can then sign up for individual groups (ones the teacher has created) using additional access codes. For additional security, educators can change all access codes once students are signed into groups; in this way, even if students share access codes later, the codes won't work.

Edmodo pages can include hypertext links, embedded videos, documents, and more. Students can set up fictitious or coded user names and avatars or pasted images rather than their actual pictures. The good news is the teacher is able to see it all!

Figure 6.8. Edmodo Communities

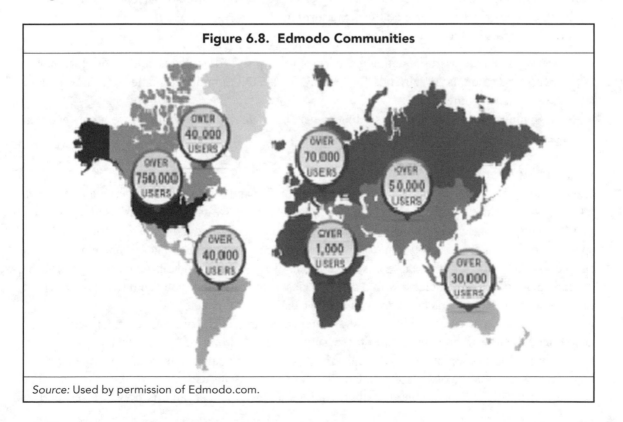

Source: Used by permission of Edmodo.com.

Simple Guidelines

As you begin working on Edmodo, it is important to set up guidelines. Some samples include:

- Do not reveal any personal information on Edmodo: no telephone numbers, addresses, or other students' names. To check someone's username, click the class group (science1, spanish5, etc.).
- Do not post photos or videos showing yourself or classmates.
- Keep conversations on topic. There is a proper place (group) for almost anything you'd like to share.
- Use appropriate language. If you're not sure if a word or joke is okay, then it's not.
- Refrain from posts that tease, bully, annoy, spam, or gossip about any other member.
- If someone posts an inappropriate remark, ask them to edit or remove it.

Discussion groups may include artwork, curriculum-related videos (one video at a time) surveys, monthly project discussions, fun stuff (videos and links unrelated to curriculum), recommended sites, reminders, stories and poems, and prompted discussions based upon class topics and themes, to name some.

It's a good idea to draft a parental consent form for Edmodo and require students to agree to established guidelines for conduct. Check the Edmodo Guide at http://www.edmodo.com/guide/.

Examples Using Edmodo

A number of examples with Edmodo, including nine states and five countries, varied from using Edmodo to jot down notes for the class to creating global classroom connections to facilitating elaborate historical event role-plays.

For example, in an American History class in their History Edmodo group, students collaborated with Thomas Jefferson and other founding fathers in talks of separation from England. Class members took excerpts from the Declaration of Independence and rewrote the document in kid terms, submitting the draft via Edmodo for Jefferson's approval. Jefferson accepted and penned it all night, and the parchment arrived the next morning.

Other examples include:

- Setting up a co-classroom with a teacher from Spain so ESL students could work together
- Informing students of activities for the day—graded assignments, homework, and links to help with assignments
- Assigning a second-grade class a link to watch a video so they could create a conversation between the dog and deer seen in the video

What Is Twitter?

Instant and to the point, Twitter is a free social networking and micro-blogging service that allows its users to send and read other users' updates (known as tweets), which are text-based posts of up to 140 characters in length. You can broadcast short messages to your friends or "followers" and specify which Twitter users you want to follow so you can read their messages in one place. With a simple hashtag (#name), it becomes easy to compile tweets, giving students an easy way to follow the information that is associated with a specific class. Note, too, that you can have only protected tweets, meaning that no one but those you approve can see your tweets.

It's easy to get started. Go to http://www.twitter.com/ and click "Join for free." For best results, use your real name when signing up; otherwise your friends won't be able to find you easily. It's also helpful to upload a picture. If you select the "Protect my updates" box, people won't be able to read your tweets unless you authorize them. Tell your friends your username, or send them the link to your Twitter page. Some common abbreviations include: @username is how you respond to

Figure 6.9. Twitter Page

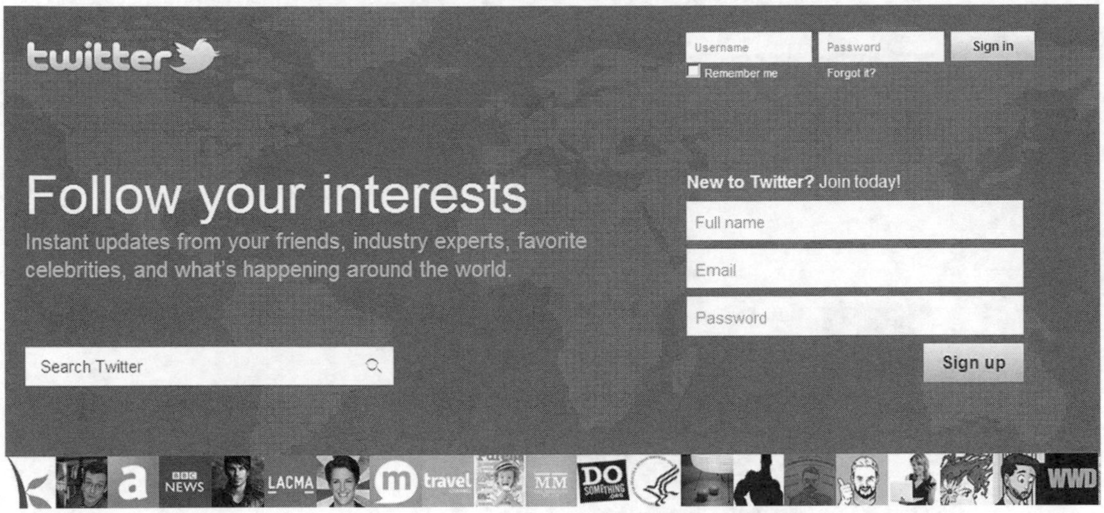

someone else directly; #topic_name is how you designate a topic for a chat; and RT means re-tweet, which is someone passing along a tweet that was generated by someone else (see Figure 6.9).

What Is Facebook?

Founded in 2004, Facebook is a social utility that connects people and lets you share with the people in your life. Anyone over the age of 13 with a valid e-mail address can become a Facebook user. The homepage includes News Feed, a personalized feed of your friends' updates. The Profile displays information you have chosen to share, including interests, education, work background, and contact information. Facebook also includes core applications—Photos, Events, Videos, Groups, and Pages— that let you connect and share in different ways. Additionally, you can communicate with others through Chat, personal messages, Wall posts, Pokes, or Status Updates (see Figure 6.10).

What Is SchoolTube?

Although YouTube is one of the largest sites on the Internet, it is often blocked by school districts for fear of unsavory content. SchoolTube.com is the nation's largest K–12 moderated video-sharing website, providing students and educators with a safe, free, video-sharing website. Teachers and students use SchoolTube for demonstrations, newscasts, digital storytelling, class projects,

> ➤ Review Bev's website at http://www.neal-schuman.com/webclassroom to learn more about social networking sites.

virtual field trips, and more. On the Educators' page (http://www2.schooltube.com/Educators.aspx), you can find best practices for videos and digital stories, as well as educational and technology resources (see Figure 6.11).

The URLs in Table 6.1 may be useful for starting social bookmarking and social networking in your classroom.

Teacher Exercises: Now You Try It . . .

It's always a good idea to try your activity first before conducting it with your students. Before reviewing the unit plan incorporating social networking in Part 3, complete the following exercises:

Figure 6.10. Facebook Page

facebook

Search

Beverley Crane
Edit My Profile

- News Feed
- Messages   1
- Events
- Friends   1

- Create Group...

- Apps
- Games
- Questions
- Photos
- Groups
- Notes
- Deals
- Places Editor
- Ads
- Links
  Less

News Feed

Top News · Most Recent 3

Share: Status   Photo   Link   Video   Question

What's on your mind?

Natalie Johnston commented on their own photo.

Profile Pictures

18 minutes ago · Like · Comment

8 people like this.

View all 10 comments

Natalie Johnston hey i wuz just stalkin ya..... miss ya shrimp
18 minutes ago · Like

Katy Wilson hehee miss ya too
17 minutes ago · Like

Write a comment...

Figure 6.11. SchoolTube Homepage

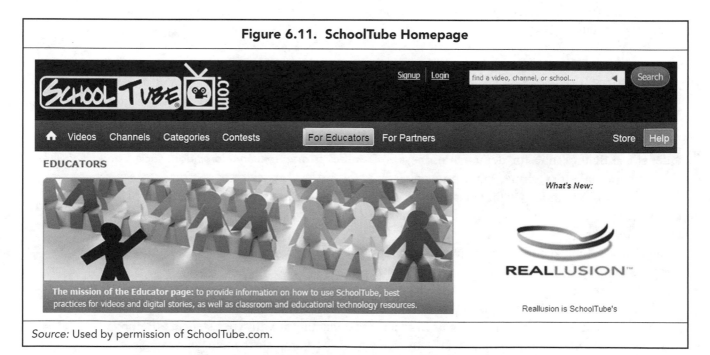

Signup | Login   find a video, channel, or school...   Search

Videos   Channels   Categories   Contests   For Educators   For Partners   Store   Help

EDUCATORS

What's New:

REALLUSION™

Reallusion is SchoolTube's

The mission of the Educator page: to provide information on how to use SchoolTube, best practices for videos and digital stories, as well as classroom and educational technology resources.

Source: Used by permission of SchoolTube.com.

Table 6.1. General Social Bookmarking and Social Networking URLs	
URL	**Description**
http://commoncraft.com/twitter	Twitter in plain English tutorial
http://www2.schooltube.com/Educators/AboutST.aspx	SchoolTube how-to videos and guides
http://www2.schooltube.com/Educators/videoproduction.aspx	Video tutorials, along with lesson plans and URLs to royalty-free movies and images
http://www.slideshare.net/iteachyoucomputers/edmodo-in-your-classroom	Edmodo in the Classroom PowerPoint
http://help.edmodo.com/teacher/	Help Center for Edmodo
http://support.twitter.com/groups/31-twitter-basics/topics/104-welcome-to-twitter-support/articles/215585-twitter-101-how-should-i-get-started-using-twitter	Twitter 101—how to get started and review of basics
http://www.youtube.com/watch?v=MpIOClX1jPE&feature=related	Social media in plain English
http://www.youtube.com/teachingchannel	YouTube Teaching Channel
http://cybersmartcurriculum.org/tools/	Safety and security with social networking
http://www.education.com/reference/article/facebook-privacy-setting-internet-safety/	How to set privacy setting on Facebook
http://www.youtube.com/watch?v=NGXElviSRXM&feature=related	Social bookmarking video tutorial

1. Review resources using Twitter for Educators at http://edudemic.com/2010/06/the-ultimate-twitter-guidebook/. Then sign up for #edchat (http://edchat.pbworks.com/w/page/219908/FrontPage). You may also want to join #edtech.
2. Check several of the top educator Twitter sites at http://wefollow.com/twitter/edtech and follow the ones that seem most interesting to you. (e.g., SherllTerrell, stevehargadon, web20classroom, kathyschrock, joycevalenza). Create several tweets to join the discussion.
3. Look at educator Facebook sites; then sign up for your own.
4. Begin your social bookmarking by viewing the YouTube video at http://www.youtube.com/watch?v=HeBmvDpVbWc.
5. Sign up for Delicious, Diigo, or another social bookmarking site you have heard about.
6. Select an upcoming topic you want your students to research. Review a number of websites on the topic and bookmark at least five sites. Add one or more tags to each bookmark.

You now have your own social bookmarking and two social networking sites. Become familiar with your sites so that you can incorporate the technology, as well as other social networking tools discussed in earlier chapters.

PART 3: PRACTICAL APPLICATIONS

Viewing current events or world situations is an advantage to using the Internet. For example, history textbooks, even those most currently published, will not reference nor describe the 2011 conflict in the Middle East where leaders of countries such as Egypt and Tunisia were overthrown and other countries are still crying for democracy. Using the Internet and social networking sites, students can witness events as they unfold, giving them a chance to examine a controversy from both sides, reading for bias, making predictions, and supporting their own opinions with facts.

> **Clip on Twitter**
>
> A commentary on using Twitter illustrates some of the means the Middle East revolutionaries used to forward their ideas and actions.
>
> Classes will be using Twitter to reflect on learning. As a class they will share, reflect, engage, inquire, and report. This doubles nicely as a means of informal formative assessment. Classes will also use the Twitter accounts to connect with other classrooms and experts. Students will not be permitted to post to the accounts without teacher permission because of the Twitter age limit. Students should be involved in the tweeting not only for the learning opportunities, but also for the opportunity for teachers to model proper use of social media.

Interdisciplinary Unit Plan for Secondary Students

This multidisciplinary unit discusses the role of social media in a history topic—the revolution that ousted both Tunisian president Ben Ali and Egyptian president Hosni Mubarak in early 2011. It encompasses history, geography, social media, and English in writing across the curriculum. A question to discuss: Has social media influenced this important time in world politics?

The unit is designed to make students think critically about both sides of this controversial Middle East issue. Students will work individually, in small groups based on aspects of the topic, and with a partner to respond specifically to their writing. They will use the Internet for research, including Facebook, Twitter, Edmodo, and blogs, as well as traditional media such as CNN. They will write blog posts and comment upon other students' writing using the blog.

Step 1: Connect to the Standards—What Should Be Taught?

This unit supports content and NETS, providing a challenging curriculum for students.

Content Standards

Secondary frameworks in history, civics, and language arts contain the following standards relevant to the assignments in this unit:

- Understand the impact of significant political and nonpolitical developments of the United States and other nations.
- Understand how participation in civic and political life can help citizens attain individual and public goals.
- Illustrate interdisciplinary connections through research.
- Use analysis and evaluation—critical thinking skills—to look at a topic from a variety of points of view, identifying bias and authoritative sources.
- Develop students' research skills on the Internet to find answers to curriculum-related questions.
- Use viewing skills and strategies to understand and interpret visual media.

NETS for Students

In addition to curriculum standards, the *National Educational Technology Standards for Students* (ISTE, 2007) include the following technology standards appropriate for this unit. Students will:

- communicate, collaborate, and publish with peers, experts, or others employing a variety of digital media;
- practice digital citizenship by ensuring safe, legal, and responsible use of information and technology;

- locate, organize, analyze, evaluate, synthesize, and ethically use information from a variety of sources and media; and
- process data and report results.

As a result of engaging in the activities in this unit and working together using social networking, social bookmarking, and social media, students will become information literate in using the Internet and social networking in history/social studies.

Step 2: Identify General Goals and Specific Objectives

The goals and main objectives for this unit are based on national standards for history and English and current NETS. After completing this unit, students should be prepared to do topical research, present opinions supported by authoritative research, question Internet content based on bias, and collaborate with and provide helpful responses to their peers on contemporary issues using social networking.

Goals

Goals for learning about worldwide events in general should include the following:

- Reviewing traditional and nontraditional websites for research purposes.
- Analyzing and evaluating what they read, view, or listen to, thus building critical thinking skills.
- Collaborate with classmates and, if possible, classes and/or students in other regions of the world to understand all sides of an issue.

Objectives

More specifically, as part of each goal, students will:

- define social media and identify its uses in current events;
- create and use social networking to write and comment on this contemporary political issue;
- check news, releases, newswires, TV stations such as CNN and Al Jazeera, as well as blogs, Facebook, Twitter, and other social networking sites to research all sides of the Egyptian uprising;
- question the validity and accuracy of information from news sources and social media;
- determine the role played by social media in the Egyptian uprising and others in the Middle East; and
- describe the role of the United States and European countries in this conflict.

Step 3: Gather Materials

Students will be gathering information from mainstream news sources, including CNN, the Associated Press, and Al Jazeera and comparing and contrasting that information with social media sources such as Facebook, blogs, and Twitter. Some of the resources listed in Table 6.2 can be used in the activities in this unit to learn more about modern Egyptian political history and other Middle Eastern countries.

Note: At the end of the PBS reports in Table 6.2 are additional articles, timelines, country profiles, and more. These can also provide important information for students to review.

Step 4: Introduce the Unit

This unit analyzes worldwide political issues and how an incident in one country can affect events in countries worldwide. Students will look at both sides of the revolution, from websites containing opinion only to factually based sites. Each search students complete will require they employ increasingly higher levels of critical thinking—from merely finding information to analyzing it for currency and concrete support, to synthesizing information from numerous sources and evaluating their own and other students' writing on the blogs through their comments.

Table 6.2. URLs for Unit Plan	
URL	Description
http://www.pbs.org/newshour/bb/international/jan-june11/ tunisia2_01-14.html	Explosion of frustration in Tunisia
http://www.pbs.org/newshour/bb/international/jan-june11/tunisia2_01-17.html	Tunisia's upheaval continues
http://www.pbs.org/newshour/bb/international/jan-june11/tunisia1_01-17.html	Interim government announced
http://www.pbs.org/newshour/bb/international/jan-june11/tunisia2_01-17.html	Will Tunisia's upheaval spread?
http://www.pbs.org/newshour/bb/world/jan-june11/egypt1_02-14.html	Debate on social media's role in Egyptian and other Arab protests
http://www.pbs.org/newshour/extra/teachers/lessonplans/world/jan-june11/socialmedia1.pdf	PBS cartoons illustrating social media role in Egypt
http://www.foreignpolicy.com/articles/2011/01/14/the_first_twitter_revolution?page=0,1	Lesson plan—Demonstrations in the Middle East
http://www.pbs.org/newshour/bb/world/jan-june11/egypt2_02-14.html	How did social media factor into protests?
http://www.pbs.org/newshour/bb/world/jan-june11/egyptcommunica_01-31.html	Social media a catalyst?
http://www.foreignpolicy.com/articles/2011/01/14/the_first_twitter_revolution	The First Twitter Revolution?
http://www.pbs.org/newshour/extra/features/world/jan-june11/egypt_02-01.html	Demand for Mubarak to step down
http://www.pbs.org/newshour/rundown/2011/02/revolution-online.html	Egypt unrest
http://www.pbs.org/newshour/bb/world/jan-june11/egyptitn_01-31.html	Massive demonstrations for Mubarak to step down
http://www.pbs.org/newshour/extra/features/world/jan-june11/syriaturkey_06-10.html	Syrian role in Middle East
http://www.pbs.org/newshour/news/egypt/	Later news from Egypt
http://www.nevillehobson.com/2011/02/12/which-arab-state-will-be-the-next-falling-domino/	Which Arab state is the next to fall?
http://mashable.com/2011/02/25/facebook-egypt/	Facebook's role in the Middle East

In groups of four, students will research one aspect of the topic:

- Political policies of Egyptian leaders Sadat and Mubarak
- Economic conditions and issues arising from them during this time period
- Youth movements and their leadership
- Political and economic policies of neighboring Middle Eastern countries (e.g., Syria, Bahrain, Tunisia, Libya)

Essential questions to ask:

- Why are Egyptians and citizens from other Middle East countries revolting against their governments?
- What role did social media and traditional media serve in the revolutions in Egypt and Tunisia?
- What other factors, such as strong organization and nonviolent dissent, contributed to the Egyptian revolution?

The Product

The product for this unit will be divided into the following parts and include answers to the essential questions posed. Using Edmodo, each group will:

- post information identifying what they want to know about the problem. The first posts will contain what they know, what they assume they know, or what they imagine about the topic. This information will be posted during the introduction to the unit.
- research the topic to test their previous assumptions. All sources must be documented as they proceed. They will also include important links to sites they visited containing valuable information about the topic. These activities will be conducted during the unit, and all information will be posted to their group sites on Edmodo.
- describe what they learned in posts assuming the role they are investigating, for example, relating policies of Mubarak as if he were speaking. Other groups will regularly write comments to each group's posts. These posts and comments will be completed just before follow-up to the unit.
- formulate a visual presentation (e.g., video on SchoolTube) that summarizes their understanding of the situation in Egypt and Tunisia, offer some personal comments, and draw conclusions as follow-up to the unit. They must select an audience (e.g., their congressman, students in the Middle East) to try to persuade the person or group to a particular point of view—that social media does/does not have value to world affairs.

Step 5: Create Sample Activities

Activities at the beginning of the unit will stimulate students' prior knowledge of the Middle East—its upheavals, dictatorial policies, economic policies, and more. A number of tasks will enable students to learn more about the current situation.

Activities to Begin the Unit

At the beginning of the unit, students must assess their prior knowledge about the world situation in the Middle East, most specifically Egypt and its aftermath and how social networking might have had a part to play in the uprising. Parts 1 and 2 of this chapter provide background information on social networking.

As a class, students will:

- analyze political cartoons that depict the revolution in Egypt at http://www.pbs.org/newshour/extra/teachers/lessonplans/world/jan-june11/socialmedia1.pdf and answer the following questions:
  ○ Why are Egyptians and citizens from other Middle East countries revolting against their governments?
  ○ What does the cartoon suggest about the Internet and social media's effects in Egypt?
  ○ Did social media and traditional media serve as a tool in the revolutions in Egypt and Tunisia? Why or why not?
- brainstorm other factors that may have contributed to the Egyptian revolution and create a cluster of factors and other causes for the uprisings (see Figure 6.12).

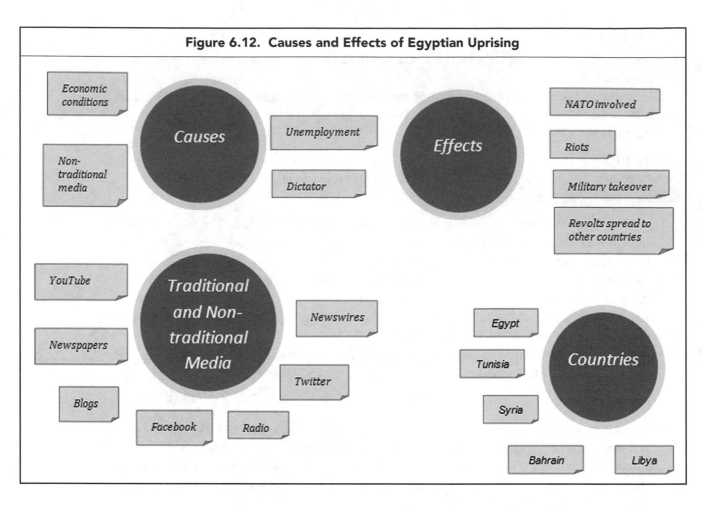

Figure 6.12. Causes and Effects of Egyptian Uprising

In teams of four, students will:

- review vocabulary in Part 1 about social networking and social media;
- create a KWL chart displaying their knowledge of the situation in Egypt in the K column (see Figure 6.13), identify what they need to find out in the W column, and post the chart on their Edmodo group site; and
- select a team leader and have each team member identify comments and questions in the W column that each student will tackle.

Figure 6.13. KWL Chart		
K—What I Know	**W—What I Want to Know**	**L—What I Learned**
Revolt in Tunisia and Egypt	Why are citizens revolting?	
Citizens want Mubarak to resign	What has the president done to prompt the revolution?	

Activities to Use during the Unit

Teams are now ready to start the research process. Each team member must do the following:

- Gather a list of websites, news sources, and social media resources (e.g., Facebook, Twitter, MySpace, blogs) that represent both sides of the issue for the entire group to discuss. Table 6.2 (p. 124) provides a sampling of resources.
- Bookmark relevant sites using Delicious or Diigo and provide the class with a running news feed. Bookmarks should be organized and available to others in the class.
- Continue to follow the situation and update events. Subscribe to relevant hashtags and accounts from all perspectives and compile an updated resource collecting as much research as possible. Students can facilitate their research by typing keywords into Twitter's search engine to find all blog entries on the subject, providing an excellent way for students to research ideas, opinions, and movements as they happen.
- Collect all material for final projects on Edmodo and complete student and group progress reports (see Figure 6.14).

> ➤ *Review Bev's website at http://www.neal-schuman.com/ webclassroom to view more activities using social networking tools.*

Figure 6.14. Student Progress Report

Name: _____   Date: _____

Tasks accomplished this week on my topic:

_____

_____

_____

Problems encountered this week and ways I resolved them:

_____

_____

Successes I had this week:

_____

_____

The most exciting thing I learned/did this week:

_____

_____

Questions I have for my teacher this week:

_____

_____

Status of my progress:

_____ My team is progressing on schedule and we will be ready to turn our assignments in on time.

_____ My team needs more time because _____

_____

I am having trouble completing my part of the assignment because _____

- Complete the KWL chart by filling in what students have learned in the L column.
- Complete the final project (see Chapter 8 for video projects).

Activities to Be Used as Follow-Up to the Unit

As follow-up to the unit, students should answer questions about what they learned and reflect on using social networking and bookmarking in their assignments. To complete these activities, students will:

- compare/contrast entries posted by each group after research on the Middle East uprisings with those that were placed on Edmodo when the unit was introduced;
- comment on how using social media made or did not make a difference in the project—did they enjoy the activity? why or why not?—; and
- complete a checklist about using social networking in the curriculum (see Figure 6.15).

Step 6: Evaluate What You Learned

When implementing a social media plan, it's important to evaluate your results and see what impact they have had. You need to evaluate both student work (the product) and students' working (the process). There are several tools available to measure social media outcomes. For this unit evaluation will be based on the following:

Figure 6.15. Research Evaluation Checklist

1. **Is it clear who has written the information?** Who is the author? Is it an organization or an individual person? Is there a way to contact them?

2. **Are the aims of the site clear?** What are the aims of the site? Who is it for?

3. **Does the site achieve its aims?** Does the site do what it says it will?

4. **Is the site relevant to me?** List five things to find out from the site.
   a. _____
   b. _____
   c. _____
   d. _____
   e. _____

5. **Can the information be checked?** Is the author qualified to write the site? Has anyone else said the same things anywhere else? Is there any way of checking this out? If the information is new, is there any proof?

6. **When was the site produced?** Is it up to date? Can you check to see if the information is up to date and not just the site?

7. **Is the information biased in any way?** Does the site have a particular reason for wanting you to think in a particular way? Is it a balanced view or does it only give one opinion?

8. **Does the site tell you about choices open to you?** Does the site give you advice? Does it tell you about other ideas?

- Assessment of the Edmodo posts by each group

  For example, comments were thoughtful, encouraging more research or stretching thinking; team members contributed required number of posts; and posts exhibited standard American English. Evaluation will also take into account (a) content (the information was thorough and accurate), (b) process (students were able to use the Internet for research and blogs and other social media for research and collaboration), (c) ability to differentiate fact from bias, and (d) ability to support views with valid information (see Figure 6.16).
- Student self-evaluation for Internet research and social media skills (see Chapter 5 to adapt self-evaluation checklist)
- Thoroughness with which students responded as peer evaluators

Figure 6.16. Evaluation Rubric			
ELEMENT	**Exemplary** **3 points**	**Proficient** **2 points**	**Unsatisfactory** **0 points**
Content	Original tweets or posts consistently provide new resources or ideas that add value to the discussion.	Most original tweets or posts provide new resources or ideas that add value to the discussion.	Original tweets or posts do not provide any new resources or ideas, and add no value to the discussion.
	Tweets or posts are creatively and succinctly written to stimulate dialogue and commentary.	Most tweets or posts are written to stimulate dialogue and commentary.	Tweets or posts are poorly written and do not stimulate dialogue and commentary.
Frequency	Exceeds the required number of responses per week.	Meets the required number of responses per week.	Fails to meet the required number of responses per week.
	Creates and sends responses more frequently than required.	Creates and sends responses as often as required.	Creates and sends responses too infrequently to meet the requirements.
Hyperlinks	Responses include accurate hyperlinks to resources that enhance the topic.	Responses include hyperlinks to resources relevant to the topic.	Responses either contain no hyperlinks or selected resources have no relevance to the topic.
	Selects hyperlinks representing the most current resources about the topic.	Usually selects hyperlinks that represent the most current resources about the topic.	Most or all hyperlinks connect to out-of-date resources.
Mechanics	Writes with no errors in grammar, capitalization, punctuation, and spelling.	Writes with minor errors in grammar, capitalization, punctuation, and spelling.	Writes with numerous major errors in grammar, capitalization, punctuation, and spelling (more than 5 errors per tweet).
Comments and Contributions	Consistently responds to tweets and posts with positive, respectful, and succinct comments while providing a meaningful addition to the discussion.	Most responses to tweets and posts are positive and respectful while providing some meaningful additions to the discussion.	Responses to tweets and posts are negative and disrespectful and provide no value to the discussion.

Summary

This unit considered important contemporary issues for which information is found more easily online or by interviews or listening to news on television and radio than from reading textbooks. To complete the assignments, students had to collaborate verbally, read critically, express their opinions using support in writing, and evaluate others' opinions and writings using a social media format. Using social networking tools at school that students already use outside of class enables them to see how school and their everyday lives coincide and makes what they learn in school seem more authentic and relevant.

Teacher Exercises: Now You Try It . . .

Using the unit plan as a model, try the following exercises:

1. Teach a mini-lesson on how to comment on a social networking site.
2. Use the social bookmarking site you created; select a lesson you plan to teach in the near future and create at least ten bookmarked sites.
3. Go to your Facebook and Twitter sites at least twice a week; add several tweets and posts to the pages, ask a question.
4. From your social networking sites, check three or more suggestions from those you are following.
5. Write a brief lesson using social networking either on a real site, a fake site, or a post-it site you create in your classroom. Reflect on the lesson: how did the students respond, were your objectives met, did/did not the social networking aspect enhance the lesson.

CONCLUSION

Many schools initially banned or restricted Internet use, only to ease up when the educational value of the Internet became clear. The same is likely to be the case with social networking. Safety policies remain important, as does teaching students about online safety and responsible online expression— but students may learn these lessons better while they're actually using social networking tools.

Social networking is a part of students' lives. Children cannot use any of these tools responsibly if schools block them. If educators are blocked from exploring these tools, they will not begin to understand them. Educational leaders' sole responsibility is to do the best they can to create learners. In order to do that, teachers and school librarians must learn what tools their students are using and provide an environment where they can receive guidance, make mistakes safely, and be prepared to learn long after they leave school.

According to the National School Boards Association (2007), "Our challenge is to harness that informal learning, bringing it to school settings as each of those activities contains opportunities for learning, creative expression, civic engagement, political empowerment, and economic advancement. There are many ways to be social; there's more than one way to learn, and definitely a nearly infinite number of ways to form a network. But, a winner puts all three together in a social learning network in schools."

Albert Einstein had it right when he said: "I never teach my pupils; I only attempt to provide the conditions in which they can learn."

REFERENCES AND FURTHER READING

Deubel, Patricia. 2009. "Social Networking in Schools: Incentives for Participation." *THE Journal*, September 16. http://thejournal.com/Articles/2009/09/16/Social-Networking-in-Schools-Incentives-for-Participation.aspx?Page=1.

ISTE (International Society for Technology in Education). 2007. *National Educational Technology Standards for Students*. Eugene, OR: International Society for Technology in Education. http://www.iste.org/standards/nets-for-students/nets-student-standards-2007.aspx.

National School Boards Association. 2007. "Creating and Connecting: Research and Guidelines on Online Social—and Educational—Networking." National School Boards Association. http://www.nsba.org/Services/TLN/BenefitsofMembership/Publications/Creating-and-Connecting.pdf.

Pew Research Center. 2010. "Millennials: Confident. Connected. Open to Change." *Millennials: A Portrait of Generation Next* (blog), February 24. http://pewresearch.org/millennials/.

Romeyn, Sara. 2011."Using Facebook to Engage with Historical Figures." TeachingHistory.org blog, March 4. http://teachinghistory.org/digital-classroom/beyond-the-chalkboard/24152.

Wikipedia. 2011. "Social Bookmarking." Wikimedia Foundation. Last modified October 11. http://en.wikipedia.org/wiki/Social_bookmarking.

Wikipedia. 2011. "Social Networking Service." Wikimedia Foundation. Last modified November 2. http://en.wikipedia.org/wiki/Social_networking.

YouTube. 2010. "Social Media Revolution Socialnomics 2011" (video). YouTube. Uploaded September 2. http://www.youtube.com/watch?v=QzZyUaQvpdc&feature=related.

CHAPTER 7

Using Google in the Science Classroom— Tools That Work

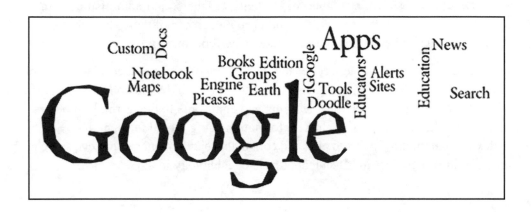

PART 1: IDEAS AND INSIGHTS

When the public first heard of Google, it was as a search engine for research. Educators and students alike could search for anything from a medicine they were taking to information on the Iraq War to something as current as the 9.0 earthquake in Japan. They just "googled" it to retrieve thousands of entries about the topic. Next, Google used its creativity and technological strength and created an array of tools especially useful to the educational community. Google has continued to enhance the tools they have, as well as to add new ones, such as Google Sketch Up or Public Data Explorer. Google provides Google Apps for Educators at no charge to K–12 and now to university educators as well. With more than 10 million students using Google Apps, educators love it:

"I created a library lesson using Google Earth for Earth Day.... The students were practically jumping out of their seats with excitement." (Google Earth; Librarian, Encinitas, CA; http://www.google.com/librariancenter/librarian_tot.html#stories)

"Using Google Docs, one poem was being written by two students in different locations at 11:00 p.m.! To me that means learning is happening at all times of the day." (Teacher at Diamante High School)

"Goggle Docs has given my students control over their education to a higher degree than they've ever had before." (Science teacher, Kennedy Junior High School)

"Students can become publishers on a worldwide level. It raises the level of their work because they understand how many people are seeing what they've done and they want it to be the best they can do." (Technology teacher, Acalanes Union High School)

"When I talk with students about their projects and they say, 'I'll share you in, Mr. Levy,' it really makes my day. It's great to see how well they actually get it, and how excited they are to be here." (Principal, Bronx middle school)

Objectives of This Chapter

The tools in this chapter can be used by school librarians and content teachers at both the elementary and secondary levels. By the end of this chapter, educators will be able to:

- differentiate among the Google tools, especially those in Google Apps Education Edition, describing them and identifying their uses in the classroom;
- get started using some of these tools;
- collaborate in cross-curricular learning activities; and
- create a unit plan that incorporates Google tools.

The International Society for Technology in Education (ISTE) revised its *National Educational Technology Standards* (NETS), available for students, teachers, and administrators in 2007 and 2008. Using Google tools offers students the ability to meet some of these standards.

After using tools described in this chapter, students will be able to:

- think creatively, construct knowledge, and develop innovative products using technology;
- employ digital media and environments to communicate and work collaboratively (including at a distance) to support individual learning and contribute to the learning of others;
- access, retrieve, manage, and evaluate information using digital tools; and
- employ critical thinking skills to plan and conduct research, manage projects, solve problems, and make informed decisions using appropriate technology tools.

Glossary

Review the following terms before starting the chapter to fully understand the concepts discussed in relation to Google and the earthquake unit plan.

earthquake: Result of a sudden release of energy in the earth's crust that creates seismic waves.

epicenter: The point on the earth's surface immediately above the place where the energy was released during an earthquake.

fault: Fracture in a volume of rock in the earth's crust across which there has been significant displacement.

Google Alert: Notifies users (by e-mail) about the latest web and news pages of their choice.

Google Apps: A service from Google containing a number of web applications, including Gmail, Google Calendar, Google Talk, Google Docs, Google Sites, and more.

Google Apps Marketplace: Integrated applications from grade book to bibliography to haiku for Google Apps from the Google Apps Marketplace Education category (http://www.google.com/enterprise/marketplace/).

Google Docs: A combination word processor, spreadsheet, and presentation tool, as well as forms and a timeline, that enables students to share their work easily, access it from any device that has Internet access, and save their work automatically so they won't lose what they have written.

Google Earth: A free, downloadable application that enables users to explore oceans, the sky, historical images of the Earth, sights around the world, and more.

Google Groups: A free service from Google where groups of people have discussions about common interests.

Google Maps: A free web-mapping service application and technology that powers many map-based services.

Google News: Access to thousands of news sources, including archives going back 200 years.

Google Reader: A web-based aggregator, capable of reading Atom and RSS feeds online or offline.

Google Sites: A tool that can be used to centralize all types of information, such as videos, documents, spreadsheets, presentations, photo slideshows and calendars, directly onto Google Sites pages from other Google tools.

placemarker: A marker placed on a map on Google Earth or Google Maps to identify a specific location.

plate tectonics: A scientific theory that describes the large-scale motions of the earth's crust.

Richter Scale: A mathematical device to quantify the energy contained in an earthquake.

seismic activity: Frequency, type, and size of earthquakes experienced over a period of time in an area.

seismometer or seismograph: An instrument that measures the continuous motion of the ground during an earthquake.

Introduction

The list of Google tools is too long to comment on each one in this chapter; however, Google for Educators (http://www.google.com/educators/tools.html) contains a comprehensive list. The site also describes the different tools and provides tutorials and videos showing how to get started using them. Some tools include: Google Books (http://books.google.com/) to preview a growing list of books, Picasa (http://www.google.com/educators/p_picasa.html) to find, edit, and share pictures, and Google Custom Search Engine (http://www.google.com/educators/p_cse.html) to search across only sites you specify and display results you know will be right for your students. The webpage also contains examples that illustrate how educators are incorporating multiple tools into their own classroom instruction. It is a site you will want to bookmark and check often so you don't miss new tools from Google and projects like Doodle 4 Google.

This chapter describes some of the Google tools, illustrates how educators are integrating them into the curriculum, and demonstrates ways the tools can be used together to create exciting and interesting lessons for students. A sampling of tools—Google Docs, Google Earth, Google Maps, Google News, Google Sites—is highlighted in the unit plan in Part 3.

Although Google tools can be used in different subject areas, the focus of the unit in this chapter will be on earthquakes, a subject that is part of the science curriculum and can also be incorporated into social studies, writing, and communicating across the curriculum. By reviewing the classroom examples and the detailed unit, educators will see how easy the Google tools are to use in their lessons.

What Are Google Tools?

In an attempt to support educators, Google has created not only a site specifically for educators but a group of tools that will help them do their jobs better and increase students' interest in learning. A newsletter and a discussion group (http://www.google.com/support/forum/p/Google+Apps), designed to keep teachers and school librarians up to date on educational initiatives at Google, are just some of the ways Google is supporting K–12 education. Several of the tools used as part of the unit later in this chapter are described here.

Google Docs (http://www.google.com/educators/p_docs.html) is a combination word processor, spreadsheet, and presentation tool that enables students to create and share documents easily, and access them from any device that has an Internet connection. It also makes collaborative editing easy.

- The word-processing tool lets students collaborate during the revision process and keep track of the changes and who is making them through a Revision History tool.

- The spreadsheet helps educators organize grades, projects, or attendance sheets. Students can also use the spreadsheet, for example, to create a budget in math, keep track of the details of how a seed grows in a biology class, watch candidates for a presidential election, or use forms to create surveys (see Figure 7.1).
- The presentation tool enables students to work together to create group presentations from any location and jointly present the topic.

Educators find Google Docs helpful because they can monitor student work while they are in the process of writing or revising in class and identify and work with students who are having major problems. Check the demos and click the download button to install Google Docs on your computer.

Google News (http://www.google.com/educators/p_news.html) provides access to thousands of news sources, including a 200-year archive. Students can search for events, people, or ideas and see how they have been described over time. They can search articles in order of relevance to the query and see a historical overview of events and articles associated with the search on a timeline that is automatically created. The latter allows students to discover a variety of viewpoints across time periods. And, Google News is updated continuously throughout the day.

Teachers, librarians, and students can also set up Google Alerts, e-mails automatically sent whenever there are additional news results about their saved search. Alerts enable students to track developments in the news on an ongoing basis. Along with news alerts, there are five other types of Alerts: "web," "blogs," "comprehensive," "video" and "groups." Figure 7.2 illustrates how to set up an Alert.

Figure 7.1. Google Docs—Spreadsheets

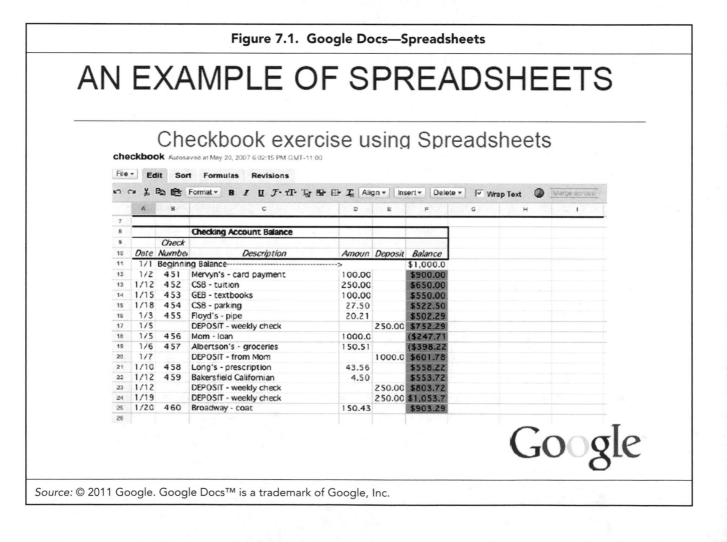

Source: © 2011 Google. Google Docs™ is a trademark of Google, Inc.

Figure 7.2. Google News Alerts

Web Images Videos Maps News Shopping Gmail mor

Google alerts
beta

Search   earthquakes
terms: Preview results

Type: Everything

How often: Once a day

Volume: Only the best results

Your email:

Create Alert

Source: © 2011 Google. Google News Alerts™ is a trademark of Google, Inc.

Google Groups (http://www.google.com/educators/p_groups.html) enables educators to set up their own place to communicate and collaborate safely and securely with their students. It is easy and quick to get started: create an account, name the group, and invite people to participate in private or public groups. Teachers can customize the look of the page and upload files to share students' work with others. Group members can also participate from any device with an Internet connection. Teachers and librarians may also want to join the Google for Educators Discussion Group (http://groups.google.com/group/google-for-educators?lnk=gschg) to share ideas, ask questions, or tell their colleagues about teaching ideas they have created that have worked well.

Google Earth (http://www.google.com/educators/p_earth.html) is a free, downloadable application combining satellite imagery, maps, 3-D terrain, and 3-D buildings to create a realistic virtual globe. Educators can create inquiry-based lessons using Google Earth to enhance understanding of topics such as earthquakes, volcanoes, erosion meteorite impacts, and more. See Figure 7.3 for a view of Google Earth Earthquakes.

Google Maps (http://www.google.com/educators/p_maps.html), on the other hand, can be viewed right from your browser to view satellite imagery and shaded-relief terrain in a two-dimensional (overhead) view. These tools provide an uncomplicated means of combining satellite imagery with geological and geographic information so that teachers can create learning environments that merge content, media, and geography (see Figure 7.4).

Google Sites (http://sites.google.com/) can be used to centralize all types of information directly onto webpages from other Google tools, such as videos, documents, spreadsheets, presentations, photo slideshows, and calendars. Google Sites pages can be shared with just a few people, an entire school, or the world. Designations for owners, viewers only, and collaborators who have permission to edit the pages can be set up. See Figure 7.5 for an example of a teacher's team site.

Google Reader (http://www.google.com/reader/view/#overview-page) enables educators

> Review Bev's website at http://www.neal-schuman.com/ webclassroom to learn more about the latest Google tools.

to collect all of their favorite sites in one convenient place. Google Reader constantly checks these news sites and blogs for new content. Whether a site updates daily or monthly, users can be sure

Figure 7.3. Google Earth Earthquakes

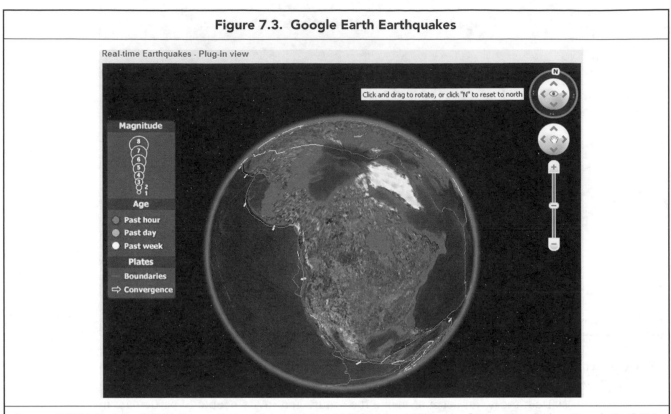

Source: © 2011 Google, © 2011 Europa Technologies, © MapLink/Tele Atlas, U.S. Dept. of State Geographer. Google Earth™ is a trademark of Google, Inc.

Figure 7.4. Google Maps

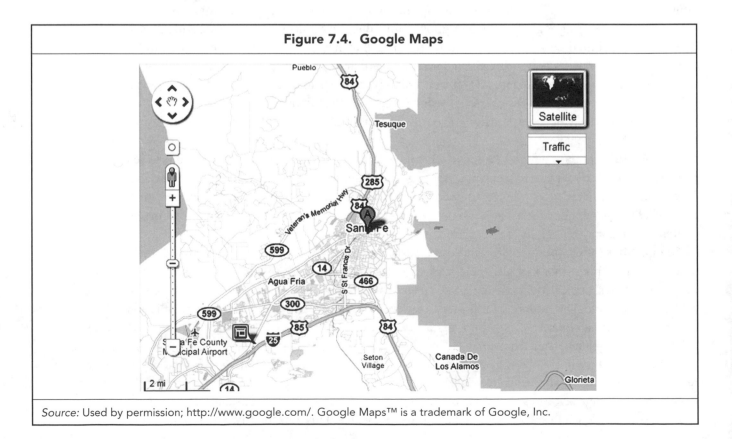

Source: Used by permission; http://www.google.com/. Google Maps™ is a trademark of Google, Inc.

Figure 7.5. Google Sites

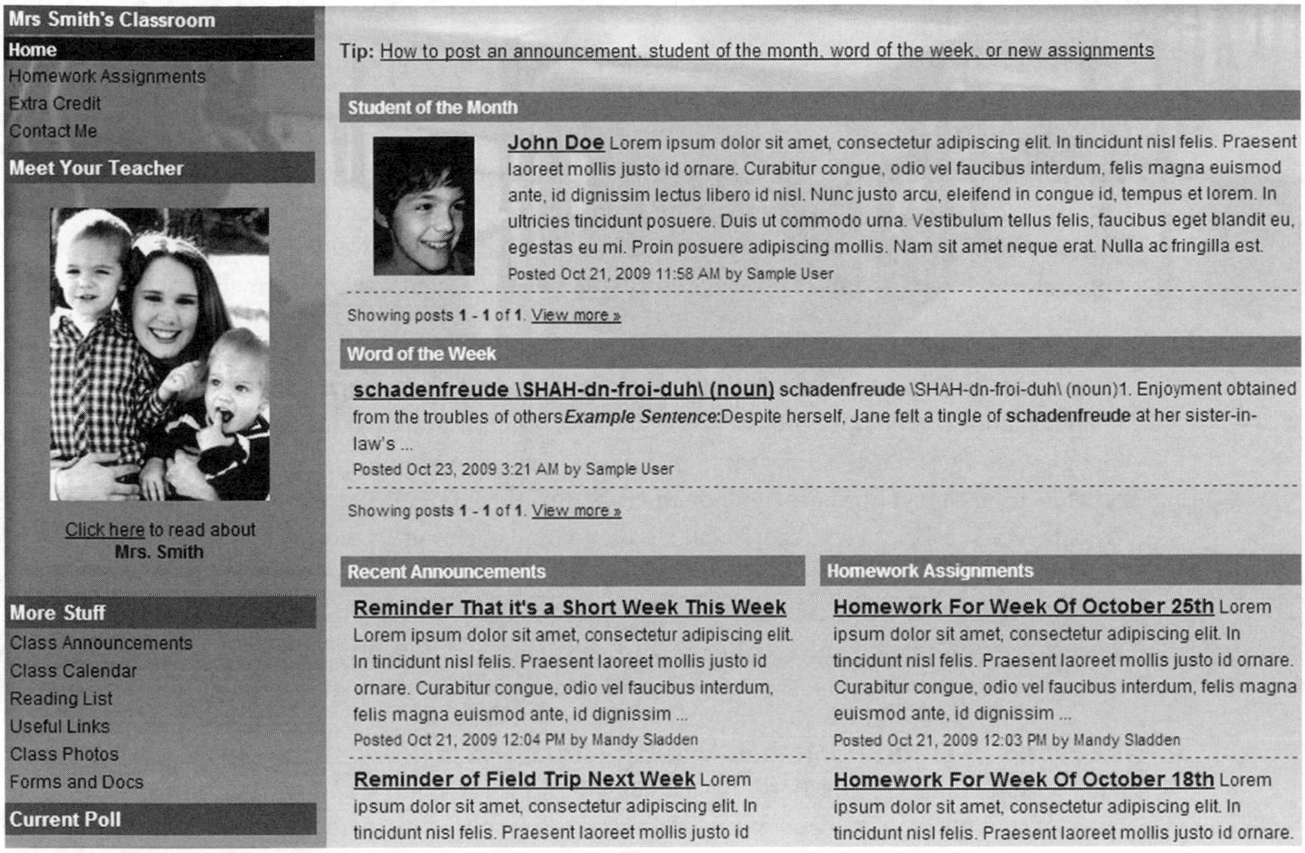

Source: © 2011 Google. Google Sites™ is a trademark of Google, Inc.

they won't miss a thing. They can access their Google Reader account from any device with online access. Sharing items from Google Reader with friends is also easy. A tour is available at http://www.google.com/intl/en/googlereader/tour.html.

Why Use Google Tools in the Classroom?

Educators have already found many uses for Google tools, both as teaching aids and for administrative tasks such as keeping track of grades. These free tools are easy to use, require little instruction, and often are available from the desktop or through a quick download from the Google website. The wide variety of offerings enables teachers and school librarians to use the tools for collaboration and presentation with all grade levels and subject areas. Google Apps for Educators is loaded with teaching ideas and examples of uses in the classroom. Google tools can be used to:

- practice research, evaluate sources, synthesize information, and formulate opinions (Google News);
- study natural and political maps; learn map reading and navigation (Google Earth, Google Maps);
- practice each phase in the writing process by getting quick feedback from many people, demonstrating editing skills, and writing for an authentic audience (Google Docs);
- analyze and organize data and share data sets (Google Docs—spreadsheet);

- study geography and mapping by finding locations all around the world (Google Maps); and
- share schoolwork such as book reviews with peers, parents, and others; collaborate on projects and get feedback from others (Blogger).

The list of ways to use Google tools in the classroom is extensive. As you proceed through this chapter, you will see illustrations of other ideas for Google tools.

Examples of Google Tools for the Classroom and Library

Besides the lessons on the Google site for each tool, several other sample lessons created by students illustrate how easy the tools are to use, as well as emphasizing how well they can be integrated into the curriculum. A brief synopsis follows describing the lesson, and the URL provides more information at the site.

Example 1: Digital Storytelling and Google Apps in High School History

A high school U.S. history project about Vietnam used a variety of Google tools. Each group set up Google Calendar pages to organize due dates. From the Google Docs template gallery, groups created their storyboards for videos to embed in their Google Sites pages. Using Aviary from Google Marketplace, they recorded and edited voice-over and created video with Microsoft Photo Story. As each group assembled the final project, members had worked together both in class and at home. The teacher even created a Google Custom Search Engine so sites visited were ones the teacher felt confident about (see Figure 7.6). See a video of this project and others at http://google-monthly.com/google-apps/using-google-apps-for-digital-storytelling-projects.html.

Example 2: Google Earth in English Literature

This lesson using Google Earth has students build a Lit Trip as part of the process of reading a work of literature. By collecting Lit Trip content throughout the reading, students can focus on the kinds of details that make for rich classroom discussions during the reading. Group assignments include question discussion starters, as well as speculations and suggestions of connections to current

---

Figure 7.6. Digital Storytelling Project with Google Tools

Source: Used by Permission of Kevin Randolph, Department Chair for History/Social Studies and Vincent Vrotny, Director of Academic Technology, North Shore Country Day School.

real-world situations. Students also collected URLs for images to enhance comprehension of the setting, characters, plot, and themes, as well as images that improve comprehension of the historical, geographical, social, political, and other relevant subjects associated with the reading assignment. They also put placemarkers on locations mentioned in the chapters. Many works of literature for all ages are listed on the site at http://www.googlelittrips.com/GoogleLit/Home.html (see Figure 7.7).

Example 3: Google Docs and Survey Forms in Fifth Grade

A fifth-grade teacher used Google Docs as part of a unit on recycling. Using a Google Form survey, the class gathered data about the items in their recycle bins at home. The goal was to compare the data students collected with information about recycling in other parts of the world. The class created a survey, using Forms, part of Google Docs spreadsheet. Students were to look at their recycle bins to find out the types and how many recyclables were in the bin. The teacher sent the survey out through Twitter and received responses worldwide. Students were extremely excited to receive so many answers, especially from outside the United States. Other student-generated

> ➤ Explore other examples of educator websites using Google tools at Bev's website at http://www.neal-schuman.com/webclassroom.

surveys concentrated on whether viewing video games, computers, and television related to amount of sleep and if playing video games influenced grade point average (GPA) (see Figure 7.8). Read

Figure 7.7. Google Lit Trips

Figure 7.8. Google Forms Survey

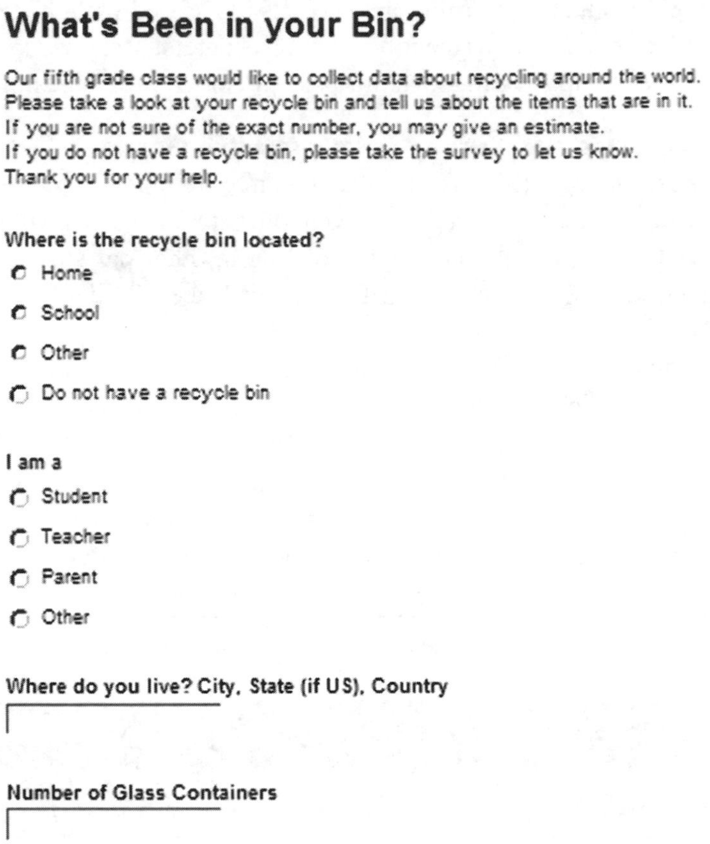

What's Been in your Bin?

Our fifth grade class would like to collect data about recycling around the world.
Please take a look at your recycle bin and tell us about the items that are in it.
If you are not sure of the exact number, you may give an estimate.
If you do not have a recycle bin, please take the survey to let us know.
Thank you for your help.

Where is the recycle bin located?

○ Home

○ School

○ Other

○ Do not have a recycle bin

I am a

○ Student

○ Teacher

○ Parent

○ Other

Where do you live? City, State (if US), Country

_____

Number of Glass Containers

_____

Source: Used by permission of Karen Bosch; http://ififth.edublogs.org/2009/11/01/invitation-join-the-whats-been-in-your-bin-survey/.

more about the project at http://ififth.edublogs.org/2009/11/01/invitation-join-the-whats-been-in-your-bin-survey/.

Teacher Exercises: Now You Try It . . .

Now that you've learned about the different Google tools and ways they can be used for instruction, it is time to practice using them.

1. Go to Google Maps (http://maps.google.com/), which you can view through your browser, and enter your home address. Then select a destination you want to visit in the United States or elsewhere and enter that name. Get directions taking you from one location to the other.
2. Download Google Earth (http://www.google.com/earth/download/ge/agree.html) and then use it to take a virtual tour to China. Take notes on your Google Blog (http://www.blogger.com/) about how you might use this tour with students.
3. Select two Google tools you are especially interested in; go to each website and review tutorials on how to use them.

➤ *Try other exercises using Google tools at Bev's website at http://www.neal-schuman.com/webclassroom.*

PART 2: GETTING STARTED WITH GOOGLE TOOLS

You, as a busy educator, have so many technology options to work with that it can be exhausting at times. Google makes it easy to get started. To implement a number of Google tools at once for the entire school, Google has an education version of Google Apps for Education for K–12 and higher education.

Getting Started with Google Apps

Google Apps for Education (K–12 Edition) enables a school to have its own account with free communication, collaboration, and publishing tools. Google Apps provides access to a number of Google tools, including Google Docs, Google Calendar, Google Sites, Google Talk, e-mail accounts on your school's domain (like student@your-school.edu), and help support (see Figure 7.9).

Note: Students can also get started for free with the Google Team Edition. A school e-mail address is needed to sign up.

To get started:

1. Go to the Google Apps page (http://www.google.com/a/help/intl/en/edu/k12.html). Click the Compare Editions button, review the Education version features, and sign up. You can see that the Education version contains many of the features of the Premier version, the difference being that the Education version is free to schools.

2. Access the administrative control panel and sign in at http://www.google.com/a/help/intl/en/ admins/resources/setup/step_one.html. Replace "your-domain.com" with your school domain

---

Figure 7.9. Google Apps for K–12

Build your 21st century school, starting today

Google Apps' advanced collaboration and communication tools make it easy to help your students acquire the skills that will help them soar, in their education and out in the world. There's no hardware to maintain or software to install, no ads, and no cost for schools.

Get Apps for your school

Google Message Security is included free for K-12 schools.

Resources for administrators

Guide to going Google
Apps FAQ
Resource Center (English)
Customer Case Studies
Education Community Site
Security & Privacy

Downloads

Google Apps for K12 [pdf]
Security white paper [pdf]

In the classroom:

K-12 Lesson Plans
Improving the writing process with Google Docs

Stay Connected:

Quarterly EDU Newsletter

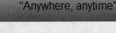

Integrated communication

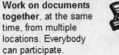

7+ GBs of email storage lets you stop worrying about a full inbox.

Integrated calendar manages your schedule, and reserves resources like lab rooms or laptop carts.

Web-based applications are accessible from any computer, so students can work outside the classroom.

"Anywhere, anytime"

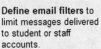

Work on documents together, at the same time, from multiple locations. Everybody can participate.

Sharing and privacy controls include domain-level security, to protect student information.

Build class or project websites without using HTML, so everyone can contribute and learn.

Security and protection
powered by Postini

Define email filters to limit messages delivered to student or staff accounts.

Customized email policies for different groups like faculty, staff and students.

Email archiving available at a 66% discount with Google Message Discovery.

Source: © 2011 Google. Google Apps™ is a trademark of Google, Inc.

name. Then verify your domain name. The Google site at http://www.google.com/a/help/intl/ en/admins/resources/setup/step_two.html provides two tests to verify the name.

3. Customize Google Apps by applying a school logo, creating and publishing webpages, and configuring the Start Page. Instructions and demonstration tours are available to help in the process.
4. Add users to your account either individually or all at once.
5. Turn on the e-mail so messages will be routed to your school domain. A number of instructive links provide all the information you need.
6. Get your classes and students started with Google Apps.

Now that your account is set up, Google encourages educators to get started with sample lesson plans, a quarterly newsletter, teacher-conducted Webinars, and more. Explore and bookmark the Google K–12 website.

Starting with Each Tool

Another method to get started is for teachers or librarians to select only those Google tools that meet the goals and objectives of their education program or classroom lessons. Many of these tools were discussed in Part 1 of this chapter.

Each tool has its own process to set it up. For some tools you must download the application to your computer (e.g., Google Earth); for others you can use your web browser to get started (e.g., Google Maps). So, just follow these five simple steps to begin using one or more Google tools.

- *Step 1:* Go to Google for Educators, click "Tools for the Classroom," and scan the list of tools (http://www.google.com/educators/tools.html). Select those that you think you can use with your subject area and grade level. For example, Google Earth or Google Maps, ideal for science or social studies, allow you to explore the sky and see an exploding star; Google Docs enhances collaborative writing in English/language arts, enabling students to help classmates revise their work. Select at least two or three tools.
- *Step 2:* Read the description of each tool you selected, follow additional links, and read the Frequently Asked Questions (FAQs).
- *Step 3:* If the tool needs to be downloaded, follow the instructions to download the tool. For Google Earth you must download the program onto your computer from http://earth.google .com/. Take a virtual tour at http://earth.google.com/tour/index.html to see how to maneuver around the globe.
- *Step 4:* Practice using the tool with some simple exercises, for example, use Google Earth to identify your house or plan a trip you have wanted to take. Experiment with some of the features including a visual overlay, add a placemark (a marker placed on the map), and share your work with a colleague.
- *Step 5:* Create a simple lesson that uses the tool, test it, and use it with your students. Following the experiment, ask students to comment on the lesson. Of course, if you want to set up a blog (Blogger is a Google tool), you can use it for the class dialogue about the new Google tool. (See Chapter 2 for more on blogs.)

Note: Check these websites for additional support for Google tools.

- If you want to set up a blog, you can set up an account at Blogger at http://www.blogger .com/start?utm_source=en-cpp-edu&utm_campaign=en&utm_medium=cpp.
- To set up Google Docs, go to http://www.google.com/educators/p_docs_start.html.
- Take a tour of Google Reader at http://www.google.com/intl/en/googlereader/tour.html.

Now that you know about the many Google tools and how to set them up and use them, it's time to turn to the task of creating interesting, educational, creative lessons to motivate students and enhance their learning.

> ➤ Learn more about each Google tool at Bev's website at http://www.neal-schuman.com/webclassroom.

PART 3: PRACTICAL APPLICATIONS

The unit chosen for this chapter will primarily illustrate using Google Earth and Google Maps in high school science, as well as other Google tools to connect learning to social studies and language arts. Designed to incorporate a hands-on approach to learning, the unit can be adapted for other grade levels.

Cross-Curricular Unit Plan Using Google Tools

The activities in this unit focus on the topic of earthquakes. Few countries are free from the terror a sudden, devastating natural disaster can bring to its population and infrastructure, and many regions of the world live in fear of earthquakes. In fact, a number of severe quakes have occurred in the last few years. Using Google Earth to mark earthquake locations, Google News to find out about the magnitude of quakes and effects worldwide, and Google Alert to continue to identify new severe tremors provides inquiry-oriented, engaging activities. Tasks are designed to support learners' thinking at the levels of analysis, synthesis, and evaluation on Bloom's Taxonomy (see Chapter 1). Students will look at a variety of resources and use their creativity and critical-thinking skills to analyze why earthquakes have continued to be a most devastating natural disaster. This problem is "real world"—that is, one that affects a large global population.

Today's students face a challenging world. In their jobs they will work in teams. Masses of information will be available to them, and they will have to sift through it, filtering the authentic from the opinion from the lies. Issues facing them will become more and more complex, and societal problems will resist easy solutions. Practice in identifying problems and finding innovative solutions helps build a solid foundation to prepare students for their futures. Google tools will facilitate the process, offering inquiry-based, collaborative learning opportunities.

As we have seen in previous examples of classroom activities using Google tools, educators integrate them into many subject areas at different grade levels. In this science unit at the secondary level, students will use a number of

> ➤ See other examples of using Google tools in different subject areas and grade levels at Bev's website at http://www.neal-schuman.com/webclassroom.

Google tools described earlier to delve into the scientific phenomena of earthquakes, studied at varying levels of sophistication according to content standards in elementary, middle, and high school.

To compile this information, students will test the following Google tools:

- Google Earth and Google Maps
- Google News, archived news, and Google Alerts
- Google Docs
- Google Sites
- Blogger

Step 1: Connect to the Standards—What Should Be Taught?

This unit incorporates standards in science, history/social sciences, and English/language arts, as well as taking into account NETS, discussed in Part 1.

Science Standards

Students will be able to:

- summarize and make generalizations from content and relate them to earth processes;
- use information to form, explain, and support questions, and produce reasonable explanations about plate tectonics;
- understand the processes of scientific inquiry and technological design to investigate questions, conduct experiments, and solve problems;
- collect data about the earth's changes using scientific process skills including observing, estimating, and measuring; and
- report and display the results of individual and group investigations.

Social Studies Standards

In social studies, students are asked to consider historical events through a variety of perspectives and recognize how economic and social turmoil can affect ordinary people. The California History–Social Sciences framework, for example, states that "history should be treated as a skill to be developed rather than as knowledge to be acquired" (California Department of Education, 2009). In other words, students should be taught to understand past and present connections in history so they can make meaning out of the future.

Teachers will:

- integrate the teaching of history with other subjects, such as language arts and science;
- engage students actively in the learning process through collaboration, role-playing, and writing projects;
- include critical thinking skills at every grade level to learn to detect bias in print and visual media, to recognize illogical thinking, and to reach conclusions based on solid evidence; and
- enhance content using technology.

English/Language Arts Standards

Teachers will:

- encourage an integrated curriculum in which students practice language skills in meaningful contexts; and
- improve communication skills, both oral and written, through intensive practice.

Step 2: Identify General Goals and Specific Objectives

The goals and specific objectives that follow form the basis for the content and skills to be mastered in the unit.

Goals

Students will:

- link past to present;
- learn about tectonic movements at plate boundaries;
- make and support inferences and form interpretations on main themes and topics about physical changes of the earth;
- collect and record data accurately using consistent measuring and recording techniques from the U.S. Geological Survey about earthquakes happening throughout the world in a given time period; and
- use Google tools for research and for individual work, collaboration, and presentation.

Objectives

The activities and materials in this unit will contribute to a greater understanding of earthquakes, plate tectonics, results of earthquakes, and how to prepare for them. The unit will provide content and strategies so students will be able to:

Content—understand earthquakes:

- compare and contrast earthquakes of different magnitudes and their effects worldwide;
- stimulate interest in the earthquake-plotting process and promote critical thinking and questions about earth science in the students;
- locate and mark earthquakes above a 4.0 magnitude on the Richter scale; and
- plot the quakes and examine the data for patterns and trends.

Technology—use the following Google tools for their assignments:

- Google Calendar to set due dates;
- Google Earth and Google Maps to discover geographic areas where earthquakes commonly occur;
- Google Maps to plot earthquake locations;
- Google Docs to create presentations incorporating research, spreadsheets, and graphs to track earthquakes, and forms to survey schools in earthquake areas;
- Google News, archives, and Alerts for research on earthquakes globally;
- Blogger to communicate and comment within and among teams; and
- Google Sites to set up a website to incorporate all work products that are part of the unit.

Step 3: Gather Materials

Students will need to explore maps, global earthquake activities, historical events, and more. Groups can check some of the URLs on earthquakes in Table 7.1 throughout the unit as they research their topics.

Table 7.1. URLs for the Earthquake Unit	
URL	**Description**
http://earthquake.usgs.gov/earthquakes	Earthquake topics
http://earthquake.usgs.gov/earthquakes/world/historical.php/	Historic earthquake data
http://www.enchantedlearning.com/subjects/astronomy/planets/earth/continents.shtml	Information about plate tectonics at elementary school level
http://earthquake.usgs.gov/learn/topics/all.php	Earthquake hazards program
http://www.pbs.org/wgbh/aso/tryit/tectonics/#	Introduction to plate tectonics
http://earth.google.com/support/	Google Earth support
http://www.earthquakecountry.info/roots/seven_steps.html	Seven steps to earthquake safety
http://urbanext.illinois.edu/earth/shakeup.cfm	Large U.S. earthquakes with pictures
http://edu.glogster.com/	Glogster for Educators to create interactive posters
http://www.exploratorium.edu/faultline/	Fault lines

Step 4: Create Sample Activities

Included are activities to introduce the unit, use during the lessons, and follow up to complete the project. Earthquakes occur all over the world. Students will accomplish a number of tasks that help them learn more about the scientific nature of earthquakes, their locations, and their intensity. The tasks in this unit enable students to accomplish goals and provide focus for student energies and inquiry.

> ➤ *Learn more about earthquakes and about the latest Google tools at Bev's website at http://www.neal-schuman.com/webclassroom.*

Activities to Introduce the Unit

Some students may have experienced earthquakes; others have read about them. It is important that students have some basic background about earthquakes and bring their prior knowledge to the discussion. As a group the class will:

- discuss what they know about earthquakes from experience, and about plate tectonics from reading and former study. Create a class KWL chart (see Figure 7.10) indicating what they know and what they need to find out. At the end of the project, they will fill in the last column with what they have learned and put it on their team website.

Figure 7.10. KWL Chart on Earthquakes		
K—What I Know	W—What I Want to Know	L—What I learned

- review plate tectonics using information and models from the PBS website at http://www.pbs.org/wgbh/aso/tryit/tectonics/#.
- learn how to find a specific location where an earthquake has taken place (e.g., 9.0 quake in Japan in March 2011) from a teacher demonstration using Google Earth.
- in teams of four, select one Google tool planned for the unit and give the rest of the class a lesson on how to use this tool.

Tracking the earthquake data provides a more constructivist or inquiry-based approach in which students collect data, observe, and analyze the patterns of earthquakes, which then appear on Google Maps. Students are using real data and studying earthquakes from all over the world that have occurred only a few days or even hours before. They can then begin to ask questions about and interpret the data. As students perform these tasks, their interest in earthquakes, their causes, and earthquake hazards should increase.

Activities to Be Used during the Unit

The following activities will provide new information and reinforce the concepts that students have already attained. In groups of three or four, students will:

- select a portion of the globe, and using Google Earth, plot all global earthquakes that happen daily during a specific two-week period (e.g., North America, South America, Middle East, Southern Europe, Japan, Northern Europe, Eurasia, Australia, etc.); and
- create a website that will incorporate research on earthquakes, past and present. In groups of four, each student will be assigned one of four roles: scientist, mathematician, reporter/photo-journalist, or historian/geographer. Each person will conduct research to provide expertise

for his/her role. Team members are also responsible for incorporating their information and visuals on their webpage.

The activities each must perform will help develop their expertise about earthquakes:

Scientist: Identifies earthquakes in their team's region (see Figure 7.11).

- Uses Google Earth to locate each earthquake their group has to track and add placemarkers at each earthquake site.
- Identifies landmarks near the major earthquakes.
- Uses Google Maps (and works together with the mathematician) to calculate the distances between earthquake locations.
- Creates a virtual tour of their region.
- Creates a map of earthquake zones with symbols for intensity of earthquakes.

Mathematician: Compiles pertinent data about each earthquake.

- Uses Google Docs to create a spreadsheet including name, date, latitude/longitude, and magnitude of each quake.

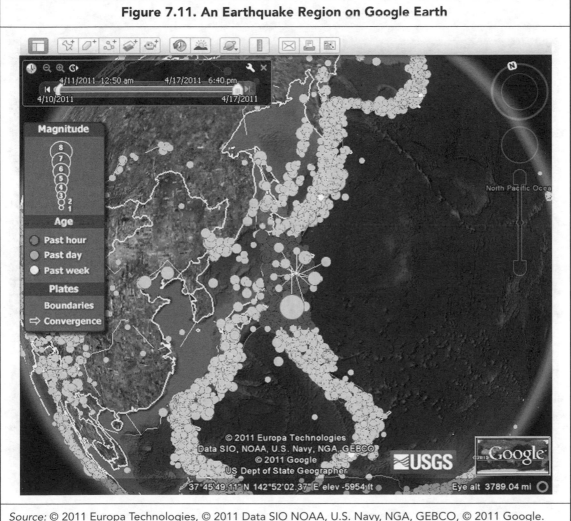

Figure 7.11. An Earthquake Region on Google Earth

Source: © 2011 Europa Technologies, © 2011 Data SIO NOAA, U.S. Navy, NGA, GEBCO, © 2011 Google. Google Earth™ is a trademark of Google, Inc.

- Calculates distances between earthquakes and landmarks (works with the scientist).
- Creates a timeline containing each earthquake.
- Selects a chart type (e.g., line, pie, bar) and plots earthquakes based on magnitude.

Photojournalist/reporter: Researches news about earthquakes both current and historic.

- Uses Google News, archive news, and the Google search engine to compile a historical time-line of major earthquakes (e.g., San Francisco in California, Loma Prieta in San Jose). *Note:* Teachers can create a Google Custom Search, a custom group of sites (http://www.google.com/cse/).
- Uses Google News to read articles and find pictures about earthquakes large enough to make the news. Summarize the news stories using Google Docs.
- Using Google Earth, reviews photos of places of interest near the earthquake locations (e.g., nuclear plant in Japan). With the map the scientist created in Google Earth, places pictures of the locations on the map (see Figure 7.12).
- Sets up a Google News Alert to keep up to date on effects, repercussions, and other important facts about earthquakes in the region (see Figure 7.13).

Figure 7.12. Google Map

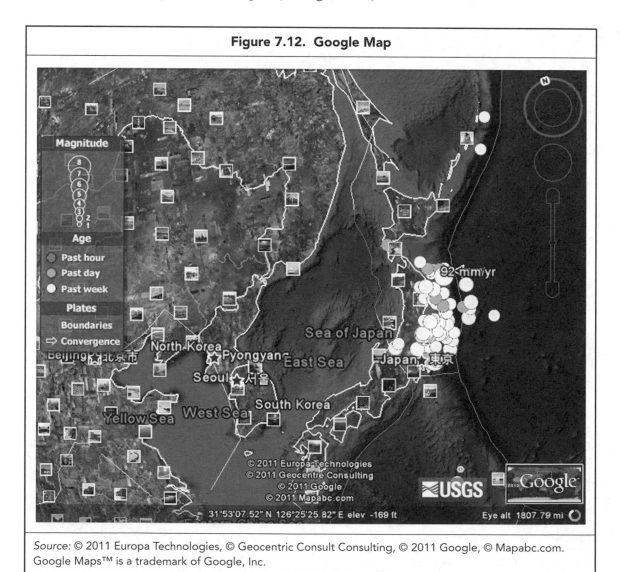

Source: © 2011 Europa Technologies, © Geocentric Consult Consulting, © 2011 Google, © Mapabc.com. Google Maps™ is a trademark of Google, Inc.

Figure 7.13. Google News Alert

Google alerts
beta

Search terms: earthquakes
Preview results

Type: Everything ▼

How often: Once a day ▼

Volume: Only the best results ▼

Your email:

Create Alert

Source: © Google. Google News Alert™ is a trademark of Google, Inc.

Historian: Researches historical earthquakes.

- Using Google News archives, creates a timeline containing earthquakes with a magnitude of 6.0+ that have occurred prior to the two-week study period.
- Creates a podcast detailing information about the ten largest earthquakes in magnitude in their region prior to the study period (see Chapter 4 on podcasts).

As a group:

- Team members discuss the information they gathered about earthquakes in their region, explaining to other group members what they learned after completing their tasks. All group members should have a basic understanding of all topics.
- Using Google Docs, "experts" share information they have collected in their area of expertise about earthquakes. Group members will edit, ask questions for clarification, visit websites via links, and identify the five most important facts from each expert to include in their group presentation.
- With Google Docs, students will design a report in the form of a digital book, incorporating all data, materials, visuals, and podcasts created during the unit.

Culminating Activities

Groups can select one of the following culminating activities to demonstrate their knowledge, ideas, and creative skills gained from participating in the earthquake project.

- Create a model showing what happens when an earthquake begins.
- Write a story in first person as though they were experiencing an earthquake at the moment they were writing.
- Design a one-page Glogster poster illustrating how to prepare for, protect themselves, and recover from an earthquake. Use a variety of media.
- Create a podcast on the team website with each "expert" writing and presenting information.

Website Contents

Using Google Sites, each group will place all information from their activities on the site the team has created. Sites must contain all information compiled by the group in an interesting, thoughtful, informative format. Each group must include the following:

- A tour of their earthquake region using the photos and placemarkers on the map that was created with Google Earth
- An individual report from each expert, as well as a group report using some of the tools in this book
- A list of resources
- Visuals that represent their findings

Activities to Use as Follow-Up to the Unit

It is important for students to reflect on what they learned. As follow-up, students will do the following:

1. Using Google Blogger, groups will post answers to the following questions about their research on their group blog pages:
   - In your region, what area seems to be having more earthquake activity than others?
   - Can you determine a pattern to the size of the quakes?
   - Which, if any, of the quakes you charted have you heard about on the news? What were the effects of the quake on the people and infrastructure?
   - Based on earthquakes charted and news, can you in any way predict where there might be another earthquake and its possible magnitude? Why/why not?
2. Each group will review other groups' blog entries and write short blog posts comparing/contrasting their data with that of other teams.
   - Write blog posts to reflect on what they learned about earthquakes in this unit. Some questions to pose might be: Have your opinions about earthquakes changed at all since the beginning of this project? If so, how? If not, what opinions have been reinforced because of your research?
   - Bring your research closer to home and complete information about the earthquake nearest your home (see Figure 7.14).

Figure 7.14. Earthquake Chart

Earthquakes are constantly occurring throughout the world. To find out what is happening in the world, go to http://earthquake.usgs.gov/eqcenter/.

1. What is the closest earthquake activity to where you live?
2. What was the Richter Scale measurement? What do you think the people experienced?
3. From today's world map, where was the largest earthquake and how many have been recorded?
   - Date _____
   - Time _____
   - Location of largest earthquake _____
   - Number of earthquakes _____

Step 5: Evaluate What Was Learned

Evaluation is vital to any unit. Because Google Docs is being used in the lesson, the teacher or library media specialist can evaluate student work as it progresses. Evaluation will include the information listed in the Evaluation Rubric (see Figure 7.15).

Summary

Science, social studies, and language arts are particularly good curriculum areas in which to use Web 2.0 tools. A variety of Google tools was incorporated into this unit to aid students in research, presentation, note taking, mapmaking, collaboration, and data collection (see Table 7.2). Using these tools provides hands-on activities to enhance student learning and make it more fun. However, the main emphasis of the learning is on the content, not the availability of the technology. Educators creating lessons using Google tools should consider:

Figure 7.15. Evaluation Rubric			
Group Project	**Excellent**	**Good**	**Needs Work**
Participation	Was involved in all parts of the project and showed leadership. 7 points	Was equally involved in the project. 4 points	Let other group members do the work. 2 points
Knowledge	Understands the material and can answer all questions. 10 points	Understands material and can answer most questions. 6 points	Some understanding of material and can answer some questions. 3 points
Research	Topic has been researched extensively; used a number of different resources. 10 points	Topic has been somewhat researched, used some different resources. 7 points	Topic has been researched very little; possible misinformation because few resources included. 3 points
Earthquake map	Map is included and contains at least 5 markers and 5 photos. 5 points	Map is included and contains at least 3 place markers and 2 photos. 3 points	Map is included with no place markers or photos. 1 point
Final Project			
Organization	Content is easy to read and well organized. 10 points	Some parts are hard to read or understand. 7 points	Difficult to read and understand. 3 points
Creativity	Presentation is extremely creative, neat with good variety of resources. 5 points	Presentation is creative but not enough diversity of resources. 3 points	Presentation isn't creative or is sloppily done with errors. 1 point
Visuals	Group has included appropriate visuals and number required. 5 points	Group has included one less visual than required. 3 points	No visuals included. 0 points

- the type of content for the lesson first and foremost;
- the abilities and prior experience of the learners;
- students' knowledge of the technology being considered;
- the relevance of Internet resources and Web 2.0 tools as related to the content; and
- evaluation of content learning, collaboration, and technology use.

The number of Google tools that could be used in the unit illustrates how versatile the tools are. Integrating one, two, or more Google apps into the curriculum will provide opportunities for students to learn science and integrate it with geography and history—past, present, and future—as well as improve their language skills at the same time.

Teacher Exercises: Now You Try It . . .

You have already experimented with Google tools. Now it is time to think about using the tools in your lessons as aids to student learning. The idea is to start simple.

Table 7.2. General Google Tools URLs	
URL	**Description**
http://www.freetech4teachers.com/p/google-tools-tutorials.html	Tutorials on how to use Google tools
http://www.google.com/educators/about.html	Google Homepage
http://earth.google.com/intl/en/userguide/v4/tutorials/index.html	Google Earth tutorials
https://sites.google.com/site/instructionaltech4u/google-apps	Google Apps tutorials
https://docs.google.com/viewer?a=v&pid=sites&srcid=ZGVmYXVsdGRvbWFpbnxpbnN0cnVjdGlvbmFsdGVjaDR1fGd4OjMzODA5MzlzMjY5ZmJhMDY	Google search tools guide 1
http://issuu.com/richardbyrne/docs/google_for_teachers_ii/1	Google tools guide for teachers 2
http://earth.google.com/support/bin/static.py?page=guide.cs&guide=22550&topic=23455	Game to learn how to use features on Google Earth
http://www2.lhric.org/eastchester/schools/hs/teachers/fermann/documents/GEforESmanual.pdf	A Google Earth User Manual for Earth Science Teachers
http://www2.lhric.org/eastchester/schools/hs/teachers/fermann/GE.htm	Geological Society of America Google Earth ideas
http://www.googleguide.com/	Guide to Google searching
http://www.schooltube.com/video/f9cb3a948ae14456bb86/Google-Docs-in-Plain-English	Google Docs in Plain English

1. Based on the examples where educators used Google tools in the classroom or library, identify one tool you think would be useful in a lesson.
2. Go to Google Tools for Educators (http://www.google.com/educators/tools.html), click the tool you have selected, and read the material on the tool. Follow all of the links so you have a good overview of what the tool can do and how to use it. *Note:* if a download is required, download it now.
3. If the tool is incorporated into the previous unit, use the tool yourself to model what students will do as part of their unit tasks.
4. Check the classroom activities for your grade level and subject area for the selected tool at http://www.google.com/educators/activities.html.
5. Create one activity appropriate for a unit you are teaching that incorporates your selected tool.
   a. Share it with a colleague.
   b. Try it with your class or a small group.
6. Reflect on your blog about how the activity went, what you would do differently, how students reacted, and what your next steps are.
7. On the Google search page, try some other Google tools such as Google's Sketch Up to build 3-D models or use Translator Toolkit to translate information into another language if you're teaching a foreign language or ESL.

> ➤ *Use the additional exercises at Bev's website at http://www.neal-schuman.com/webclassroom to practice what you have learned about Google tools and how you can use them in different subject areas.*

CONCLUSION

Google tools have provided an incentive for educators to use technology in everyday classroom activities. The goal is to equip young people who will be effective learners, collaborators, and innovators for the twenty-first century:

- Twenty-first-century learners continue to learn throughout their lives because they have "learned how to learn." They are independent and intrinsic learners and focus on self-improvement.
- Twenty-first-century collaborators are effective communicators, socially and culturally aware, flexible, and take responsibility for their role at their job in the community and the world. They appreciate and internalize the essential interdependence of being part of society.
- Twenty-first-century creators synthesize and analyze and are innovative and creative contributors to society. They are goal-oriented and demonstrate ethical responsibility.

Using Google tools and other Web 2.0 technology to enhance instruction, educators are teaching students how to be learners, collaborators, and creators for the twenty-first century.

REFERENCES AND FURTHER READING

California Department of Education. 2009 (draft approved). *History–Social Science Content Standards for California Public Schools, Kindergarten Through Grade Twelve*. California Department of Education. http://www.cde.ca.gov/be/st/ss/documents/histsocscistnd.pdf.

California Department of Education. 2009 (draft approved). *Science Content Standards for California Public Schools, Kindergarten Through Grade Twelve*. California Department of Education. http://www.cde.ca.gov/be/st/ss/documents/sciencestnd.pdf.

ISTE (International Society for Technology in Education). 2007. *National Educational Technology Standards for Students*. Eugene, OR: International Society for Technology in Education. http://www.iste.org/standards/nets-for-students/nets-student-standards-2007.aspx.

ISTE (International Society for Technology in Education). 2008. *National Educational Technology Standards for Teachers*. Eugene, OR: International Society for Technology in Education. http://www.iste.org/standards/nets-for-teachers/nets-for-teachers-2008.aspx.

CHAPTER 8

Creating Motivating Lessons with Video

PART 1: IDEAS AND INSIGHTS

According to *The Huffington Post*, "Three billion views on YouTube a day represents a 50 percent increase over last year. Uploads have spiked as well. Over 48 hours of video are uploaded to the site each minute, a 37 percent increase in the past six months, and a 100 percent increase from 2010" (Lee, 2011). Today's students are creating and viewing video as an integral part of their everyday lives, and they're also looking to draw on those same technologies at school. Video can be used in the classroom in lieu of or to enhance traditional assignments, while creatively incorporating different subjects, from math to English. This chapter explores a variety of video uses and their importance in teaching and learning.

Storytelling has been a part of culture from the time cavemen wrote on walls, Native Americans passed oral stories down through the generations, and the Egyptians wrote their hieroglyphics. Each culture has its own stories. But, why do we tell stories? What motivates us to tell and listen to stories?

Stories are a way to engage the imagination of a reader or listener. Stories can teach lessons. Stories warn us of the consequences of our actions to ourselves and to others. Stories help us understand ourselves a bit better. Stories provide insight into someone's history and culture, forcing one to look at a situation from another's point of view. These and many more reasons illustrate why storytelling is so popular. It is how we share experience, understand one another, and create community.

Although digital storytelling has been around for a number of years, educators are now implementing the process with the availability of easy-to-use technology. Many books have been written describing this new writing process, and there is a wealth of material on the Internet about it. In this chapter we want to review the basics of storytelling, emphasize the importance of storytelling as a writing process, familiarize educators with digital storytelling, and illustrate how digital media can enhance writing for K–12 students and integrate other content areas as well.

Objectives of This Chapter

This chapter has two major components: (1) it describes digital storytelling and illustrates ways to create digital stories as part of content instruction; (2) it incorporates the use of video technology as an integral part of the curriculum. By the end of this chapter, educators and school librarians at both the elementary and secondary levels will be able to:

- define digital stories and describe the components comprising them;
- create a video product from preproduction through postproduction; and
- create a digital storytelling unit that includes writing storyboards and scripts, making puppets, filming a video, and more.

Background as it relates to storytelling is also included so that all curriculum areas understand the basics of writing stories and how they can be incorporated across the curriculum in subject areas such as science and social studies, as well as language arts.

Glossary

Review the following terminology to become familiar with terms used in the unit plan and words related to working with video and creating digital stories.

digital story: A short, often first-person video narrative created by combining recorded voice, still and moving images, music, and/or other sounds.

digital storytelling: Uses new digital tools to help ordinary people tell their own "true stories" in a compelling and emotionally engaging form.

dissolve: In filming, a gradual transition from one still image to another.

fade: A camera shot where the scene gradually darkens and disappears.

glog: An interactive, multimedia poster.

Glogster: A Web 2.0 tool to create posters using photos, videos, and text.

iMovie: Video-creating and -editing software bundled with a Mac computer.

Movie Maker: Video-creating and -editing software bundled with the Microsoft Windows operating system.

pan: A camera shot in which the photographer moves slowly from one side of an image to the other side.

protagonist: The main character or the central figure of a story.

soundtrack: Recorded music accompanying and synchronized to the images or the physical area of a film that contains the synchronized recorded sound.

storyboard: Graphic organizers such as a series of images displayed in sequence for the purpose of visualizing an interactive media sequence.

zoom: A camera shot where the photographer moves in for a closer shot of the subject.

What Is Digital Storytelling?

Digital storytelling is an engaging means of integrating technology into the curriculum, whether the technology includes digital movies or online storybooks. This phenomenon uses technology to accelerate students' oral, visual, and written communication skills to express what they know and understand to others. Stories can be created by people everywhere, on any subject, and shared electronically all over the world. Storytelling projects help improve students' reading and writing skills. These same projects can also enhance cross-curricular learning to improve math, social studies, and science learning.

Story Elements

Good stories contain essential elements, and digital stories are no different. However, because digital stories are so short, usually from two to five minutes, authors do not have the same space to expand upon their message; therefore, some components become more important than others when creating stories digitally.

- *Digital stories are personal.* The creator of the digital presentation is in the story in a key way—as the narrator and sometimes also as the protagonist. The story is usually written using the "I" point of view. Although many digital storytelling projects feature third person, the narrator is encouraged to personalize the tale, making it clear how the people or events in the story impacted his or her life. The audience should be able to sympathize with the character's feelings, and the story should be appropriate to listeners.
- *The story or script is most important.* Each story should have a single theme that is clearly defined. The plot should be well developed with a beginning, middle, and end. Furthermore, the story should be told in a way that allows the audience to identify with it, remember it, and be changed by it.

  Other aspects of the story include: developing intrigue or tension around a situation that is posed at the beginning of the story and resolved at the end, sometimes with an unexpected twist. Using a unique event to start the story provides a hook that leaves the viewer wondering how the story will unfold and how it will all end. The tension of an unresolved or curious situation engages and holds the viewer until the story reaches a memorable end. Pacing helps to sustain story tension. Figure 8.1 provides a general story outline.
- *"Show—don't tell."* Students should write using "observations." They must describe the characters and settings and help the listeners sympathize with the characters' feelings. Stimulating the audience's senses so they feel, smell, touch, and listen enables them to see vivid pictures. This is also the art of good writing.
- *Collaboration is involved.* Once participants have a draft of the story, they give and receive feedback on their scripts. Peer revision is crucial to the final product.
- *Technology enhances story meaning.* A good story incorporates technology so it communicates with images, sound, voice, color, animations, design, transitions, and special effects. All media elements are selected to illustrate the meaning of the tale rather than being used to "decorate" the story.

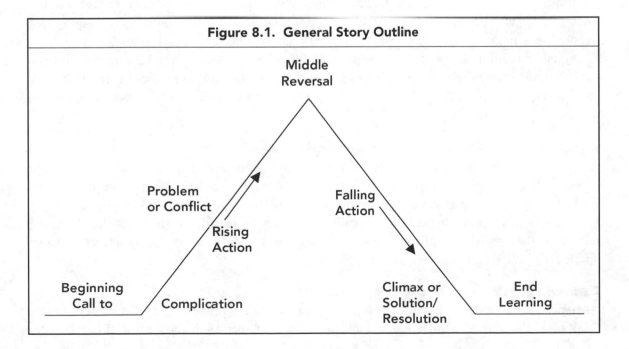

Figure 8.1. General Story Outline

Middle
Reversal

Problem
or Conflict

Falling
Action

Rising
Action

Beginning
Call to

Complication

Climax or
Solution/
Resolution

End
Learning

Creating digital stories, students can connect the past with the present, relate personal narratives, and improve their reading, writing, and technology skills, while enjoying themselves at the same time. Since these stories can focus on a scientific event or a historical figure or understanding a culture, they lend themselves to cross-curricular connections as well.

> ➤ *Learn more about digital storytelling at Bev's website at http://www.neal-schuman.com/webclassroom.*

Story Types

- Personal narrative
- Fictional story
- Movie or book trailer
- Adventure story
- Movie or book review
- Interview
- Memorial story
- Place in my life
- Very short documentary
- Reminiscence
- Poem
- Photographic journey
- Character story
- Accomplishment story

Story Types

There are a variety of story types that educators can use as assignments for their students in the classroom or library.

Examples of Digital Storytelling in the Classroom and Library

Many digital stories have been created in the last few years with a number of teachers and librarians pioneering the technique. Students in health classes have written public service announcements on addiction; English classes have created visual poetry; and history students have interviewed their parents about their own ancestors. As part of preparing the digital story, students develop critical questions to address in their presentations. Digital stories can have many purposes: relating a personal story, describing a place, examining a historical event, informing or instructing, taking a position on a current issue, and more. Educators have embraced this technology at all grade levels and in different subject areas as shown in the following examples.

Example 1: U.S. History Vietnam Studies Project

At North Shore Country Day School, north of Chicago, Illinois, an eleventh-grade U.S. history class integrated digital storytelling into their Vietnam studies culminating project, incorporating imagery, audio, and motion picture. The essential question they were to answer was what meaning does the Vietnam War have 35 years after its end, especially in relation to wars in Iraq and Afghanistan. Read about the project on the wiki at https://sites.google.com/a/nscds.org/reflections/. Figure 8.2 shows a scene from one of the Vietnam stories created in the North Shore Country Day School Vietnam Project (http://nsreflectionssupport.wikispaces.com/Final+Projects).

Digital storytelling has widespread support at this school. Students from kindergarten through twelfth grade create digital projects. An environmental sustainability project by middle school students included embedded maps and spreadsheets. Students also view each others' projects and comment upon them.

Example 2: The Story of the Horned Owl

At the Parish Episcopal School in Dallas, Texas, eighth-graders in groups of three created their science projects using iMovie. For example, one group of three created a video about the horned owl. Each student played a part in an entertaining, humorous interview between a professor, intimately knowledgeable about the horned owl, and a PBS reporter. As part of the video, captions included facts about the bird. In addition to the video, students built a model of the owl and wrote a newspaper article they posted on their class blog (see Figure 8.3).

Example 3: Henrico County Public Schools

At Henrico County Public Schools in Virginia, video is an integral part of the district curriculum. Examples illustrate how different schools are using video in their instruction. In a Glogster

Figure 8.2. North Shore Country Day School Vietnam Project

Group C2

Source: Used by permission of Kevin Randolph, Department Chair for History/Social Studies, and Vincent Vrotny, Director of Academic Technology, North Shore Country Day School.

Figure 8.3. Story of the Horned Owl

Source: Used by permission of Mark Johnston, parent at Parish Episcopal School.

multimedia poster (http://ryantstein.glogster.com/american-revolution/), teachers and students represent aspects of the Revolutionary War, from embedded video about battles such as Lexington and Concord, to events leading up to the war, to a play designed, written, and created by fourth-graders. "Live from the American Revolution" features ten acts highlighting important events of the war. Students dressed as newscasters and reporters interviewed the characters. Patriots argued at the "MVP" table for their title as "Most Valuable Patriot" of the American Revolution. Other students even created a video commercial about "J-Wigs" those worn by Thomas Jefferson. "The whole unit is about the students searching for a deeper understanding of the American Revolution and showing what they know," explained their teacher Mr. Ryan Stein (see Figure 8.4).

Each month the Henrico district website Student Zone features videos in which students speak out on a controversial topic such as texting and driving. Another video illustrates how to grow plants at home or make an omelet. View these videos at http://henrico.k12.va.us/Newsroom/Student ZoneFebruary.html.

Example 4: A High School Personal Story

Silvia Jeong, a ninth-grader at San Francisco School of the Arts, was awarded first place for her digital story describing her experiences when she arrived in the United States from South Korea. She explains through her character—a potato—the differences between herself and her American classmates with the most difficult task being communicating in a new language. Silvia used audio and pictures to create her digital story at http://www.leslierule.com/C2C05/Silvia_Jeong.mov (see Figure 8.5).

Figure 8.4. Glog on the American Revolution

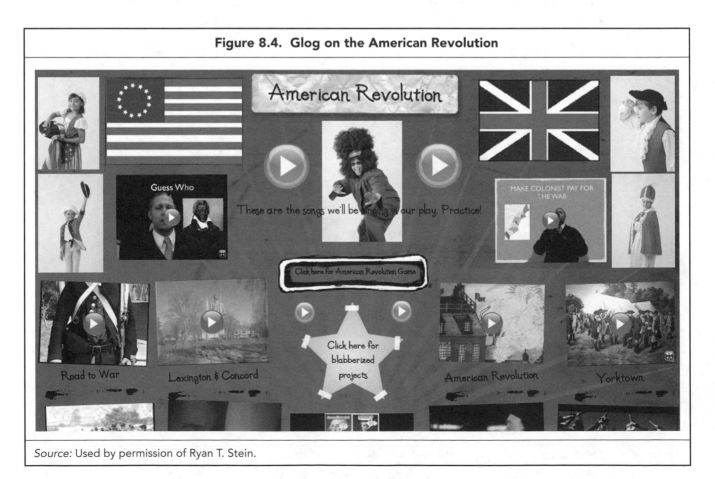

Source: Used by permission of Ryan T. Stein.

Figure 8.5. The Potato Story

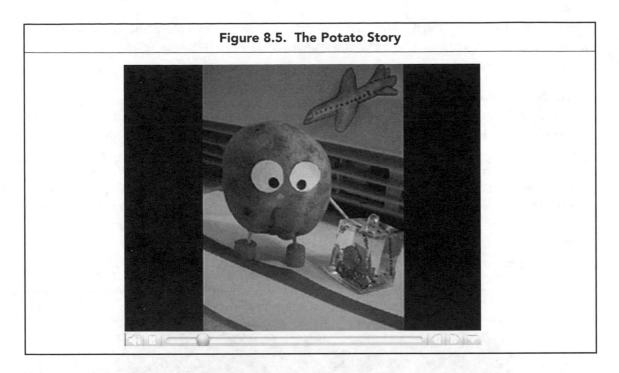

Example 5: Podcasts, Vodcasts, iMovies, Photo Story

Using different media from podcasts to pictures, classes at Village Elementary School in New York create digital stories. For example, students in a kindergarten class created "Bears in Winter." Each student illustrated and stated one fact about bears. See other videos at https://villagewiki.pbworks .com/w/page/13226814/FrontPage (see Figure 8.6).

Other media presentations include Penguins, animal reports on lemurs, the life cycle of plants by second-graders, and solar system facts by first-graders. There is a great diversity of story lines. For

Figure 8.6. Village Elementary Digital Stories

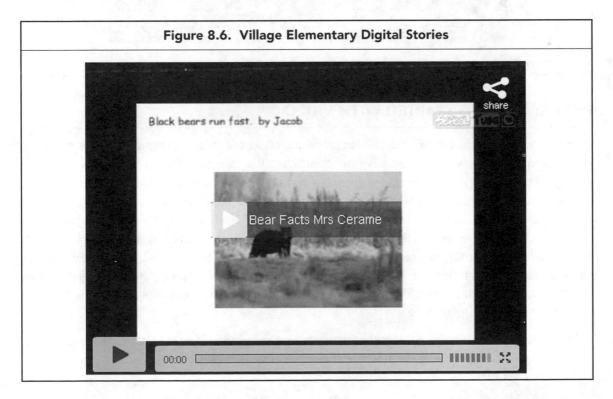

example, a sixth-grader created a story about World War II using, pictures, audio, and music. Read the stories at https://villagewiki.pbworks.com/w/page/25994761/Podcast,%20Vodcasts,%20I-Movies,%20Photostories%20page%202.

Example 6: My Best Friend's Girlfriend

Seventh- and eighth-grade classes at Millikan Middle School in Los Angeles Unified School District produced an award-winning video "My Best Friend's Girlfriend," which can be seen at http://ito .lacoe.edu/dva/dva_view.pl?entry=1630&run_mode=view.

> ➤ *Visit URLs and read more about how educators are using digital storytelling at Bev's website at http://www.neal-schuman.com/webclassroom.*

The assignment was to create a narrative film based on a strong conflict between two characters. The well-written, humorous, 10-minute script has an outstanding plot and notable character development (see Figure 8.7). This video combines writing standards in seventh- and eighth-grade English/language arts with visual arts to create an original work of art using film, photography, and video.

Figure 8.7. My Best Friend's Girlfriend

Source: Used by permission of David Guest, Head of the Academy.

PART 2: GETTING STARTED WITH VIDEO

Although writing stories in English and language arts classes is an essential part of the curriculum, writing across the curriculum is equally important. Thus, the curriculum tie-in to digital storytelling is integral to the activity. As mentioned, the most important aspect of digital storytelling is the story and how students interact in creating the parts of it. However, the technology can enhance the story and motivate students to create a story they otherwise would never have been excited to begin.

A digital story encompasses three phases of production. First and foremost is the preproduction, which includes creating the story itself. Second is the production stage where all elements are gathered together and media is introduced. Finally, during postproduction, students put the story together and present it to the audience. Figure 8.8 describes the steps in the process.

Usually the best digital stories:

- Begin with a script that focuses the writing before audio and video are created or manipulated.
- Are quite personal, with the narrator making it clear how something or somebody impacted her or his life.

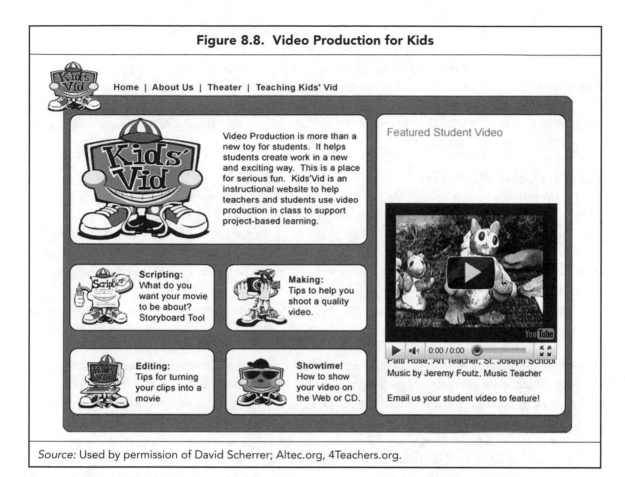

Figure 8.8. Video Production for Kids

Source: Used by permission of David Scherrer; Altec.org, 4Teachers.org.

- Are concise at two to five minutes long with a story narrowed down to a single central idea.
- Use easily available source materials such as still photos, hand drawings, scanned images, transition effects, recorded narrative, and video.
- Include story elements of conflict, transformation, and closure so that the audience can identify and be changed.
- Involve collaboration in which students give and receive feedback during scripting and production.

Preproduction

Preproduction forms the basis of building a digital story. Idea-sharing takes place, responsibilities are assigned, and sketches and text evolve as students write the storyboard. This phase is most important to the rest of the production and usually takes the longest to complete. During this phase it is helpful if the educator develops a set of steps, promotes expectations for each step, and assigns roles and responsibilities.

Step 1: Draw Upon Prior Knowledge

Assigned to groups, students should review several examples of digital stories and participate in cooperative learning activities to discuss the stories. These tasks allow them to gain confidence in sharing their own ideas.

Step 2: Start with an Idea

Students should begin with an idea that is both personal and meaningful to them. They must also think about the purpose of the story: Are they trying to inform, convince, provoke, question, persuade?

How has this particular topic touched the author's life? The idea can also focus on their interests in a content area. For example, a young boy who loves insects can create his story around his interest in science; a student fan of the Civil War can use the historical period as a backdrop for a digital story; or a young girl with a new baby sister in the house can pour out her personal feelings in a story. One's imagination is the only limiter to the story. The primary concern, however, is encouraging thoughtful and emotionally direct writing. Often the story is told in first person so students' own storytelling voices narrate the tale.

Step 3: Gather Resources

Finding resources entails researching on the web, reading articles, interviewing, or going to the library. In addition, the digital story includes sounds and images. For example, a personal story might need photos of a family member. Besides gathering the sources, it is also necessary for students to evaluate what they have obtained, selecting only those images that enhance the story quality. Students must also consider whether they plan to use live actors or representations of characters.

Copyright rules must be adhered to, and checking Creative Commons licenses is important at this stage (http://creativecommons.org/) (see Chapter 1). Remember, too, that government resources are usually in the public domain, meaning they can be used without specific permission, although the owner should be identified. Some sources have a more lenient copyright (fair use) if they are used for educational purposes. Nonetheless, it is still important to ask and credit the source.

Images can take the form of photos, pictures, or video clips. For a three-minute story, students should select a maximum of fifteen images or a short video. This achieves two goals: first, it forces students to make decisions on the value of the images to the story and results in the use of only the best photos, drawings, or video. Second, it focuses their attention back to the story. Students must rely on the story driving the images, instead of the images taking over the story. Flickr (http://www.flickr.com/) is a good place to look for vivid artistic images. Students should create individual folders on the class computer in which to place all sources they have gathered.

Step 4: Create a Storyboard

When students have written their stories, discussed them with their classmates, and made the necessary revisions, they are ready to create a storyboard. It is important to plan out their stories and using a storyboard helps to coordinate all parts of the story. Storyboard templates are graphic organizers that allow authors to visualize and detail all aspects of their story—narration, images, titles, transitions, special effects, music, and sounds. The storyboard lets them organize their thoughts before they go to the computer to type the story. When an idea for the digital story is firm, the storyboard starts and continues throughout the process. As students connect their ideas in the storyboard, they will see where they need new resources and how the direction of the story is proceeding.

Storyboarding allows students to "structure" their stories and synchronize the images to words. It is a place to plan out the visual story in two dimensions. The first dimension is time: what happens first, second, and last. The second is interaction: how does the audio, the voice-over narrative of the story, and the music interact with the images or video. In addition, a storyboard can be an effective road map of where and how visual effects, transitions, animations, and organization of the screen will be used. The storyboard also promotes revision of the story when students see how the words work with the images.

The storyboard starts with the actual text from the script along with the images and titles being planned. Transitions and special effects fill in the storyboard. Sound effects and music are added last, even though ideas may be forming along the way. Finally, good storyboards display pictures and text and lead each group into production.

There are several effective methods of storyboarding. The storyboard can be as simple as a poster board with sticky notes placed where photos will be in the story. Using Google Docs can provide a quick and easy version, or creating a template using text and image boxes will also work. All students need to do is insert images in order and copy and paste the corresponding narration (see Figure 8.9; http://www.jakesonline.org/storyboard_side.pdf).

Step 5: Organize the Resources

Managing all the files—text, images, sound, music, and final product—is an important and often overlooked piece of the process needed to ensure everything can be located for each student's product. Each student needs his or her own folder containing all media elements. If preproduction has been successful, students are ready to "produce" the digital story. This includes delivering the written script as voice-over and combining it with visual and audio effects as shown on the storyboard.

> ➤ See additional tips to use in preproduction of digital stories at Bev's website at http://www.neal-schuman.com/webclassroom.

Production

During the production phase, students will use the media to film and/or photograph; download files, if necessary; digitize images or sound; draw pictures; construct characters; and select music. Editing media resources also occurs during this phase.

Step 6: Practice the Delivery of the Voice-Over

Part of any delivery is enthusiasm, animation, variety in the voice, facial expressions, pacing, and sincerity. Students should practice their narratives a number of times before recording. Their narratives will become the voice-overs for their stories. The delivery is important because the audience needs time to process images, and a slower pace—at least most of the time—is more effective. Also, blocks of time with *no* narration can add dramatic appeal. The voice-overs should be created first as separate audio files.

Step 7: Use the Tools

One of the appealing features about digital storytelling is the ability to use a variety of tools. Students should gather, create, or edit images, sound, music, and other media with the intention of extending understanding and increasing the power of their message. If they plan to film a live presentation, they must practice and synchronize what their characters do and say. There are also a number of techniques they can use.

1. *Soundtrack.* A soundtrack can have a dramatic impact on the entire story. Pacing, emotion, and point of view are all enhanced with appropriate music.
2. *Visual effects.* Less is best. Effects should enhance the story instead of dominating it.
   - ○ *Transitions* between images help tell the story. Various transitions signal different pauses in the action of the story. For example, having no transition serves to quickly move between two closely related ideas. A "dissolve" suggests a change to a related idea. A "fade" suggests a change of topics or passage of time. A particularly effective technique is the use of a black screen for several seconds, with or without sound.

> ➤ Learn more about visual effects to produce digital stories at Bev's website at www.neal-schuman.com/webclassroom.

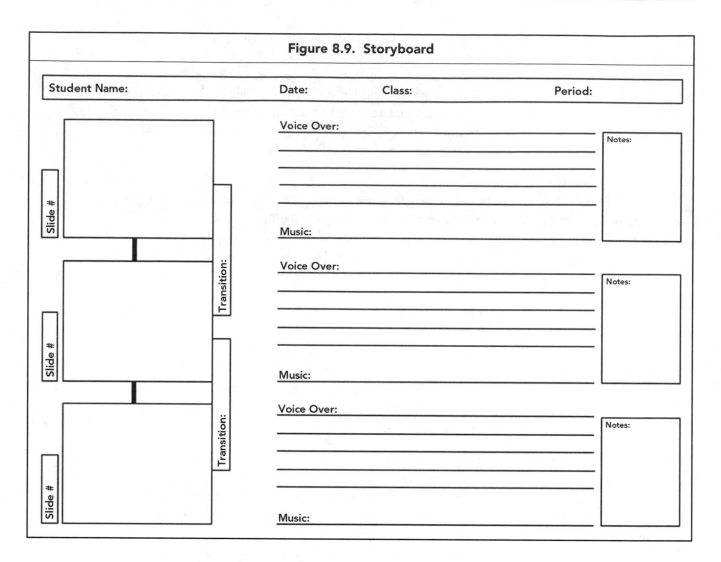

Figure 8.9. Storyboard

- ○ *Pans and zooms* can add movement to static images, focus the audience, or give a sense of place for an object. In most cases, slow movement is best so as not to distract the audience.
- ○ *Text* can be an effective method for focusing the audience on a particular line, for example, by using actual text on the screen. Selected lines that are particularly important can be used in lieu of narration.

Note that if these digital projects are to be distributed outside the classroom, it is very important to adhere to copyright standards. Setting up a copyright-free library for sounds and pictures is helpful.

Postproduction

While a storyboard provides the initial decisions and elements, the postproduction phase is the time to combine the elements together in a compelling and memorable story that illuminates understanding for the audience.

Step 8: Put It All Together

There are two parts in postproduction. The rough draft provides the author with the first view of the story, which includes the voice-over and sequencing of images/video and titles. It illustrates how the story will flow. This draft has no music or sound, no transitions or special effects. Authors can review the draft to determine if anything is missing or if additional material or text is needed. Now is the time, too, to have other students provide feedback about the tone and design of the story.

The final product contains all parts—music, sounds, transitions—that appeared in the storyboard. Authors should review their effects as they relate to the purpose of the story, remembering that each element illustrates and extends the message.

Teacher Exercises: Now You Try It . . .

Part 1 focused on the digital story itself and Part 2 on how to create it. Review the following exercises to familiarize yourself with both stories and media.

1. Review at least three or four types of digital stories. You can use the stories given as examples or check some of the other URLs in Table 8.1. On your blog jot down what you like best about each story, what you like least. Evaluate how well you think your students would handle writing a digital story.

2. Think about an experience you've had and would like to share with your students and/or colleagues. Write a two-minute script using one of the storyboards listed in Part 2.

> ➤ Visit Bev's website at http://www .neal-schuman.com/webclassroom for more exercises on creating digital stories.

3. Explore at least two or three music and image sites to see what the sites contain and what is needed to use them in your classroom.

Table 8.1. General URLs for Digital Stories	
URL	**Description**
http://files.wlcsd.org/aal/digstorytelling/Directions.pdf	Using Movie Maker to create digital stories
http://chs.smuhsd.org/bigue/art_of_video/index/gallery.html	Video poems, news, life stories, and more
http://www.youtube.com/watch?v=EDWM7oua2k4	North Carolina fourth grade class video to celebrate Martin Luther King Day
http://www1.teachertube.com/viewVideo.php?title=Digital_Storytelling&video_id=221008	Sample digital story by seven-year-old about her baby brother
http://www.schooltube.com/	Examples of videos created by students from recycling to butterflies
http://www.yudu.com/item/details/239521/Using-SchoolTube-to-View-YouTube-Videos	Shows how to import a YouTube video to SchoolTube (Only shared videos can be imported.)
http://www.edutopia.org/digital-generation-youtube-teaching-video?page=1	Tutorial on using YouTube
http://www.dtc.scott.k12.ky.us/technology/digital storytelling/studentstories.html	Scott County digital story examples K–12
http://its.ksbe.edu/bcredit/b1001/projects/kaimi/pages/themovie.html	Example story of working together
http://www.digitales.us/	Story-making tools, projects, and examples
http://www.digitales.us/	DigiTales: The Art of Telling Digital Stories

4. Write blog posts to reflect on the following questions:
    a. How can you incorporate digital storytelling into your curriculum?
    b. What areas of the curriculum could be most effectively taught through digital stories?
    c. What challenges would you face as you implement this instructional approach in your school?

PART 3: PRACTICAL APPLICATIONS

Digital storytelling topics range from personal tales to the recounting of historical events, from exploring life in one's own community to the search for life in other corners of the universe, and literally, everything in between. Stories can be created by people everywhere, on any subject, and shared electronically all over the world. Video clips can be used along with still images to tell a story and, hopefully, inspire viewers to think about how they can use digital media to tell their own stories.

Lesson Clips

A good way to get started using video is to go slowly. These short clips offer suggestions on using specific technologies in short lessons.

*   Use the Zimmer Twins at http://www.zimmertwins.com/about/teachers to get elementary students started producing animated movies. It's easy to use. In groups or individually, students begin with a story starter or create their own movie from scratch. By clicking "Make a movie," they create a timeline (see Figure 8.10) with action clips, talk bubbles, close-ups, and other fun things. Try these short clips as an alternative to journal writing and book reports, and to accustom kids to producing videos.

Figure 8.10. Make a Movie with Zimmer Twins

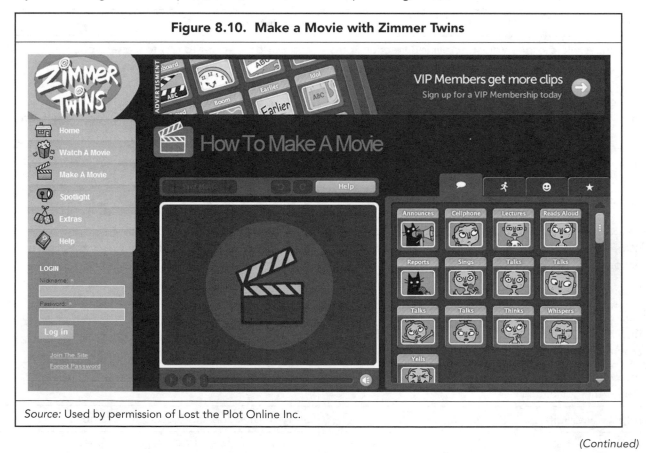

Source: Used by permission of Lost the Plot Online Inc.

(Continued)

Lesson Clips *(Continued)*

- Use Kerpoof (http://www.kerpoof.com/#) to create a collaborative tall tale, a clip about a historical figure or inventor you are studying. Activities with Kerpoof—a great tool for elementary students—promote state content standards and the National Educational Technology Standards (NETS). For example, in fourth grade students study angles in math. Use Kerpoof movie maker to illustrate rotations of benchmark degrees (e.g., 90 or 180 degrees) or show a desert scene where a cowboy is looking for his friend (see Figure 8.11).

Figure 8.11. Cowboy in the Desert Created with Kerpoof

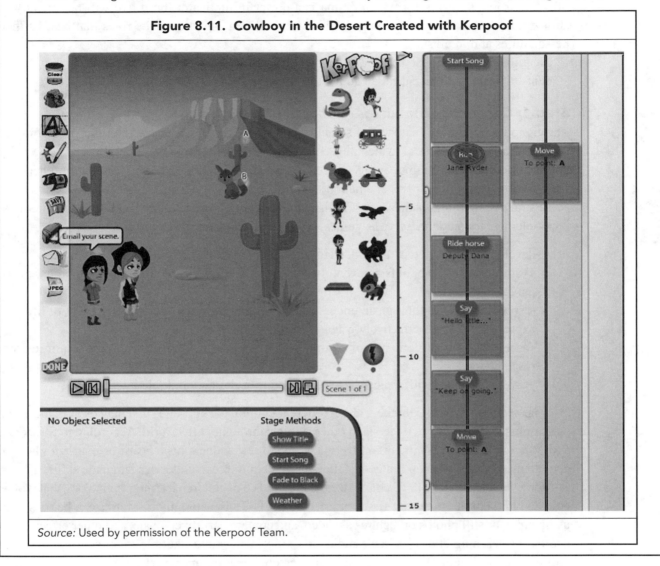

Source: Used by permission of the Kerpoof Team.

Thus, digital storytelling lends itself to cross-curricular activities at all grade levels because stories are so versatile. In this unit, groups of students will investigate a culture that interests them. As a result of their exploration, each group will become "experts" on that society and its people. Groups will demonstrate their expertise by creating and performing puppet shows illustrating myths or folktales that represent their chosen cultures. Team members will also create a video to share their stories with a global audience.

Unit Plan for Cross-Curricular Cultural Study

The United States has long been identified as the "melting pot" because it has become the home to so many different cultures. Some states such as California have more minority students in their classrooms than Anglos. Therefore, it is important to start early to teach young children about different cultures.

In elementary schools, children should also learn to express themselves in a clear and interesting fashion. One way to achieve this goal is through classroom drama, and puppetry is a good way to introduce dramatic work. For instance, some shy children find it easier to project their language through puppet actors, since puppets can provide masks that allow students to open up. You will often see some students for whom drama is a powerful motivator, but there will be others who shrink from the idea of performing. In this unit, children can choose the roles that best fit their personalities and interests.

Creating a visual representation of the story lends itself to different learning styles and motivates students to write and present for an authentic audience.

Step 1: Connect to Standards—What Should Be Taught?

Throughout elementary history and social sciences students must understand the rich, complex nature of different societies. To meet this end, children need to learn about their history, geography, politics, literature, art, drama, music, dance, education, and more. They must also comprehend the interrelationships among parts of a nation's culture.

Several state content standards—English/language arts, social studies, and art—for middle to upper elementary students serve as guides for this unit. Students will:

- develop cultural literacy by understanding the complex nature of different cultures;
- examine peoples' beliefs as exemplified in their legends, folktales, myths, poems, plays, dance, and visual art.
- respect all peoples through an understanding of their different societies and ways of life;
- express themselves effectively when speaking and writing;
- share a variety of content, for example, stories, poems, and information acquired from research; and
- address individual differences based on learning styles and multiple intelligences.

This unit starts students thinking about different cultural backgrounds that may exist in their own classrooms and helps them understand other cultures throughout the world. According to Strickland and Morrow (1989), it is important to follow up stories students have heard or read with an oral activity. Digital storytelling is a good follow-up to help improve children's language skills.

Moreover, the revised NETS emphasize the importance of children learning technology that will be essential to them in the twenty-first century (ISTE, 2007). Because digital stories can be presented using video or still photos or pictures as video, and contain narrative, music, and other effects, they address all learning styles—visual, audio, and kinesthetic—and multiple intelligences, including musical, verbal-linguistic, visual-spatial, interpersonal, and intrapersonal.

Step 2: Identify General Goals and Specific Objectives

Use the goals and specific objectives that follow as a basis for developing content and improving skills.

Goals

Students will:

- learn about the mythology, legends, values, and beliefs of different cultures;
- improve expressive language skills and inventive thinking; skills in listening for appreciation and understanding;
- work cooperatively on a project while communicating in small groups;

- improve self-esteem and build self-confidence and poise as they work and share together;
- identify and appreciate cultural differences; and
- use technology for research and presentation.

Objectives

This unit provides content and strategies for students to achieve the following objectives in social studies, language arts, and art while using video technology to enhance their learning. As a part of this unit, students will:

- read with a specific purpose in mind and learn how to make judgments about stories;
- learn to be respectful listeners and give constructive criticism;
- use their voices and movements to communicate messages;
- use visuals and props to add clarity to an oral message;
- gather and organize ideas for communicating with others; and
- learn basic Internet research and video production skills.

Step 3: Gather Materials

First, students must gather materials that represent different cultures, such as photographs of themselves or their relatives, pictures of native dress, information about the country they have chosen, and maps. By exploring specific countries, children can find information on African, Chinese, or Mexican culture to name a few. Next, they need to search for ideas on how to make their own puppets and collect bits and pieces to create them. Finally, other technological materials are needed: a microphone, perhaps a digital camera or video recorder, plus software to create and edit the movie. Of course, it is a good idea to review any websites you are planning to use as part of the unit and create a list of URLs so that students can just click the URL links to go to individual sites. Sample URLs are included with specific activities.

From their research, students will gather ideas to create their own puppets and perform puppet shows for the videos they will create. Many of the sites in Table 8.2 (p. 176) are used in the activities that follow.

Reading literature about countries students choose to depict will help children imagine what their puppet characters may look like and provide examples for the puppets' actions and speech. Legends, myths, and folktales are good starting points, since they appeal to all ages and demonstrate diversity. Sample titles may provide some ideas:

- *Why Mosquitoes Buzz in People's Ears: A West African Tale*, by Verna Azardema
- *Tales of a Korean Grandmother*, by Frances Carpenter
- *Listen to the Wind*, by Greg Mortenson

Teachers should collaborate with the school librarian to find titles once groups have selected the cultures they plan to dramatize.

Step 4: Create Sample Activities

Activities will be divided into the three phases of production—preproduction (activities to introduce the unit), production (activities during the unit), and postproduction (activities as follow-up to the unit). Specific tasks may also address students' specific learning styles.

Writing assignments have often taken the form of an assigned essay, a book, or a report to be completed by the end of a unit to test students' understanding. Digital storytelling, on the other hand, provides a powerful way for students to personalize their learning. Stories are designed to be engaging, to be personal, and to help viewers draw conclusions about their own lives or actions.

Whether they are talking about their own experiences or something they have learned about in history or science, digital storytelling teaches them to ask important questions like: "Why am I telling this story?" "What is the main point I want to make?" "Where am I in this story?" "How do I relate to it?" Knowing their writing exists for more than just the teacher can also be very motivating.

Activities to Introduce the Unit

As part of the project, students also make choices about the roles they want to play within their groups. For example, two or three students may like to speak and act in the video. These children can choose to be performers in the puppet shows. Others may feel more comfortable in the role of creating the playhouse in which to hold the plays. At least one child from each group will need to assume the role of director to help coordinate the activities and act as narrator for the video. Whichever roles students assume, they will be involved in language arts, social studies, and art activities. Students will also be reading myths and folktales, accessing the Internet to learn more about individual cultures, and participating with other children to achieve common goals. In addition, each group member will have a role in creating the video of their presentation.

At the beginning of any storytelling unit, it is important to stimulate students' prior knowledge of how stories are put together, already learned in their language arts classes. A brief review of story types with examples, such as similarities, differences, which story is better and why, and writing patterns that repeat in each story, provides a model for students before they create their own story. Figure 8.12 illustrates the components to any story, as well as those parts needed in a digital story.

Students should establish the parameters of the topics—what they are going to investigate—and explore their prior knowledge about the cultures they have chosen. If students in the classroom belong to different ethnic groups, they should choose cultures different from their own; however,

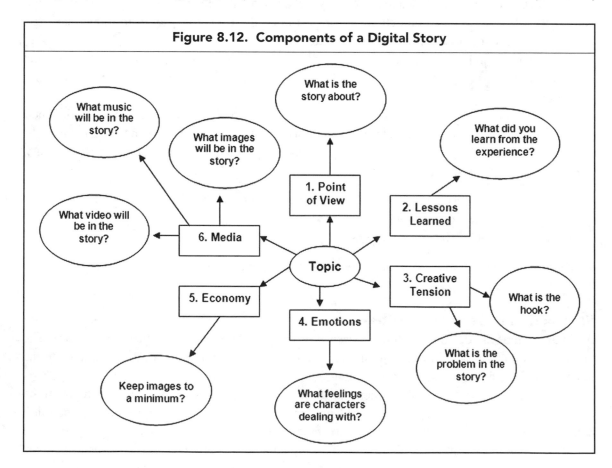

Figure 8.12. Components of a Digital Story

they can still contribute special information and personal experiences about their own countries of origin to their classmates.

Initial tasks ask students to think generally about the concept of "culture" and then to narrow down choices to the specific groups they want to research; African culture will be the example used throughout this unit. To draw upon their prior knowledge, students will:

- explore the concept of "belonging to a group." Have students list on the class blog all the groups they belong to, then draw a hierarchy similar to the one in Figure 8.13. Teachers should give some examples of how society categorizes people into different groups, such as by age, gender, religious belief, and nationality. This will help to extend the concept of diversity and to break down stereotypes.
- clarify terminology by discussing and writing definitions and examples as blog posts for culture, diversity, and stereotype.
- interview each other or friends and neighbors from different ethnic groups to compile firsthand information about cultures.
- create a Glogster poster (http://edu.glogster.com/) with pictures of themselves representing the different groups they belong to and information compiled about the ethnic group.

As a result of completing these activities, students will have reviewed and reflected on their prior knowledge about culture and be ready to start their tasks to find out more about the one they have selected.

Activities to Be Used during the Unit

In student-selected "culture" groups, children will begin research to accumulate information on the culture they have selected. Their research should include data, myths, and folktales on the selected countries. Ten sample tasks can be selected for the following projects.

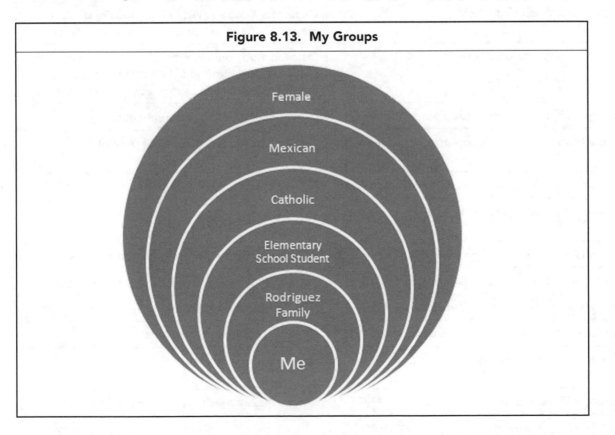

Figure 8.13. My Groups

Female

Mexican

Catholic

Elementary
School Student

Rodriguez
Family

Me

Project A—Research in Order to Write a Script about Their Culture. Each group will:

- *study maps of their country.* Draw maps and locate major cities, rivers, mountain ranges, provinces, bordering countries, and bodies of water. See Chapter 7 on Google for more on Google Earth and Google Maps.
    - See a virtual class trip to Africa at http://www.hardin.k12.ky.us/upton/NewFolder/Wyatt safari/sld001.htm.
    - Review facts and data about African cultures at http://www.hardin.k12.ky.us/upton/Africa.html.
- *collect information on their ethnic group.* Select five facts and post them to their blog.
    - http://www.wartgames.com/themes/countries/southafrica.html
    - http://africa.pppst.com/countries.html
- *read folktales about their culture.* These will give students ideas to use in their own presentation.
- *look at different types of digital stories.* Models created by others will help students begin thinking about their own stories. Show the following stories or some from Table 8.2.
    - http://its.ksbe.edu/dst/iMuaMovies.html
    - http://its.ksbe.edu/dst/Ke%27eiMovies.html
    - http://its.ksbe.edu/dst/movies/jacob,brian,kady,chris.mov—movie on Hawaiian culture
- *collaborate to write the script for their presentation.*
    - Contribute at least two facts for the script about their culture and write them on the group storyboard (see Part 2 on storyboards); review and edit the script into final form.

Table 8.2. Puppet Information URLs	
URL	**Description**
http://www.puppet.org/videoroom.shtml	Center for Puppetry Arts with videos of puppets playing Cinderella, Beauty and the Beast, and more
http://www.puppet.org/edu/guides.shtml	Detailed study guides with other web resources for grade levels K through 6. Some represent culture from different countries such as China and Greece
http://www.sagecraft.com/puppetry/traditions/index.html	Explore cultures from different countries
http://familycrafts.about.com/od/puppets/tp/Puppet-Crafts-For-Kids.htm	How to make different types of puppets
http://familycrafts.about.com/od/royalcrafts/a/cbbcastle.htm	How to create a puppet theater
http://video.about.com/familycrafts/How-to-Make-Shadow-Puppets.htm	Video showing how to make shadow animal puppets
http://familycrafts.about.com/lr/puppets/514948/3/	How to make different types of puppets easily
http://www.teacherfilebox.com/Unit/Detail.aspx?F=392	Korean folktale—Tales of a Korean Grandmother
http://www.teacherfilebox.com/Unit/Detail.aspx?F=4432	Listen to the Wind—Shadow play
http://www.teacherfilebox.com/Unit/Detail.aspx?F=3069	How to make types of puppets
http://www.teacherfilebox.com/Unit/List.aspx?S=african+puppets	How to make African puppets
http://www.teacherfilebox.com/Unit/Detail.aspx?F=1178	How to make types of African animal puppets

- Divide the work in pairs so one of the pair finds or creates visuals while the other looks at music sites for background music and other transition effects.
- Practice presenting the script in their group, making sure each student has a part in the oral presentation. Present their script to at least one other group who will provide comments and suggestions.

Project B—Work on the Puppet Presentation. The teacher will conduct a mini-lesson for the class to include how to get started creating a puppet presentation, examining construction methods, materials, and different types of puppets. Team members will choose one of the following roles: performers in the play, set designers, or directors. Each group will now get together to prepare its part of the performance (see Table 8.2 for ideas).

- Actors will create a puppet for their own characters.
- Set designers will gather as a group and create a stage or playhouse in which all "culture" groups will perform. This group will also create a Glogster poster to advertise the video. The poster should include the URL where the video will reside and visual images that represent the culture groups students have chosen to depict.
- The directors will consult with all groups on special needs and write the announcer's script, including background on their culture.

Project C—Create the Video. As a finale to the unit, each group will create a video that includes their puppet presentation. The set designer for the group will take the lead and film the final show.

1. Prior to filming, each group will review the storyboard to make sure all parts—music, sounds, transitions—are incorporated.
2. Group members will edit the video and upload it to the class blog.

Walled Lake School District teachers have written detailed, step-by-step instructions on using Movie Maker 2 at http://files.wlcsd.org/aal/digstorytelling/Directions.pdf, and Silvia Tolisano has also created a guide to digital storytelling (Tolisano, 2009). Use these as guides to help create the video.

Activities to Be Used as Follow-Up to the Unit

As a result of completing activities in this unit, students have had the opportunity to practice speaking, listening, reading, and writing. They have also learned about cultures different from their own. In addition, they are now familiar with creating a video presentation. By working in small groups, they have practiced socialization skills. It is important, too, that they reflect on the tasks they have just completed:

- Reflect on the following:
  - What are some of the differences and similarities they noticed among the cultures?
  - Why did they assume the roles they did? Would they choose the same roles again? Why/why not?
  - What difficulties, if any, did they encounter working with their groups? What could they have done to make the performances go more smoothly?
- Fill in "culture" charts following each group presentation and place it on the class blog (see Figure 8.14).
- Write three facts they now know about their cultures that they did not know before they began their investigations.
- Write blog posts in which they explain why they would like to visit specific cultures. Include at least three reasons based on their research and the presentations given.

Figure 8.14. Culture Chart

My Name is: _____

Fill in your culture chart after each puppet video.

	Culture Name China	Culture Name Japan	Culture Name Africa	Culture Name Mexico
History				
Location				
People				
Traditions				
Dress				
Art				
Music				
Government				
Literature				

Step 6: Evaluate What Was Learned

Evaluation will be based on five aspects: (1) the products they produced in their roles as performers, set designers, and directors; (2) the writing on the blog; (3) their knowledge of different cultures as exemplified through the "culture" charts and other writing; (4) their abilities to use the Internet; and (5) their abilities to perform their roles in creating the videos.

Assessment will comprise the following elements:

- A handout for teachers to use to assess puppet performances, stage construction, narrative texts, and the scripts (see Figure 8.15).
- Review of student blog posts and comments periodically throughout the unit for completeness and creativity to gain insight on students' day-to-day progress.
- Student self-evaluations of their use of technology tools (see Figure 8.16).
- Review of culture charts for completeness and content.
- Evaluation of written information for clarity, coherence, and command of standard English conventions.

Summary

This unit is designed to enable students to work independently or in groups to explore the concept of culture. As a result, children should have a better understanding of their community and the similarities and differences among the people in it. By allowing students to research cultures of their own choosing, children have had to make decisions about their learning. In addition, they have gained skills in language arts, social studies, and art.

> ➤ For activities to create other types of digital stories, go to Bev's website at http://www.neal-schuman.com/webclassroom.

Puppetry provided an excellent vehicle for practicing speaking and listening skills, and it was also an effective way to teach content. Using the project approach for the unit provided students with a wide range of learning opportunities. Students should now understand that people

---

Figure 8.15. Puppet Project Assessment

Name: _____

_____

Direction: As you watch the puppet presentations, evaluate each of the roles—performers, set designers, and director in each play—according to the following criteria. Fill in your comments after each puppet presentation on the following.

The Performers

Criteria	Agree	Disagree	Why/Why Not
The puppets were well made and represented their characters.			
The puppets represented the culture through their costumes, dialogue, and performances.			
The puppets' dialogues helped me to understand the culture better.			
The characters expressed emotion in their voices, movements, and dialogue.			
The Set Designers			
The stage was sturdy and accommodated the presentations.			
The poster was visually pleasing, presented a clear message, and was grammatically correct.			
The Director			
The narrative helped the flow of the show, identified the characters, and brought the show to a conclusion.			
The narrative presented facts about the culture that helped me to understand the story events, the characters, and the moral of the story.			
The director directed the other performers.			

are unique human beings who have varied characteristics not limited by gender, race, class, or ethnic backgrounds.

A digital story can cross curriculum areas. It requires that students work together, think critically about the process of putting all aspects of the story on the storyboard, research, write, read, speak, and listen. Students who create digital stories and use other technologies such as video have succeeded in real twenty-first-century learning.

Teacher Exercises: Now You Try It . . .

It is important to reinforce how to create digital stories, including writing stories and producing them digitally. Before going on to Chapter 9, try some of the following activities:

1. Review Part 2 and how it fits together with the unit plan. Review Chapter 4 describing podcasts to become more familiar with using audio in a project.

Figure 8.16. Digital Story Evaluation Rubric				
Category	**4 points**	**3 points**	**2 points**	**1 point**
Purpose of Story	Establishes a purpose early and maintains clear focus throughout.	Establishes a purpose early and maintains focus for most of presentation.	A few lapses in focus exist but purpose is fairly clear.	Purpose is unclear.
Clarity of Voice	Voice quality is clear and consistent throughout.	Voice quality is clear and consistent through the majority of the story.	Voice quality is clear and consistent through some of presentation.	Voice quality needs attention.
Pacing of Narration	Pace fits story line and helps draw audience into story.	Occasionally speaks too fast or slow for the story.	Tries to use pacing but noticeably does not always fit story.	No attempt to match pace of the telling to the story or audience.
Meaningful Audio Soundtrack	Music matches story line well.	Music somewhat matches story line.	Music is OK and not distracting but not coordinated well.	Music is distracting, inappropriate, or not used.
Quality of Images	Images create distinct atmosphere.	Images create an atmosphere that matches some parts of story.	An attempt was made to use images to create a tone.	Little or no attempt to use images to create tone.
Economy of Story Detail	Exactly right amount of detail throughout.	Composition is generally good but seems to drag somewhat.	Story needs more editing.	Story needs extensive editing.

2. Follow the process that students will take to complete the tasks in the unit. This will give you a feeling for what your students will experience as they complete each activity.
3. Take the story you wrote as part of the exercises at the end of Part 2 and create the actual story to use as a model. Include all components such as music, audio, transitions, and effects on a storyboard.
4. Identify several issues you want students to explore (e.g., energy conservation, recycling, etc.). Divide students into groups and have them follow the process in the unit plan to create a storyboard they can use for the issue.
5. Reflect in a blog post to other educators by answering the following questions:
   a. How will digital storytelling improve students' reading, writing, speaking, and listening skills?
   b. Is digital storytelling a good interdisciplinary project? Why or why not?
   c. What are some of your ideas for using digital storytelling in your school?
   d. How does video add to the ultimate product?

CONCLUSION

Advancements in technology have given everyone the opportunity to be a digital storyteller for an online, worldwide audience. Digital storytelling is an engaging means of integrating technology into the curriculum, whether students are creating digital movies or online storybooks.

Teachers who bring digital storytelling into the classroom are discovering what makes this vehicle for expression worth the effort. They watch students gain proficiency in writing and research, visual literacy, critical thinking, and collaboration. They see students learn through a range of learning styles. Of course, they also see students make authentic use of technology, and they hear students discover the power of their own voice.

Moreover, integrated instruction lends itself to more than one curriculum area to reinforce the idea that all subject areas have value and are interrelated in students' lives. Schools must continue to focus on interdisciplinary teaching, and teachers and school librarians must bring their special talents together to create cross-curricular units. Web 2.0 provides tools to enable educators to cross curriculum boundaries more easily.

REFERENCES AND FURTHER READING

Discovery Education. 2011. "Digital Storytelling 2.0: Connect, Create and Collaborate." April 27. Discovery Education. http://web2010.discoveryeducation.com/blog/index.cfm/2011/4/27/Digital-Storytelling-20-Connect-create-and-collaborate.

Gardner, Howard. 1983. *Frames of Mind: The Theory of Multiple Intelligences.* New York: Basic Books.

ISTE (International Society for Technology in Education). 2007. *National Educational Technology Standards for Students.* Eugene, OR: International Society for Technology in Education. http://www.iste.org/standards/nets-for-students/nets-student-standards-2007.aspx.

Lee, Amy. 2011. "YouTube Shares Surprising Statistics on 6th Birthday." *The Huffington Post.* May 25. http://www.huffingtonpost.com/2011/05/25/youtube-statistics-birthday_n_866707.html.

Strickland, D. S., and Morrow, L. M. 1989. "Emerging Readers and Writers/Oral Language Development: Children as Storytellers." *The Reading Teacher*, 43, no. 3: 260–261.

Tolisano, Silvia. 2009. "How-to Guide: Digital Storytelling Tools for Educators." *Langwitches Blog.* http://langwitches.org/blog/wp-content/uploads/2009/12/Digital-Storytelling-Guide-by-Silvia-Rosenthal-Tolisano.pdf.

CHAPTER 9

Enhancing English Language Learning with Web 2.0 Tools

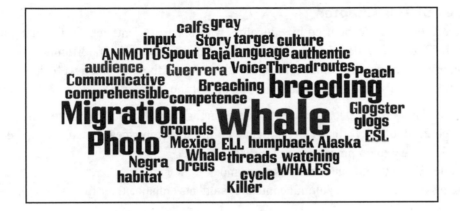

PART 1: IDEAS AND INSIGHTS

Envision nonnative English-speaking students being journalists in English, the target language, fulfilling an authentic task of interviewing a native speaker. Imagine students using their cell phones to record a message in the language they are learning that will be published on a blog or incorporated into a class podcast. Visualize students listening to authentic language on their own time, extending the learning time beyond the classroom. Picture a class project where students create a culturally authentic electronic recipe book and share it with the world. These are just some tasks that second-language learners can accomplish with Web 2.0 tools while improving their language skills at the same time.

Perhaps some reading this book might wonder why we are including English Language Learning (ELL) in a book on Web 2.0 tools in the curriculum. The increase in numbers of nonnative English speakers has continued to grow at a rapid rate. Most teachers and librarians throughout the country have had contact in school with students whose first language is not English. For example, data from the National Center for Education Statistics indicated that in 2009 approximately 21 percent of children ages 5–17 (or 11.2 million) spoke a language other than English at home, and 5 percent (or 2.7 million) spoke English with difficulty (Aud et al., 2011). Approximately 73 percent of those who spoke English with difficulty were Spanish speakers. Other languages include Vietnamese, Korean, Chinese, Russian, Hmong, Arabic, and many more. These skyrocketing numbers of limited English proficient (LEP) students underscore the importance of ensuring that their academic success becomes a reality and that teachers provide these students with every opportunity to excel. Moreover, the No Child Left Behind (NCLB) Act clearly sets as a goal for LEP students to meet the same challenging state academic achievement standards and state academic content standards expected of all students (No Child Left Behind, 2001). The law also states that every student should be technologically literate by the eighth grade, regardless of student background or family socio-economic status.

Thus, educators are faced with real challenges. They must teach these students how to comprehend, speak, read, and write in English, use technology effectively, and adhere to culturally mandated goals. These tasks can be overwhelming for both educators and students. It is no wonder the dropout rate among this student group is so high.

Some of the technologies discussed already in this book provide new ways to engage English-language learners or anyone learning a new language to improve in the four skills—listening, speaking, reading, and writing. Understanding a bit about how students learn a second language will illustrate why.

Objectives of This Chapter

This chapter is designed to be used by educators who teach students whose first language is not English. Web 2.0 tools are ideal for these students because they provide opportunities for them to use authentic language to create meaningful projects that require them to listen well, speak effectively, read and think critically, and write clearly. By the end of the chapter, educators will be able to:

- understand how Web 2.0 tools can enhance the English as a Second Language (ESL) curriculum;
- use Web 2.0 tools to further LEP students' ability to listen, speak, read, and write—the four skills necessary to communicate in English;
- integrate Web 2.0 tools into their lessons; and
- create lessons that include cultural content as students enhance their English language abilities.

> ➤ Check Bev's website at http://www.neal-schuman.com/webclassroom to see how educators are using visual Web 2.0 tools in this chapter in other subject areas and grade levels.

Part 1 discusses theories that need to be considered to teach LEP students. It also discusses the reasons Web 2.0 tools can enhance the curriculum. Part 2 shows educators how to get started with different Web 2.0 tools, and Part 3 describes a unit plan incorporating VoiceThread, Glogster, Photo Story 3, Animoto, and Photo Peach technology as integral parts of the unit. Examples using these tools and exercises reinforcing what was discussed are also part of this chapter.

Glossary

Review the following terms before starting the chapter to fully understand the concepts discussed.

Animoto: An online service that allows users to upload their own pictures or video clips, select music, and then automatically create professional-quality video segments.

authentic language: Language that is appropriate and authentic to children's lives.

communicative competence: The learner's ability to understand and communicate in L2 (the target language they are learning).

comprehensible input: Information that is understandable to LEP students.

ELL students: English-language learning students.

ESL: English as a Second Language.

LEP students: Limited English proficient students, whose first language is not English.

Photo Peach: A simple free online slideshow creator.

Photo Story 3: A free program for the PC that enables a user to create multimedia presentations from digital photographs.

target language: The language being learned.

thread mode: A form of discussion where a community or group holds a conversation.

VoiceThread: A tool enabling group conversations to be collected and shared in one place from anywhere in the world.

Introduction

Today, language-learning experts emphasize input over output, listening and reading over grammar study. If you want to learn English or any other language for that matter, you need input that is meaningful, interesting, and at your level. Before you can use the language, you must get used to the language. You don't need to be in a hurry to speak English, and you don't need to speak it all the time to improve.

Stephen Krashen (1992), professor at the University of Southern California and well-known for his study of language acquisition, states that real language acquisition develops slowly, and speaking skills emerge significantly later than listening skills, even when conditions are perfect. The best methods are, therefore, those that supply "comprehensible input"—language students understand in low-anxiety situations, containing messages that students really want to hear. These methods do not force early production in the second language, but allow students to produce when they are ready, recognizing that improvement comes from supplying communicative and comprehensible input, and not from forcing and correcting production. Even if you are an intermediate learner, extensive reading and listening will increase your familiarity with the language, enrich your vocabulary, and develop your confidence.

One reason learning language with Web 2.0 tools is effective is that it is fun. The Internet avoids the tension and boredom of the classroom and increases students' motivation. For example, bloggers may post messages in their own language or in English. English becomes the medium of communication among people of different cultural backgrounds. Blogging isn't just an assignment, but a genuine, enjoyable, and meaningful activity. A contagious enthusiasm will keep learning happening because it is less like studying and more like making new friends and discovering new cultures through language.

Here is what several classroom teachers and a student had to say about using Web 2.0 tools with second-language learners:

> "In our middle schools, students are given 20 vocabulary words to learn, and they were learning 40 percent. With the use of iPods and podcasts, learning has increased to 95 percent." (El Paso teacher)

> "It's an authentic audience. It's one thing to make a product that's read by a teacher. It's a whole different picture when you're communicating to hundreds of other students around the world that really want to know what the United States is like. Another asset is that students also become teachers, representatives, and ambassadors of their countries." (Larry Ferlazzo, ESL Teacher; http://voicethread4education.wikispaces.com/EFL+%26+ESL).

> "I love, love, love VoiceThread! I use it at home, but I can't use it in my school. It's blocked! Is there any way you can help?" (Student response to VoiceThread)

To understand why these statements are important, it is necessary to understand how children learn a second language.

Attaining Competence in a Second Language

When teaching LEP students, educators must keep several principles in mind (Stevick, 1980):

1. For most learners, acquisition of a second language will only take place as learners are exposed to and engaged in contextually rich, meaningful communication.
2. Most learners are not successful when they learn grammar rules and then try to use those rules in communication.

3. Communicative competence is achieved by subconsciously acquiring the language through active participation in real communication, such as conversation that is interesting to learners.
4. Language is most effectively acquired when it is used as a vehicle for doing something else—then learners are directly involved in accomplishing something via the language and thus have a personal interest in the outcome of what they are using the language to do.
5. Teachers need to create opportunities for students to be exposed to, and engage in, real communication.

How can educators help their students gain the competence in the second language they need to succeed in school, in their jobs, and ultimately in their lives? Here are a few suggestions that activities will illustrate later in this chapter in the unit plan:

1. Provide a meaningful context for the introduction of new items in order to engage students' interest. Web 2.0 tools can provide an interesting context for students through a multimedia presentation of information and by acting as a vehicle for communication.
2. Allow students to feel their experiences are valid, important, and relevant to the learning of English. The unit plan in this chapter incorporates an interesting experience where students can use English to learn about animal migration.
3. Encourage students to use English for social reasons. Have students work in groups and talk with one another as part of completing a task to provide a vehicle for real communication for a specific purpose.
4. Provide opportunities to practice the four skills—speaking, listening, reading, and writing—while encouraging vocabulary building and grammatical competence.
5. Show respect for students' native cultures by illustrating the importance of contributions by members of their ethnic groups. At the same time, continue to familiarize students with the culture in which they are living.
6. Teach to the needs of different learning styles. It is especially important with nonnative speakers, who are struggling with language and cultural differences, to learn in the style that best suits them.

Using a variety of resources can help promote interest in learning for English-language learners and provide a change of pace in the language classroom. The Internet, especially with the introduction of Web 2.0 and social networking tools for communication and collaboration, offers creative tools even outside the ESL classroom for students to practice English skills. What better way to promote reading and writing competence in authentic situations than by communicating with a class in another part of the world. And, with blogs (Chapter 2), wikis (Chapter 3), and podcasts (Chapter 4), educators now have easy-to-use tools to reinforce all four language skills.

Using these technological tools within their inquiry-based curriculum provides visualizations and animations that allow students to become active researchers and knowledge-generating participants able to better comprehend many abstract concepts. Presentations are made using technology to communicate understanding of their new learning. The use of technology eases the LEP students' process of conceptualizing. Daily technology use in relevant applications gives them practical knowledge and twenty-first-century skills reflective of real-life applications, while enhancing their use of language acquisition skills.

Why Use Web 2.0 Tools with LEP Students?

LEP students benefit in a number of ways when they use Web 2.0 tools as integral parts of their lessons. Here are just a few:

- Web 2.0 tools engage them in learning by motivating them to listen, speak, read, and write.
- Tasks using Web 2.0 tools can reinforce their new culture and that from which they came.
- Students can expand their opportunities with technology because many will not have access to computers or these Internet tools at home.
- By expressing what they learned, LEP students show others what they are capable of doing.
- LEP students see the importance of technology and apply it to the real world.
- Web 2.0 tools provide a venue to promote meaningful content for LEP students.

When students are engaged in meaningful activities, they are constructing their own knowledge, with the teacher as the facilitator of the process. Web 2.0 tools described in this chapter are among those that are ideal for LEP students who need authentic language and the ability to use comprehensible input.

Examples of Digital Tools Used in the ESL Classroom

The Internet provides a number of examples of ESL classrooms using blogs, podcasts, and wikis integrated into lessons that emphasize language learning. To provide more awareness of different Web 2.0 tools, this chapter will discuss those not used in previous chapters. Several tools are good at producing a venue for practicing listening, speaking, reading, and writing so important to second-language learners.

Example 1: VoiceThread Projects

English-language learners at Lincoln-Eliot Elementary school designed and created a piñata for their project (see Figure 9.1). The kickoff was a discussion of what they already knew and what they wanted to know about piñatas. Children of different ages, all LEP students, were responsible for different parts of the project. They researched, determined the heart shape of the piñata, and decorated it by drawing upon math concepts to measure the width of stripes on the heart of the piñata. See a picture of their work at http://ed.voicethread.com/#u411680.b549799.i2941394. In another project for beginning English learners at the same school at http://ed.voicethread.com/#u411680.b666482 .i3524534, students learned phrases in English and recorded them in VoiceThread. They then added their own comments and questions.

Figure 9.1. The Piñata Maker VoiceThread

In addition to the VoiceThread projects just described, other schools are using this tool in numerous ways. For example, for the school year 2011–2012, the Hawaii State Department of Education made VoiceThread available to elementary and secondary schools and had students submit their VoiceThreads for a statewide contest. The winners, third-graders, created the Bully Free Zone VoiceThread at http://ed.voicethread.com/share/1814765/ (see Figure 9.2). Others are available at http://hawaiivln.k12.hi.us/vtwinners.

Example 2: Greetings from the World Glog Project

In Example 2, a wiki site, created by Arjana Blazic with the help of other K–12 educators, displays glogs showcasing students' home countries. Topics range from Easter in Portugal to Brazilian culture, music, and history to cities in Australia to a U.S. class in Texas that describes both Texas and Mexico, the homelands of her students. Students creating the glogs are second-language learners from five continents—Europe, Asia, Australia, and North and South America—14 countries, and 21 different schools. View glog examples at http://greetingsfromtheworld.wikispaces.com/ (see Figure 9.3).

Example 3: Fifth-Grade English-Language Learners Learn Idioms

The Bluebonnet fifth-graders—the Cheetahs, Blue Jays, and Sting Rays—tackled English idioms by first creating an example to explain what an idiom was. Using Photo Story 3, groups selected different idioms, wrote examples, and provided definitions. Each group was photographed illustrating the incorrect meaning and then what the idiom really meant. For example, for the idiom "hit the books" they wrote the idiom in a sentence. The next picture showed students physically hitting their books, followed by a photo where they were studying intently, thereby providing the correct definition of the idiom. Idioms are often quite difficult for second-language learners, so using Photo Story provided a fun way for all students to take part and demonstrate their knowledge of

Figure 9.2. Hawaiian K–12 VoiceThreads

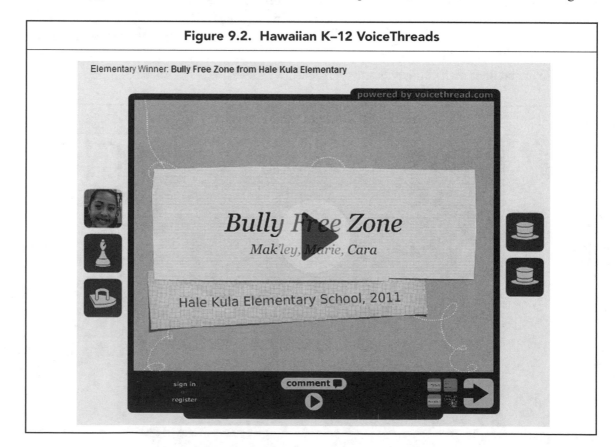

Figure 9.3. Greetings from the World

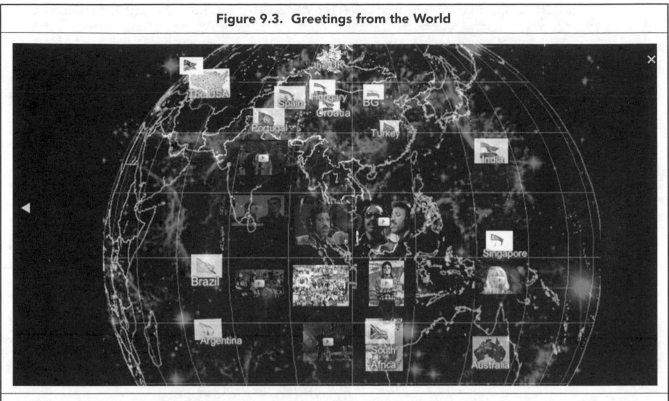

Source: Licensed by Creative Commons Attribution Share-Alike 3.0 License; http://creativecommons.org/licenses/by-sa/3.0/.

idioms (see Figure 9.4). Other examples appear at http://21stcenturyteaching.pbworks.com/w/page/833451/Photostory-3-Examples.

How did these students get started using these visual tools? Part 2 discusses how educators can begin using each tool for the benefit of LEP students.

Figure 9.4. Learning Idioms

PART 2: GETTING STARTED WITH WEB 2.0 TOOLS FOR LEP STUDENTS

Do you want a visual way to communicate a topic? Are you introducing a new topic? Are students trying to demonstrate mastery of a subject? Begin by uploading photos or bringing them in from a website such as Flickr. Arrange them in the right order to tell your story and add your music and special effects such as zooming and captions. Save your project so it can be embedded into a blog, wiki, or even Facebook. The following tools enable students as young as early elementary school to create their own digital projects.

What Is Educational VoiceThread for K–12?

VoiceThread (http://voicethread.com/) has many features that make it a useful tool for the K–12 classroom, especially second-language learners. A VoiceThread (see Figure 9.5) is an online media album that can hold essentially any type of media (images, documents, and videos). Users can make comments in four different ways—using voice (with a microphone or telephone), text, an audio file, or video (with a webcam)—and share those comments with anyone they wish. A VoiceThread allows group conversations to be collected and shared in one place, from anywhere in the world. Educational VoiceThreads (K–12), available at no cost to educators at http://voicethread

> ➤ See Bev's website at http://www.neal-schuman.com/webclassroom for more examples of video projects also ideal for second-language learners.

Figure 9.5. What Is Educational VoiceThread?

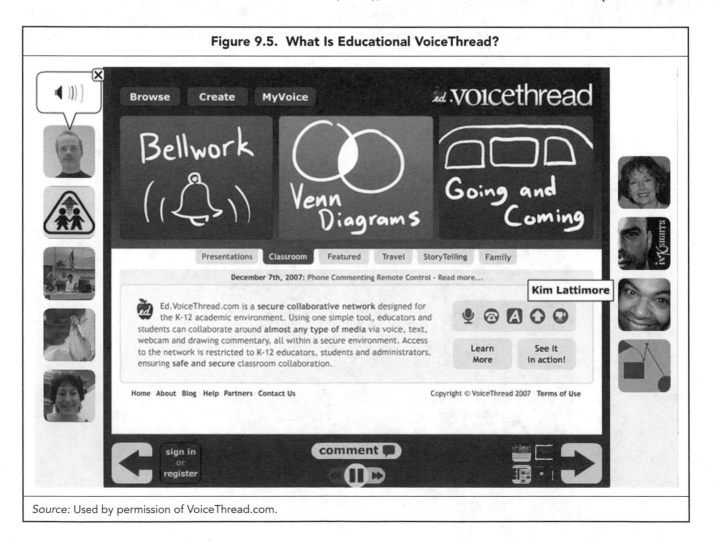

Source: Used by permission of VoiceThread.com.

.com/products/k12/, contains enhanced security and identity features, including comment moderation by educators. A video at http://voicethread.com/products/k12/# provides an overview of the tool, and tutorials at http://voicethread.com/#c28 are also available to illustrate each feature.

What Is Glogster EDU?

A collaborative learning platform for teachers, educators and schools, Glogster EDU enables students to create glogs, which are online multimedia posters with text, photos, videos, graphics, sounds, drawings, data attachments, and more. These interactive posters can be used as part of collaborative class projects in a private and safe student environment. Use this easy-to-use tool for research reports, digital storytelling, and presentations to promote student creativity and problem-solving. Take a tour of Glogster at http://edu.glogster.com/what-is-glogster-edu/ (see Figure 9.6).

What Is Photo Story 3?

Photo Story 3, a free program, allows users to create multimedia presentations from digital photographs. It is a Microsoft Windows XP program that comes installed on each computer. Using this tool, students can add panning and zoom effects, voice recording, and background music. They can also create transitions between pictures and add text with special color and texture effects. A tutorial is available at http://www.teachers.ash.org.au/hippohelper/pdfs/photostory%20tutorial.pdf (see Figure 9.7). If you have Windows 7, Windows Live Movie Maker, available at http://windows.microsoft.com/en-US/windows7/products/features/movie-maker, will provide similar features.

Figure 9.6. What Is Glogster EDU?

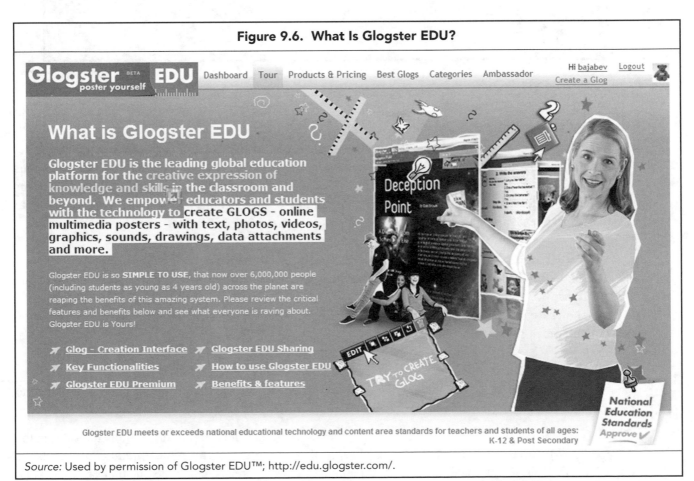

Source: Used by permission of Glogster EDU™; http://edu.glogster.com/.

Figure 9.7. What Is Photo Story 3?

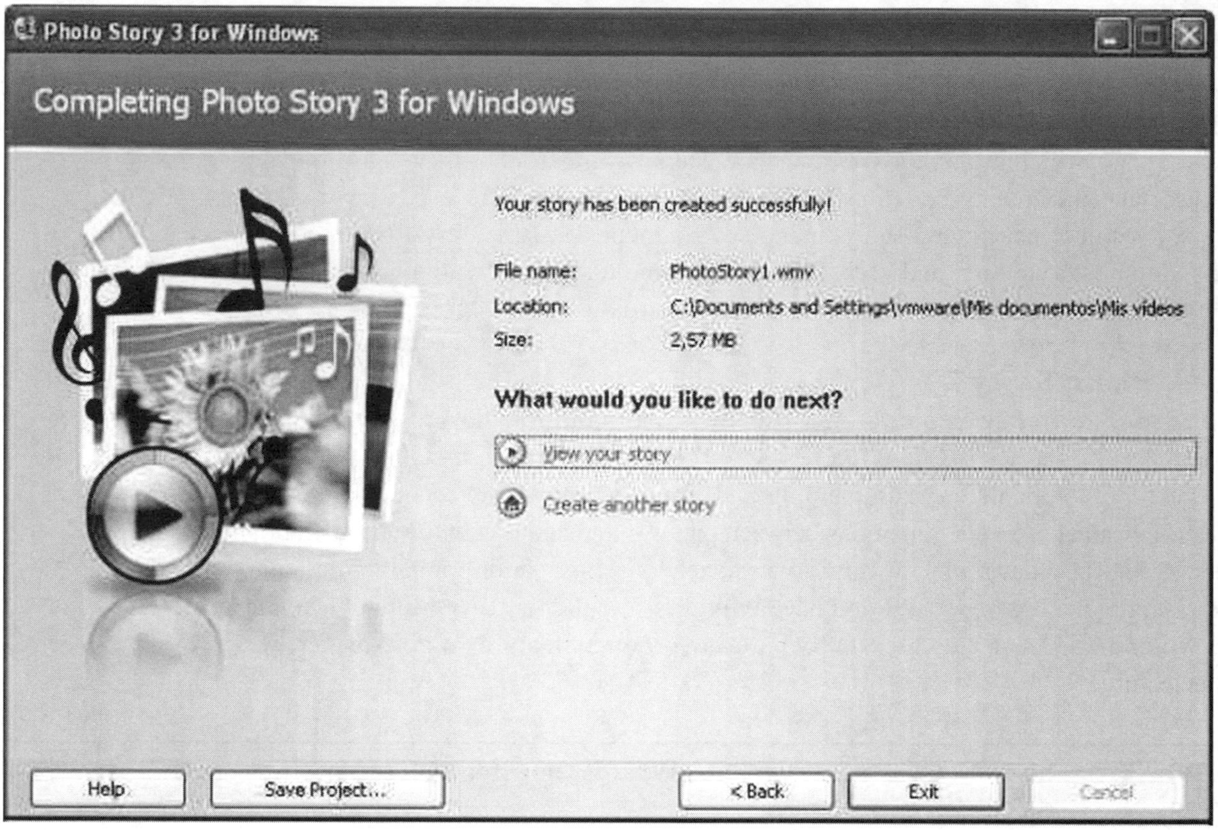

Source: Used with permission from Microsoft.

What Is Animoto for Education?

Animoto is an online service that allows users to upload their own pictures or video clips, select music, and then automatically create professional-quality video segments with elaborate transitions and special effects. Movies can then be shared online via e-mail or embedded into other websites and services. Educators can apply for a free Animoto Plus account for use in the classroom. Go to http://www.animoto.com/education/signup to get started (see Figure 9.8).

What Is Photo Peach?

Photo Peach is a simple, free, online slideshow creator that enables teachers and students to generate dynamic, zooming slideshows, digital stories, and interactive multiple choice quizzes. You can showcase students' work, document and share school events and activities, create digital stories, and much more (see Figure 9.9).

Teacher Exercises: Now You Try It . . .

Now that you have seen some of the tools available to create multimedia presentations, it is time to try using them yourselves.

1. Select one or more of the tools. Review the examples in Parts 1 and 2. Follow the steps in the tutorial for the tool you have chosen. For example, at http://voicethread.com/, click the Browse button and you will see a number of VoiceThreads. Click the one that says: "So what

Figure 9.8. What Is Animoto?

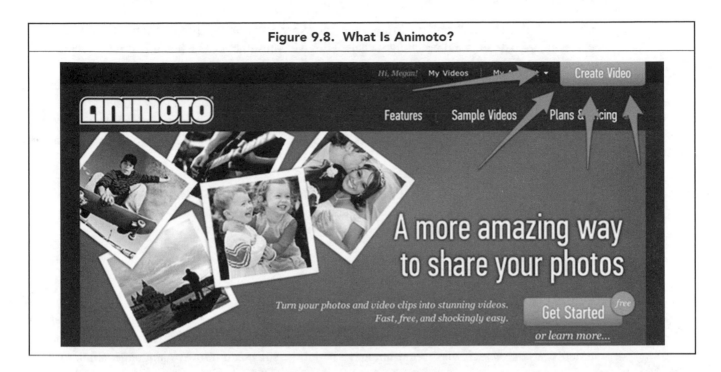

Figure 9.9. What Is Photo Peach?

Source: Used by permission of PhotoPeach.com.

is a VoiceThread?" and go through the entire presentation trying the different features while you are listening and watching it. This will give you some ideas when it is time to create your own VoiceThread. Watch tutorials for other tools to become familiar with how they work.

2. Sign up for one or more free tools and look at more examples. Try putting together a simple presentation you might use as a model when introducing the tool to your students.

3. Reflect on the tools as a blog post so you can try each one at the end of this chapter. Determine why you like one more than another. Which one seems to lend itself to your curriculum and students?

> ➤ *Interested in how to get started with multimedia projects? Check Bev's website at http://www.neal-schuman.com/webclassroom.*

PART 3: PRACTICAL APPLICATIONS

A curriculum supported through a multisensory approach of text, graphics, speech, and sounds is well suited for language learners. The collaborative project for this unit aims mainly at encouraging language learning while understanding science. By exploring the migratory paths of whales, students in two classes whose first language is not the same can improve language skills, explore science, and learn about technology at the same time. The unit also encourages collaboration between an ESL class in the United States represented by multiple languages and a class learning English in Mexico.

Cross-Curricular Unit Plan for ESL Students

This unit introduces new Web 2.0 tools—VoiceThread, Glogster, Photo Story 3, Photo Peach, and Animoto. All were described in Part 2. The unit is a collaborative project between students at a school in one country and those of similar age in another country, both of whom are learning English as a second language. At each school, students in groups of four will focus their attention on one aspect of the whale's migration. Each group will read about a specific part of the whale's journey, gather pictures, and research a particular area through which the whale travels to its breeding ground. For example, one group may learn about the beginning of the route in Alaska, another about the breeding location in Guerrera Negra in Baja, Mexico, and a third about the weather and geography of the regions. The two classes will use the new technologies to arrange presentations on their class wikis and meet online via Skype (see Chapter 5) once the presentation is completed.

Step 1: Connect to the Standards—What Should Be Taught?

When students are engaged in activities such as online collaboration with classrooms around the world or e-mail exchange and information searching, they are constructing their own knowledge with the teacher as the facilitator of the process. This unit supports the framework goal of providing a challenging curriculum for all students in several ways. Students will:

- use English to interact in the classroom;
- learn about a culture other than their own;
- use appropriate language variety, register, and genre according to audience, purpose, and setting;
- become involved in a science project that is bigger than the classroom; and
- familiarize themselves with Web 2.0 technology and how it can help to improve language skills.

Performance-based assessment will measure whether students can use the technology, with rubrics for evaluating listening, speaking, reading, and writing skill improvement. Moreover, by

ESL Clips

- *Wikipedia*'s Simple English feature (http://simple.wikipedia.org/) enables students, especially language learners or those with disabilities, to learn more about a subject using more understandable wording and vocabulary. With over 70,000 articles, learners can find topics such as Jupiter or World War II and either translate the article or go to the simple English homepage to search for a specific topic (see Figure 9.10).

Figure 9.10. *Simple English Wikipedia*

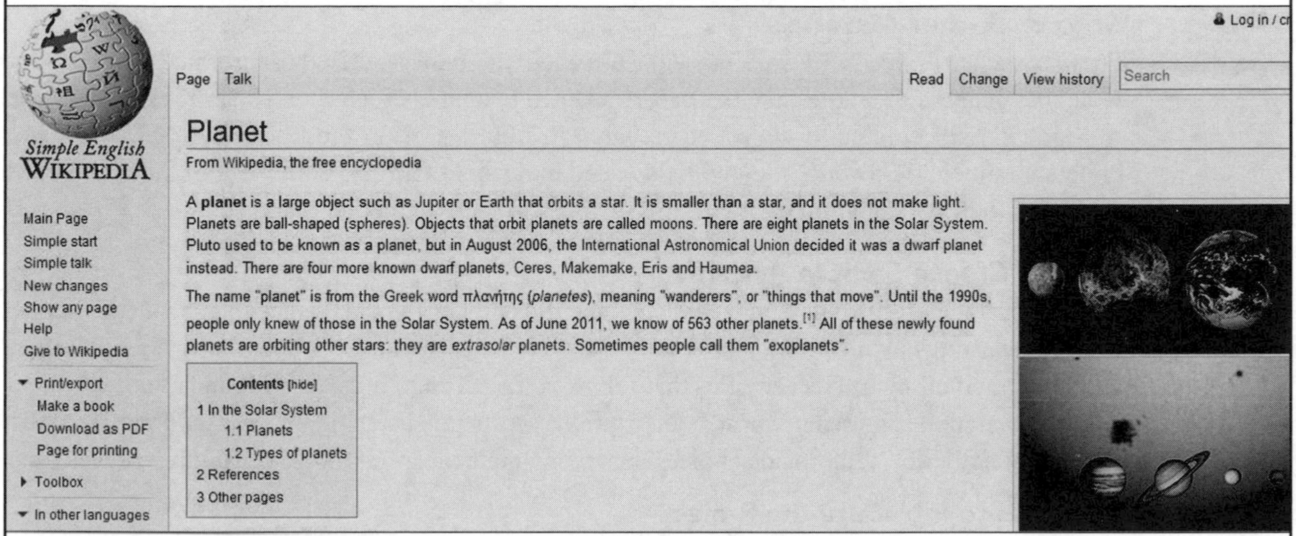

Source: Used by a Creative Commons license; http://creativecommons.org/licenses/.

- Have your students use *Simple English Wikipedia* and read about planets at http://simple.wikipedia.org/wiki/Planet. In groups, students can select a planet and create a glog based on facts and pictures they find on *Simple English Wikipedia* and any other sites supplied.
- Prior to putting the glogs on the classroom wiki, have other groups review different glogs for language.
- For an extended activity, have groups add to the articles about their planets.

engaging in the activities in this unit and working together both in classroom groups and with their partner class, students will increase their knowledge of technology tools necessary in the twenty-first century as emphasized in NETS (see Chapter 1).

Step 2: Identify General Goals and Specific Objectives

This unit is designed to engage students in learning that provides them with authentic opportunities to communicate and problem-solve, as well as to reinforce science content standards. By the end of this unit on whale migration, students will have a deeper knowledge and understanding of scientific principles and the culture of their partner class.

Goals

Students will:

- use English to achieve academically in science and participate in social interactions; and
- expand their opportunities for using English with a specific purpose for an authentic audience.

Objectives

The unit activities will provide challenging learning opportunities for students to collaborate and practice English. More specifically, as part of each goal students will:

- collaborate with each other in a group to tackle activities about whale migration that will reinforce their knowledge of animal habitats, patterns and adaptations;
- interact with students in another part of the world;
- express what they learned and show others what they are capable of doing;
- practice their public speaking and presentation skills;
- practice their writing in English by providing comments to others' writing; and
- use Web 2.0 tools to enhance language learning.

Step 3: Gather Materials

For this science project, LEP students will learn about migratory patterns using whales as an example. Note that many of the same activities can be adapted to animals such as birds, butterflies, and others.

Students will conduct background research in libraries or on the Internet to help them better understand their fieldwork. They will also need to become familiar with the tool they have chosen to use for their presentation. Part 2 of this chapter provides some ideas and sources.

Step 4: Create Sample Activities

The importance of this unit is to create an authentic audience and a chance to use L2 (the language they are learning), while at the same time meeting science standards and learning about a different culture from their own. The activities that follow can be used to improve pronunciation, vocabulary, cultural awareness, and science principles, as well as speaking, listening, reading, and writing skills. A number of activities will provide choices depending on the learner's stage of language development.

Activities to Introduce the Project

These initial tasks require students to work in groups, thus necessitating they practice language skills. They also draw upon their prior knowledge about whales and any information they have about the culture of the partner class, which in this case is that of Mexico. To initiate the project, students will do the following:

- As a class, brainstorm answers to these questions: What do they already know about whales, their habitat, and the migration process? In addition, what do they know about the culture of Mexico, especially that of Baja coastal towns? What do they want to understand more completely?
- Create two KWL charts—one on whales and another on the culture of the area where they live. Complete the "K—What I Know" column and the "W—What I Want to Know" column (see Figure 9.11).
- Select one of the Web 2.0 tools listed in Part 2. Review several examples of ways other classes have used the technology. This will also give groups ideas for creating their own presentations. See Table 9.1 for samples to view.
- Select a facet about gray whale migration from Alaska to Baja (e.g., gray whale migratory route, weather, dangers). Each group will write blog posts to explain their ideas and what they plan to research to the rest of the class. Members of other groups will write comments about different groups' ideas.

Activities to Be Used during the Unit

Students must complete two separate tasks during the unit:

- Task 1: Gather information about the aspect of whale migration they have chosen to talk about in their presentation.
- Task 2: Write a short script and record at least one or two facts about their own culture they want to present to their partner class.

Figure 9.11. KWL Chart	
Topic: Whales	**Name:**
K—What I Know	**W—What I Want to Know**
L—What I Learned	

Table 9.1. URLs for the Whale Unit	
URL	**Description**
http://www.learner.org/jnorth/tm/gwhale/jr/JnKidsOverview .html	Videos of the annual cycle of the gray whales
http://www.learner.org/jnorth/tm/spring/CreatureQuiz.html	Whale sounds
http://whale.wheelock.edu/books/ksmyth/	Day in a whale watch
http://www.swlauriersb.qc.ca/english/edservices/ pedresources/webquest/jfk/whale.htm	Facts about whales
ttp://www.learner.org/jnorth/tm/gwhale/jr/JnKids Overview.html	Overview of gray whales
http://www.learner.org/jnorth/tm/gwhale/jr/JnKids Overview .html	Learn about gray whales
http://www.learner.org/jnorth/tm/gwhale/MexSchoolTour .html	Meeting of two schools
http://www.learner.org/jnorth/tm/gwhale/sl/9/0.html	Gray whale migration
http://www.learner.org/jnorth/tm/gwhale/annual_jan.html	Annual cycle of the gray whale
http://www.cs.sfu.ca/gruvi/Projects/VirtualWhales/Whales/	Virtual Whale Watching Project
http://www.enchantedlearning.com/subjects/whales/	Enchanted Learning on Whales (Note: contains advertisements)
http://kids-learn.org/whaletales/showcase_whale.htm#	K-3 examples of whale projects—all could be used with Web 2.0 tools
http://www.youtube.com/watch?v=EBYPlcSD490&feature= share	Video of whale being freed from fishing net in Sea of Cortez

Task 1. In their groups, students will do the following to support language learning:

- Brainstorm and cluster ideas for their topic about whales. Encourage second-language learners to use words and pictures rather than phrases and sentences in their graphic organizers. See Figure 9.12 for a sample cluster.
- Create a Wordle of vocabulary and phrases they will need to describe and discuss whales. Share their Wordles with the other groups on the class wiki (see Figure 9.13).
- Have students complete the following to describe patterns, make predictions, find comparisons, share discoveries, formulate hypotheses, and ask questions.
  - I see a pattern in the migration data collected so far. My map shows...
  - Based on the patterns I see in the data collected so far, I predict that...
  - There are similarities [or differences] between...
  - I discovered that...
  - How are gray whales affected by...
- In small groups or individually, create an A to Z Whale Watch Book to improve vocabulary. Each word used must deal with whales. Publish books on the class wiki to share with other classes.
- Use Google Earth to identify gray whale sightings. Put placemarkers at each site with the day and time of the sighting. A live migration map for gray whales can be found at http://www .learner.org/jnorth/maps/gwhale_spring2011.html.

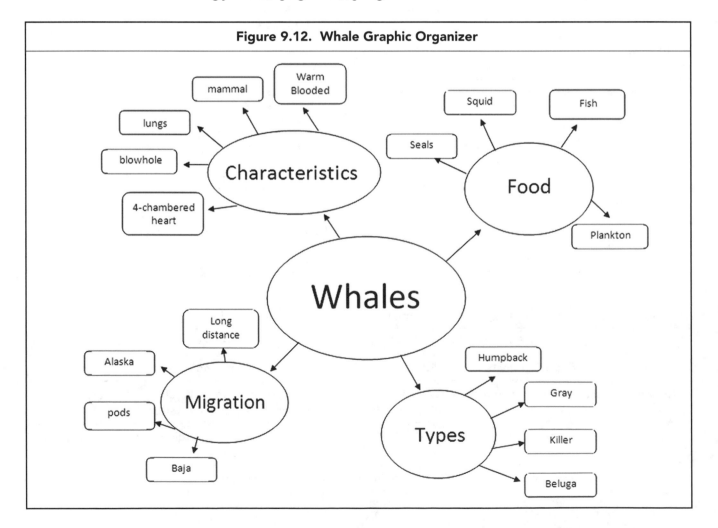

Figure 9.12. Whale Graphic Organizer

Figure 9.13. Vocabulary Whale Wordle

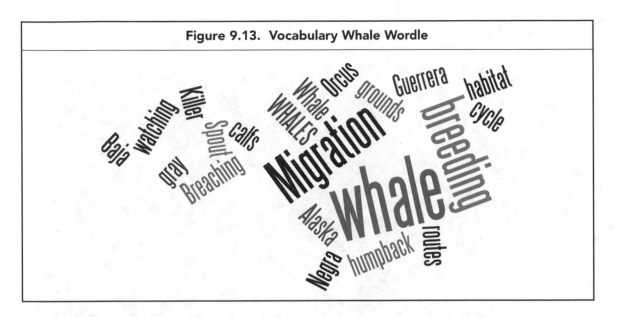

- Record discoveries for each sighting by writing fact sentences as blog posts.
- Ask questions about gray whales and their migration, and have other groups answer as they learn more from their own research.
- Create a story using one of the pictures of whales (see Figures 9.14 and 9.15).

Figure 9.14. Whales, Image 1

Source: Used by permission of June Patterson.

Figure 9.15. Whales, Image 2

Source: Used by permission of June Patterson.

Task 2. Compile facts about their own culture they want to communicate to their partner class:

- Write individual scripts incorporating at least two facts that deal directly with the group topic, then read it aloud to a partner in the group.
- Work together to select pictures and scripts for each group recording.
- Record the scripts individually using VoiceThread technology. The VoiceThreads will provide information on local culture to their partner class.

As a final project, each group will create one of the following:

- A poster using Glogster to showcase the cyclical, month-by-month events of the gray whale's annual migration (e.g., migration route, feeding grounds, mating/nursing sites). Incorporate research, photos, maps, videos, and other material they have collected and researched.
- A VoiceThread presenting facts and pictures about the gray whale.
- A presentation on a specific topic about whales: sounds, food, mammal characteristics, types of whales, and more, to include audio, photos, video, and maps. Use Animoto, Photo Story, or Photo Peach.
- A photo collage using Photo Peach or VoiceThread representing students' own cultures.
- Record or type at least three comments on pages of the partner class VoiceThreads.
- Create a VoiceThread in response to their partner school's recording. Have each group ask two or three questions they still want to know about the local culture of the partner school.

Some questions might include: What are their favorite traditions? What do people do on the weekend in their country? What is the weather like?

Culminating Activity. Each class will prepare for their Skype online meeting. Half of the groups in each class will show their presentations and explain what they learned about whales during the project. The remaining groups will collect questions from their classes to ask their partner class based on questions they still have after reviewing the VoiceThreads on culture.

Activities to Be Used as Follow-Up to the Unit

As extension activities, have groups of students try some of the following:

- Select a different Web 2.0 tool. Follow actions of a particular creature whose habitat is near their neighborhood or school (e.g., bird, hummingbird, butterfly) (see Figure 9.16; http://monarchwatch.org/). In a table identify all sightings by time and date and what they saw each time. Create a presentation representing what they learned. It should include text, pictures, charts/maps, and/or video.
- Reflect on the information from the partner school's VoiceThread, and write paragraphs showing how the cultures are similar and different. Using Photo Story, illustrate the similarities or differences. Write blog posts and comment on what they learned about the partner class culture and what was most surprising or unusual.

Note: Any or all of these presentations could be embedded into a class blog or wiki.

Figure 9.16. Monarch Butterfly

Step 5: Evaluate What Was Learned

To evaluate what was learned in this unit, each group will create a project portfolio containing their work. Use at least one of the Web 2.0 tools highlighted in Part 2 of this chapter. From Day 1 of the unit, collect, record, and display qualitative and quantitative observations, life cycle studies, weather information, maps, research findings, and more to showcase the group's work. Display it on the class wiki (see Chapter 3 for more on wikis).

Possible portfolio items:

- Concept maps and KWL charts
- Initial and revised predictions along with explanations for the revision
- Research notes
- Charts, graphs, and analysis of data
- Drawings, migration maps
- Firsthand observations
- Examples of student work/recording sheets
- Summaries of ideas and opinions on issues that have been explored
- Definitions, concepts, and problem-solving processes written in the students' own words
- Self-assessment responses

Students will place the date of entry of each item in the portfolio and put a sticky note on each item explaining what it reveals about their thinking, skills, and progress toward learning goals. Place the portfolios on the class wiki and have students identify what they think is most important, what they liked best, and what helped them most to learn about whales, a new culture, and a new language. Again, students are practicing language skills with an authentic audience for a specific purpose.

You may also have students complete rubrics. The sample rubric in Figure 9.17 contains at least one sample question to assess group work, final product, presentation, and use of technology.

Other types of rubrics you might want to create include peer rubrics to get student opinion on the workings of the groups and individual rubrics based on how students worked separately on pieces of the project. In addition, a self-evaluation rubric would help students assess their own work. These types of rubrics are available in other chapters of this book and can be adapted to use with this technology.

Summary

Technology such as VoiceThread, Glogster, Photo Peach, Animoto, and Photo Story help encourage language learners to take steps to speak out in the target language, communicate with their peers, increase their knowledge of animal migration, and demonstrate real-world skills they have achieved. These new tools emphasizing the visual and other Web 2.0 tools discussed in previous chapters can make an important difference to these struggling learners. Tasks in this unit are also applicable for elementary and middle school students in mainstream science classes.

Teacher Exercises: Now You Try It...

You are now ready to try creating your own project with one or more of the tools in Part 2 so you become familiar enough with the technology to use it with your students. Note that although this chapter addresses needs of LEP students, this technology can be used with any students at any grade level.

1. Search the web or use some of the URLs listed in Table 9.2 to become familiar with projects and lessons teachers and students have created together in different subject areas and at different

Figure 9.17. Evaluation Rubric			
This rubric contains characteristics of content, working together, technology, and presentation skills. Each of these characteristics could be split into a separate rubric, if desired.			

Characteristics	Superior 5 points	Developed 3 points	Limited 1 point
Planning	Extensive preparation of tasks for one of the Web 2.0 tools.	Adequate preparation of tasks but lacking total organization.	Preparation of tasks missing or weak.
Collaboration	Collaboration demonstrates cohesive shared leadership of tasks, decisions, contributions, group management, roles and responsibilities for project goals being met successfully; appreciation and respect for abilities of others actively communicated.	Collaboration generally performed as individuals completing tasks, assuming roles, and contributing as assigned; appreciation and respect for abilities of others adequate.	Collaboration weak or not evident; group has difficulty adjusting, communicating, and taking self-responsibility to effectively meet project goals; appreciation and respect for abilities of others apathetic.
Content	Rich imaginary and innovating task(s) create a consistent and engaging learning experience of high interest for others.	Adequate and appropriate tasks to sustain a learning experience.	Task(s) may be fun and motivating but do not sustain a learning experience for others.
Delivery	Exhibits poise, confidence, and personal style during delivery.	Exhibits relaxed delivery. Fluent with some details.	Exhibits nervous delivery. Lacking fluency, details, or originality.
Voice Quality	Quality of volume/diction/fluency/flow is high.	Quality of volume/diction/fluency/flow is acceptable.	Quality of volume/diction/fluency/flow is not acceptable.
Images	Images highly engaging for content/audience.	Images appropriate to content/audience.	Images detract or are inappropriate for content/audience.

grade levels. Write blog posts describing at least five ideas you might use for creating a project incorporating visuals with your class.

2. Look at the tutorials listed for one tool (e.g., the VoiceThread site at http://voicethread.com/#c28 showing how to set up a microphone, embed a VoiceThread, use the doodle tool, and more).

3. Create a short two- to five-minute project incorporating the tool on a topic of interest to you, one you can present to other educators and the administration in your school.

CONCLUSION

Technology as a tool to enrich learning experiences can serve as an excellent instructional tool for language learners of all ages in any language instruction program. Combining second-language acquisition principles with content instruction and using Web 2.0 tools for collaboration and teaching reading, writing, speaking, and listening provide educators with a way to motivate LEP students to improve their language skills. Activities incorporating Web 2.0 tools that were discussed in this chapter promote learning for nonnative English speakers because they:

Table 9.2. General URLs for Web 2.0 Tools in Part 2	
URL	Description
http://ed.voicethread.com/#q	More than 200 VoiceThreads created by K-12 students
http://voicethread.com/#u3968.b9458	A VoiceThread for ESL beginners with basic phrases, numbers, times, and more
http://ed.voicethread.com/about/library/	Lots of examples of student VoiceThreads
http://edu.glogster.com/glogpedia/	Examples of glogs
http://www.freeeslmaterials.com/glogster. html	List of glog blogs
http://sites.fcps.org/trt/animoto	Examples and tutorials for Animoto
http://pilaringlescole2.blogspot.com/2011/05/how-to-be-eco-friendly-on-photopeach_5719.html	How to be Eco Friendly using Photo Peach
http://web2650.grainvalley.k12.mo.us/gvsd/dreamweaver2/digital%20media.htm	Photo Story tutorials

- provide opportunities for students to use academic language in meaningful ways;
- illustrate the use of visuals to increase comprehension;
- provide opportunities for students to work together in completing academic tasks;
- promote interactive discussions among students and teacher;
- maintain cognitive challenges; and
- connect the lesson to students' own experiences.

We cannot afford to neglect the needs of this population in the twenty-first century.

REFERENCES AND FURTHER READING

American Association of School Librarians. 2009. *Standards for the 21st-Century Learner*. Chicago: American Association of School Librarians.

Aud, S., W. Hussar, G. Kena, K. Bianco, L. Frohlich, J. Kemp, and K. Tahan. 2011. *The Condition of Education 2011* (NCES 2011-033). U.S. Department of Education, National Center for Education Statistics. Washington, DC: U.S. Government Printing Office. http://nces.ed.gov/programs/coe/pdf/coe_lsm.pdf,

Krashen, Stephen D. 1992. *Fundamentals of Language Education*. Torrance, CA: Laredo.

No Child Left Behind (NCLB) Act of 2001, Pub. L. No. 107-110, § 115, Stat. 1425 (2002). http://www.ed.gov/policy/elsec/leg/esea02/index.html.

Stevick, Earl W. 1980. *Teaching Languages: A Way and Ways*. Rowley, MA: Newbury House.

CHAPTER 10

Bringing Web 2.0 and Social Networking into Elective Subjects

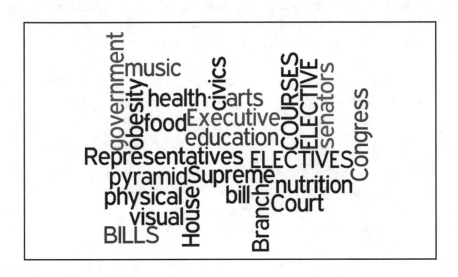

PART 1: IDEAS AND INSIGHTS

Throughout this book, each chapter has examined ways to use Web 2.0 and social networking as part of the core curriculum—science, social studies, math, and language arts. Unit plans also focused on cross-curricular learning to illustrate the connections among different subjects. These new tools have much to offer in elective courses as well, and this chapter looks at resources currently available for the visual arts, music, health education, and government.

Objectives of This Chapter

At the end of this chapter, educators will be able to:

- integrate Web 2.0 and social networking into courses in the arts, health education, and government;
- create lessons with a collaborative component in elective courses; and
- promote higher-order thinking skills by forming a relationship among other standards such as English/language arts, math, and history/social sciences.

Examples in this chapter illustrate how other educators are using the tools already described with art and music concepts, as well as nutrition and more.

Glossary

Review the following terms necessary for lesson plan understanding. Several additional Web 2.0 terms are also presented.

entrepreneur: A person who is willing to help launch a new venture or enterprise and accept full responsibility for the outcome.

immersion learning: A method of teaching a second language in which the target language, L2—the language being learned—is used as the means of instruction.

Impressionism: A nineteenth-century art movement that originated with a group of Paris-based artists who painted realistic scenes of modern life and often painted outdoors.

KWHL: An adaptation of the KWL chart for twenty-first-century skills. The new chart includes "H" for How do I find out.

majoritarian: A traditional political philosophy asserting that the majority has the right to make decisions for the population (used in art example).

Post-Impressionism: Extended Impressionism using vivid colors, thick application of paint, distinctive brush strokes, and real-life subject matter, but also emphasizing geometric forms.

Realism: The depiction of subjects as they appear in everyday life.

SchoolTube: A video-sharing site for schools, students, and educators.

Storybird: A collaborative storytelling site where students can create short, art-inspired stories to share, read, and print (especially appropriate for elementary-age students).

target language: The language being learned by a second-language learner.

The Arts

The visual arts are constructed around four components of arts education: aesthetic perception, creative expression, arts heritage, and aesthetic value. Investigating the contribution of great creators in the arts, studying the basic styles, and becoming receptive to artistic productions from different cultures foster understanding about the role the arts play in communicating the values and hopes of specific groups of people.

There are strong, natural connections among core courses and the arts. For example, students studying World Cultures in social studies may compare and contrast major themes in art throughout the world to understand better the effects of the arts on today's societies.

Example 1: Art Illustrates Science

In an elementary science class, students drew pictures of ways to conserve energy for an art contest sponsored by the California Department of Energy. See Figure 10.1 for some of their drawings illustrating energy ideas at http://www.energyquest.ca.gov/art_gallery/index.html.

Figure 10.1. Student Drawings about Energy

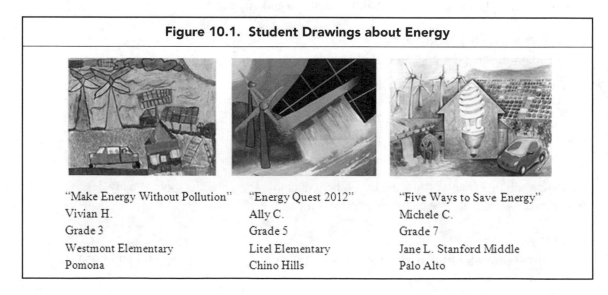

"Make Energy Without Pollution"
Vivian H.
Grade 3
Westmont Elementary
Pomona

"Energy Quest 2012"
Ally C.
Grade 5
Litel Elementary
Chino Hills

"Five Ways to Save Energy"
Michele C.
Grade 7
Jane L. Stanford Middle
Palo Alto

Example 2: Using Video for Art History/Contemporary Art Project

Burlington High School, Vermont, used video to create their self-portrait culminating activity for art history and contemporary art. Each student chose a picture of themselves after studying the techniques, color, composition, and style of an artist during their Art History class. These Art Honor 2 students created a self-portrait in acrylics to answer the question: If you could have anyone from the history of art paint your portrait, which artist would you select and how would you want yourself represented? Once students had finished their projects, they put the self-portraits together in a video on SchoolTube.

View the video at http://www.schooltube.com/video/11dec37209972aa33594/Burlington-High-School-self-portrait-art-project-for-Mrs-Conants-class (see Figure 10.2).

Example 3: Music and Technology

The music teacher at Woodstation Elementary School in Catoosa County, Georgia, has his music classes create podcasts each month, featuring music played and often created by different grades. Students also write and announce the musical segments. For example in the final thirty-third music podcast of school year 2011, three fourth-grade classes used GarageBand to create their own musical tracks. One class divided into teams—percussion, guitar, and keyboard—and collaboratively composed and arranged musical compositions.

In another project, a fifth-grade class demonstrated a little West African drumming, and other fourth-graders put together a more subdued but melodic piece. Podcasts are a great way to present what students have learned in music classes. Listen to more podcasts at http://web.me.com/lanemusic/WESPodcast/Podcast/Podcast.html. Music teacher Dr. Lane also blogs about innovate ideas for using technology in his music classes at http://web.me.com/lanemusic/WESPodcast/Tech_Ideas/Tech_Ideas.html (see Figure 10.3).

Figure 10.2. Self-Portrait

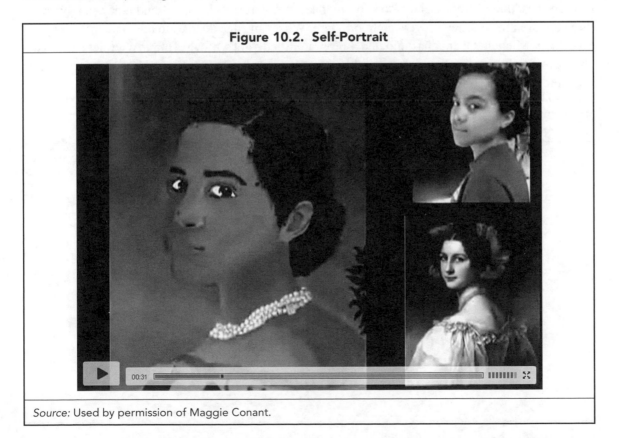

Source: Used by permission of Maggie Conant.

Figure 10.3. Woodstation Elementary School Music Podcasts

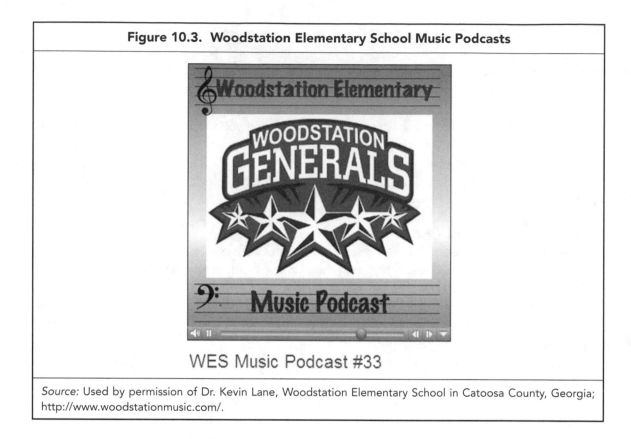

WES Music Podcast #33

Source: Used by permission of Dr. Kevin Lane, Woodstation Elementary School in Catoosa County, Georgia; http://www.woodstationmusic.com/.

Health and Physical Education

Over the past three decades, childhood obesity rates in America have tripled, and today, nearly one in three children in America is overweight or obese. What can educators do to alleviate this problem? First Lady Michele Obama has initiated a program titled "Let's Move" (http://www.letsmove.gov/about) to combat obesity and raise a healthier generation of kids (see Figure 10.4). Some projects illustrate how educators are dealing with this serious, far-reaching problem.

Figure 10.4. New Food Pyramid

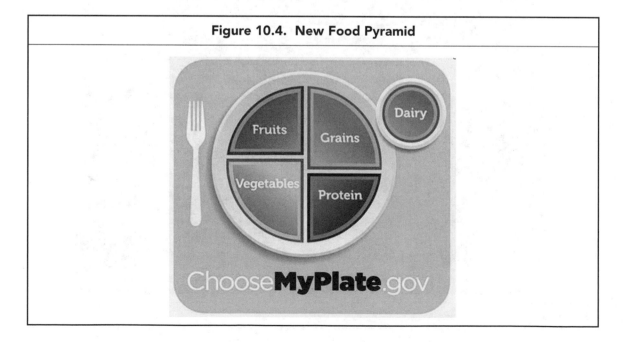

Example 4: Nutrition

Students at Lincoln Elementary School created class presentations about fruits and vegetables. In their presentations, each student tried to persuade classmates to eat a particular fruit or vegetable by providing facts about its origin and its nutritional value. The students used VoiceThread to create their presentations. See their lessons at http://www.educationworld.com/a_lesson/lesson/lesson054 .shtml.

Example 5: Exercise

The PE Geek at http://thepegeek.com/ has put together some interesting ideas on using Web 2.0 technology in physical education and health. Here are some of them:

- To assist with the presentation of content and homework requirements, the PE Geek in Australia uses a Facebook Page as the student center for his twelfth-graders taking physical education. Students "like" the page and then receive updates within their news feed. Teachers can easily post content and have discussions, which can be viewed and added to by students. Other students taking this course throughout the region can view and contribute to this site. The page at http://thepegeek.com/2011/01/09/the-facebook-page/ also has numerous other helpful fitness activities using podcasts, apps for mobile devices, and more.
- In Waterbury, Connecticut, virtual active technology equipment makes use of middle school students' appetites for games and virtual reality to encourage exercise. For example, virtual treadmills guide students on runs through cities around the world, and stationary bikes let them ride up a mountain. Brain Bikes challenge their minds and bodies with a computer game that only works if the player keeps pedaling. Some of the treadmills allow students to track how far they climbed during each class, how many calories they burned, how many miles they traveled, and how long it would take them to reach a goal. Read the entire article at http://www.educationworld.com/a_admin/admin/admin615.shtml.

Civics and Government

In the fourth grade, students start learning about government. They learn how bills become laws and identify the different branches of state governments. In ninth grade, students take a course in civics and explore the legislative, executive, and judicial branches of Congress in more depth. By twelfth grade, students have specifically learned about the government of the United States. As students examine legislative actions and our rights as citizens, they learn the fundamentals of what it means to live in a democratic society.

There are many Internet resources that contain information on government—its organization, the laws it makes, and the issues discussed among members of Congress. Using Web 2.0 resources such as Skype, students can also connect with students in other countries and learn similarities, differences, rights, and freedoms of other forms of government.

Example 6: Art and Politics = Real-World Lessons

There are strong, natural connections among subjects, and then there are those you would not suspect. For example, two classes at a high school in York, Pennsylvania, one studying art and the other advanced placement (AP) government, collaborated to create successful integrated studies projects. Both teachers worked together to design the project so that students not only gained information from one another but also maintained focus on the curricular goals of their respective classes.

Here's how it worked. Students in the sculpture class were to research a public policy, determine their position on the policy, and think of imagery that might reflect the policy. They then had to create a three-dimensional structure that portrayed their viewpoint about a government policy. The government class was studying the four major types of public policy (majoritarian, client, interest group, and entrepreneurial) and the categories of public policy (foreign policy, social welfare, economic, and environmental). AP students had to give feedback on whether or not the sculptures were portraying the public policy issues accurately; therefore, they had to understand the concepts involved with each of the policies.

All students collaborated on a wiki created by the AP government students. Both classes were responsible for including specific information so that all students could continue on with the assignment. This information also served as documentation for the entire process. Students used the wiki to share resources and collaborate about topics. Information supplied by the government students drove the creation of the art students' sculptures.

An AP history class partnering with an art class is quite unusual; nonetheless, teachers learned some important lessons from this collaboration: (1) teachers need to open themselves to new ideas by just going to the teacher in the next classroom; (2) subjects are not stand-alone, and teachers inherently start to integrate other subject matter without even thinking about it (see Figure 10.5). For more details about the project, visit http://www.edutopia.org/blog/stw-integrated-studies-video-york-high-school-teachers and http://www.edutopia.org/stw-integrated-studies-york-resources-video#Resources.

Immersion Learning

Dual Immersion programs use two languages for literacy and content instruction for all students. These programs provide the same academic content and address the same standards as other educational programs. They provide instruction in the two languages over an extended period of time, from kindergarten through eighth grade.

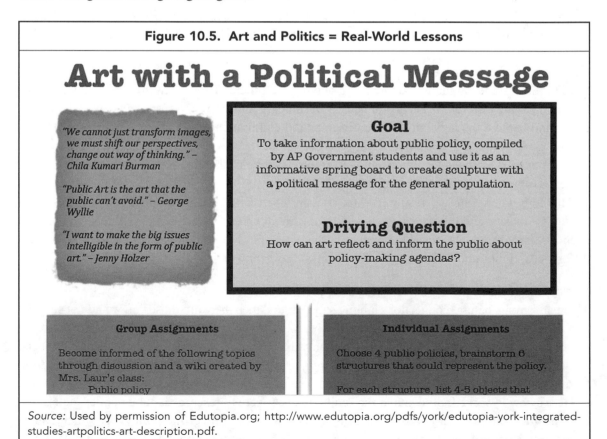

Figure 10.5. Art and Politics = Real-World Lessons

Source: Used by permission of Edutopia.org; http://www.edutopia.org/pdfs/york/edutopia-york-integrated-studies-artpolitics-art-description.pdf.

Example 7: Language Development

Beach School is a Neighborhood School and Dual Immersion (Spanish/English) School in Portland. Teachers at Beach School often use a project approach integrating different kinds of technology, including video, Flash, graphics, and electronic portfolios (see Figure 10.6). One particularly moving video, titled *The Story of Haiti*, created by a fifth-grade ESL student used her photo-editing skills, audio recording, research skills, and more. She divided the video into three parts: early history of Haiti; recent history, including the 2010 earthquake; and what Haiti means to her. Haiti is her own personal story. Born in Haiti, she was adopted from an orphanage with her three-year-old sister at the age of two and a half and brought to the United States. Not only did this youngster learn English, but also the history of an island that had special meaning for her. Ms. Haris commented that she feels very lucky to work in a school that allows her to build her curriculum and integrate her projects into classroom content.

Teacher Exercises: Now You Try It...

Try the following to learn more about using Web 2.0 and social tools in elective subjects.

1. View three examples of educators integrating Web 2.0 and/or social networking into elective courses. Look for ones in addition to those in this chapter.
2. Reach out to an educator teaching an elective subject to collaborate. Spread the word among Twitter or Facebook colleagues to see who might be interested in a collaborative project incorporating Web 2.0 tools.

Part 2 contains sample lessons in elective courses that include a Web 2.0/social networking component. These lessons model how to integrate activities with videos, VoiceThread, wikis, and other tools into elective courses.

Figure 10.6. The Story of Haiti

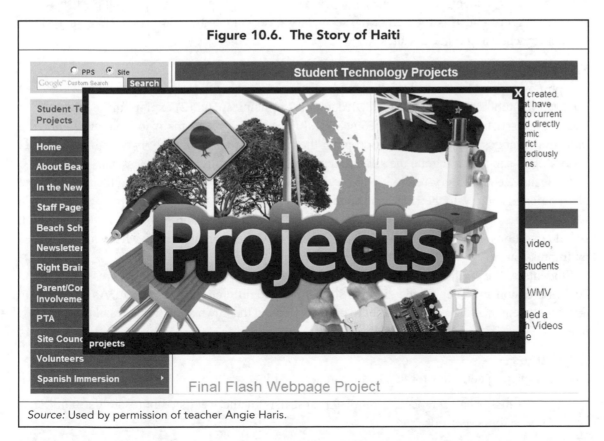

Source: Used by permission of teacher Angie Haris.

PART 2: PRACTICAL APPLICATIONS

The three lesson plans in Part 2 complement the discussion of the elective areas of the arts, health/physical education, and government in Part 1. Each web-based lesson plan, designed as part of a larger unit, contains the following components:

1. Context and purpose for the lesson
2. Objectives
3. Materials
4. Procedures
5. Evaluation
6. Extensions for further study
7. Summary

Grade levels are suggested for each lesson, although most plans can be adapted by creative teachers for students at any level. Each lesson plan explores one major concept with several activities, unlike the units in preceding chapters, which investigated larger themes.

Math Clip: Teaching Math Lessons with Animoto

Get students engaged by having them come up with the material for a lesson. Many students need to literally see how math is all around them before the concepts they need to learn are going to make any sense. For example, have students bring in photos that illustrate various math concepts such as fractions, percentages, shapes, angles, and more. Using Animoto, put together a video illustrating these math concepts in real life. Once the video is posted online, the students have a reminder of the concepts they need to learn that is easily accessible. The video is also something they had a part in creating, so there is great buy-in from the students.

Lesson 1 (Secondary Level): Learning about Art

At the elementary level, children sing, dance, paint, and draw pictures. They are exposed to art in books, and they learn to tell stories through pictures. At the secondary level, art is integral to core subjects. Students draw symbols representing themes in literature, and in social studies they learn about different cultures by studying their artwork. In many schools, art is taught as an elective subject. This lesson asks students to work together to learn about different periods in art and the artists whose styles they represent. It is focused at the secondary level but can be adapted for elementary-level students by choosing other websites.

Purpose

The purpose of this lesson is twofold: (1) familiarize students with art resources and how they can use Web 2.0 tools to expand their knowledge of art principles; and (2) explore those resources to learn about artists who paint in different styles. For example, students who have been studying industrial changes that occurred in Europe in the late-nineteenth and early-twentieth centuries in history class can also integrate the same time period in art with their history lessons.

In the nineteenth century, reforms led to revolutionary movements in art. Realism focused on direct observation of society. In the 1860s and continuing into the twentieth century, the Impressionist style began in Paris. Impressionism was concerned with direct observation of nature rather than with social conditions. Post-Impressionism denotes late-nineteenth-century artists who were influenced by Impressionism.

Students will examine artwork from these three schools of art—Realism, Impressionism, and Post-Impressionism. They should discover similarities and differences among them. As an extension activity, students will have opportunities to practice creating their own art in the styles of these periods in art.

Objectives

Upon completing activities for this lesson, students will:

• gain a historical perspective on different artists of the Realist, Impressionist, and Post-Impressionist periods;

- compare and contrast the works of artists using these styles;
- identify characteristics of these artists' works; and
- understand how earlier artists influenced later artists.

Materials

While there are many art websites available on the Internet, the sites in Table 10.1 will enable students to view paintings of artists who emerged in the late-nineteenth and early-twentieth centuries. These sites offer thousands of images of famous artwork often not available in school libraries.

Procedures

Using the URLs in Table 10.1 and any others they find in their research, students will view in groups of four different artists' works whose paintings represent styles from Realism through Post-Impressionism. Groups will select some activities from the following:

- Create timelines using Google Docs (see Figure 10.7) identifying the styles of painting in Europe in the late-nineteenth and early-twentieth centuries and the artists whose work represented those styles.
- Search The National Gallery of Art for Kids website at http://www.nga.gov/kids/kids.htm, shown in Figure 10.8, to identify artists and their works.
- Choose one of the artists from the timeline in Figure 10.7 and find paintings by these artists. The National Gallery of Art with its 100,000 images will be invaluable for this task.
- Create T-charts on their group wiki that include their chosen artists and characteristics of their works (see Figure 10.9). Answer the following questions: What is the subject matter of each

Table 10.1. Web 2.0 in the Arts

URL	Description
http://arted20.ning.com/	Connecting art educators around the globe using Web 2.0
http://www.nga.gov/kids/linkclassroom.htm	National Gallery of Arts for Kids
http://www.getty.edu/education/teachers/ classroom_ resources/tips_tools/index.html	The Getty Institute of Art classroom resources
http://blogs.getty.edu/openstudio/artist/ activities-beginning-level/	Collection of art-making ideas from artists (beginning, intermediate, and advanced)
http://www.hickorytech.net/~cshirk/k-12music/	Lists of music sites for K–12

Figure 10.7. Art Timeline

Realism Mid-Nineteenth Century	Impressionism Late-Nineteenth Century	Post-Impressionism Early-Twentieth Century
Goya (1746-1828)	Monet (1840-1926)	Seurat (1859-1891)
Courbet (1819-1877)	Renoir (1841-1919)	Van Gogh (1853-1890)
Daumier (1808-1879)	Pissarro (1830-1903)	Cézanne (1839-1906)
Manet (1832-1883)	Degas (1834-1917)	Gauguin (1848-1903)

Figure 10.8. National Gallery of Arts for Kids

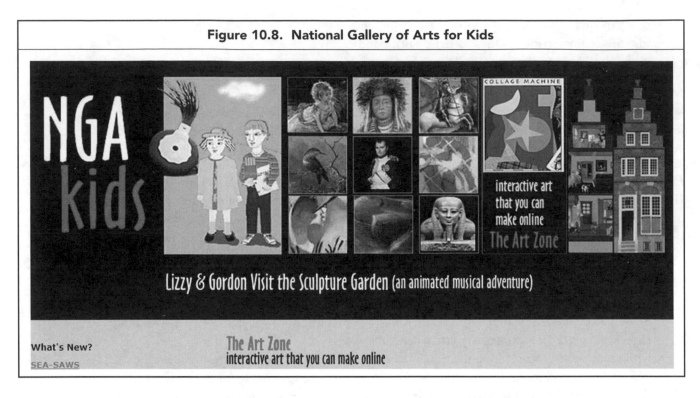

of these works? What styles did the artists use? What are characteristics of the paintings? This chart will be completed as student groups report on their artists.

- Choose two works by the same artist painted at different times during his or her career. Compare and contrast the two works based on the characteristics in the T-chart.
- Select paintings that have given them ideas for their own art-making. Write blog posts about the artists and tell what they especially like about those artworks.
- As a culminating project, create a digital story or a VoiceThread describing the artwork that appeals to them the most. Add images of the painter's work that may illustrate some of the following points: How are the shapes or elements in the picture arranged? How is the eye led around the painting? How does each part relate to other parts? Do lines define the edges of

Figure 10.9. Artists and Characteristics of Their Paintings

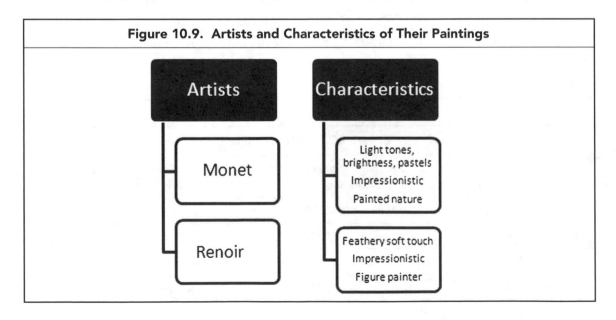

objects, or do they create abstract patterns? What are the subjects, and why were they chosen? How is color used? How does use of color compare to color in another period? What period does the picture represent? How does the painting differ from art in another period?

- Compile all work of the group and place it on the group wiki.

Evaluation

Each group will present artists they have placed on their group wiki to the rest of the class. Each member of the group will contribute to the presentation. Teachers will use Figure 10.10 to evaluate each group's wiki and presentation. Students will also complete group evaluations.

Extensions

When students are exploring other periods of art history during the school year, have them:

- identify influences that artists have on one another by comparing two artists from different styles;
- discuss similarities and differences between two styles—for example, Impressionism and Realism; and
- use paint, crayons, or pastels to create pictures of themselves that resemble the style of the artists they have chosen to research, and display their pictures on the class wiki.

Summary

Through the multimedia capabilities of Web 2.0 tools, students now have access to lifelike images and videos that would have been otherwise difficult to find. Whether students are learning to appreciate art for its own sake or to understand different cultures through their art, music, and dance in other subjects they are studying, Web 2.0 can bring resources and experts into the classroom that make art easier to understand and appreciate.

Lesson 2 (Elementary to Middle Levels): Keeping Fit

For this lesson, students will apply what they learn about nutrition in order to maintain their own health. This lesson can easily be adapted for any age level.

Figure 10.10. Evaluation Checklist

Directions: Fill in the checklist below to assess students' final projects. These can be returned to students.

1. Shows advanced familiarity with the subject matter for students' ages. _____
   _____

2. Reflects a superior level of quality. _____
   _____

3. Reflects care, attention to detail, and overall pride. _____
   _____

4. Shows a commitment of time, effort, and energy. _____
   _____

Other comments:
_____
_____
_____

Purpose

Students will have already studied food groups and what constitutes a healthy diet and lifestyle in their health classes. This lesson shows students' understanding of nutrition and its relationship to core subjects. It also requires students to apply these concepts to their own health.

Objectives

Students will:

- create one-week diets that suit their height, weight, age, and gender;
- demonstrate the ability to practice health-enhancing behaviors and reduce health risks;
- identify calories in food;
- use safe and sanitary food preparation and storage techniques with emphasis on how food handling and preparation practices affect safety and quality of food; and
- plan their own exercise programs.

Materials

Information on the web for health and nutrition is voluminous. The sample websites in Table 10.2 offer medical data for consumers and health safety and nutrition sites for children and teenagers.

Table 10.2. Web 2.0 in Health and Physical Education	
URL	**Description**
http://www.mypyramidtracker.gov/planner/sitetour/USDASiteTour.html	Tour on how to plan your menu
http://www.choosemyplate.gov/tracker/trackertutorial.html	Tutorial to assess your food intake and physical activity using MyPyramid Tracker
http://www.clipartguide.com/_search_terms/food.html	Free clip art pictures of food to use in presentations
http://www.educationworld.com/pe_health/	List of articles with free physical education teaching materials
http://www.shapeup.org/	Info on weight management and physical fitness
http://www.fda.gov/Food/ResourcesForYou/Consumers/KidsTeens/default.htm	FDA Kids Homepage on all aspects of health issues
http://www.fightbac.org/cornellvideos	Short videos on food safety
http://www.fightbac.org/storage/documents/flyers/cook_fightbac_factsheet_2010_color.pdf	Flyer factsheet on safe cooking
http://www.fightbac.org/storage/documents/flyers/clean_%20fightbac_factsheet_2010_color.pdf	Sanitary rules to fight bacteria
http://www.fightbac.org/storage/documents/flyers/chill_%20fightbac_factsheet_2010_color.pdf	How to keep bacteria down
http://www.canleyvale.hs.education.nsw.gov.au/Faculties/english/7N/peter%20lion.htm	How the Lion Got Its Roar
http://www.youtube.com/watch?v=FZ79rwDMXo0	Video of primary children acting out How the Lion Got Its Roar

Procedures

Individually, students will:

- use the Food Guide Pyramid at http://www.fns.usda.gov/eatsmartplayhardhealthylifestyle/ tools/mypyramidtracker.htm to review the different food groups to determine what USDA Dietary Guidelines say they should eat each day (see Figure 10.11); and
- track for one week the number of servings they eat from each food group (see Figure 10.12).

Figure 10.11. MyPyramid

Figure 10.12. Food Groups

Food Groups	Day 1	Day 2	Day 3	Day 4	Day 5	Day 6	Day 7
Bread, Cereal, Rice, and Pasta (6–11 servings)							
Vegetables (3–5 servings)							
Fruits (2–4 servings)							
Milk, Yogurt, and Cheese (2–3 servings)							
Meat, Poultry, Fish, and Eggs (2–3 servings)							

In groups of four, select one of the following tasks:

1. Using Google Docs, poll classmates and chart the results to a nutrition-related question. Develop their own questions or choose one of the following:
    ◦ What's your favorite fruit juice—orange, apple, grape, grapefruit, or cranberry?
    ◦ Which of these sandwiches do you prefer—peanut butter and jelly, bologna, ham and cheese, bacon/lettuce/tomato, or turkey?
    ◦ What's your favorite sandwich bread—white, wheat, Italian, multigrain, rye, or pita?
    ◦ What's your favorite snack—potato chips, apple, banana, grapes, orange, candy bar, carrots, or pudding?
2. Plan a balanced menu for one day. Include foods from all groups on the food pyramid. For younger students, the number of servings from each group might be on the lower end of the range listed for the group. Use the Calorie Database (http://www.caloriedatabase.com/), Calorie King Foods List (http://www.calorieking.com/), or MyPyramid Tracker (http://www.mypyramid tracker.gov/) to determine how many calories they will take in if they follow their menus. Keep a tally of calories as they go along (see Figure 10.13).
3. Select at least two food chain restaurants and compare food choices using Fast Food Facts (http://www.foodfacts.info/) and The Fast Food Nutrition Fact Explorer (http://www.fatcalories.com/). Create a spreadsheet of their choices in Google Docs. Graph the data in Google Docs. Create a group spreadsheet and place on their group wiki.
4. Assume a role and act out a short scene identifying one safety precaution when cooking, avoiding bacteria, or handling food. Use Photo Story or another video program to film the video. See Chapter 8 for more on video programs.

Figure 10.13. Menu Planner

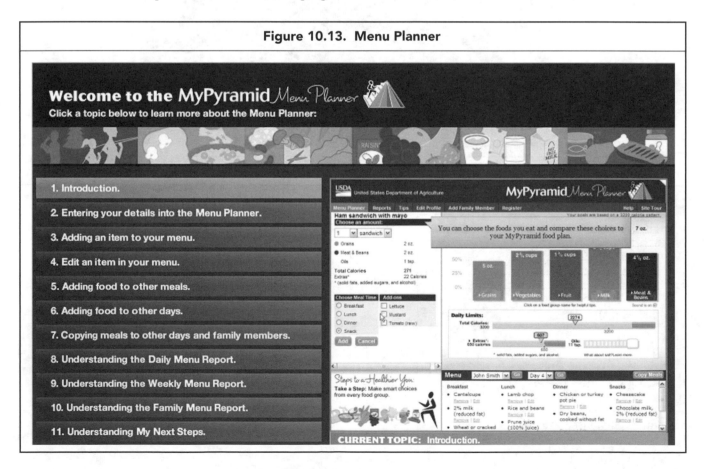

5. Write group folktales to explain a fact about the nature of fruits or vegetables, such as how the raisin got its wrinkles, how the tomato got its color, or how the peach got its fuzz. Read a story or show a video first such as *How the Lion Got Its Roar*. Use Storybird or Photo Peach (see Chapter 8), depending on the student's age, to illustrate the story.

Evaluation

Use the Rubric in Figure 10.14 to assess the different activities in this lesson.

Extensions

Students will:

1. create a glog (interactive poster) containing tips for food safety to put on the class and school websites or wikis, using Glogster at http://edu.glogster.com/;
2. continue daily blog entries for at least a week on what they ate for each meal and chart on their spreadsheet;

Figure 10.14. Rubric for Evaluation		
Evaluation for Nutrition Lesson Using Web 2.0 and Social Networking Tools		
To What Extent Has the Student Shown Ability	**Points Possible**	**Points Awarded**
Web 2.0 and Social Networking		
Uses blog and wiki effectively		
Completes a multimedia glog		
Effectively uses a video option		
Writing Samples		
Organizes ideas		
Writes clearly		
Uses evidence to support points		
Presentations		
Content complete		
Presentation (enunciation, volume, gestures, posture)		
Group Work		
Works well with others		
Participates equally		
Other Comments		

3. plan a healthy menu for one week, post it on their blog, and ask for comments from their classmates; and

4. keep track of their physical activity using MyPyramid Tracker at http://www.mypyramid tracker.gov/. Compare this score to the physical activity recommendation for health at their age. Graph the comparison with Google Docs.

Summary

When students check their diets, exercise habits, and places where they eat frequently—such as McDonald's or Taco Bell—they are actively involved in staying healthy. Setting and sharing nutrition goals and encouraging one another are ways to promote healthy eating and hopefully curtail the number of obese children. The activities in this lesson reemphasize to students the importance to their daily lives of nutrition and maintaining good health.

Lesson 3 (Middle to Secondary Levels): Protecting Your Rights

A free society must rely on the knowledge, skills, and virtue of its citizens and those they elect to public office. Civic education is the primary way our citizens acquire the knowledge and skills necessary for informed and engaged citizenship. Knowing who members of the House and Senate are and how they serve their constituents in Congress is fundamental to developing civic literacy in today's students. As students study civics and government, educators need to keep them informed and engaged, and help them become participatory citizens.

Purpose

How much do students know about the halls of Congress and the activities that transpire there? Do they know what effects the actions of representatives and senators have on them? Do they even know how many people are elected to Congress and when? This lesson requires students to learn about officials in their state—find out about their actions, including their voting records, what they stand for, and how they are representing the voters who elected them. Once they are informed, they will need to make decisions about their own ideas and how they relate to those of elected officials. This will require teamwork, critical thinking, and shared responsibilities.

Objectives

Students will:

- develop critical-thinking, problem-solving, and decision-making skills;
- understand the local and global implications of civic decisions;
- explore ideals, principles, and practices of citizenship in a democratic republic;
- recognize and respect different points of view;
- research members of Congress using a variety of sources; and
- use Web 2.0 tools to enhance, share, and present their findings.

Materials

Use Table 10.3. to find historical background on the Capitol and elected officials, political positions, voting records, and differing viewpoints to complete the tasks in this lesson.

Procedures

As a class, students will:

- review the video at http://www.icivics.org/subject/legislative-branch about the legislative branch of Congress and how bills become laws, as well as the student documentary titled

Table 10.3. Resources about Congressional Elected Officials	
URL	**Description**
http://www.c-spanarchives.org/program/ID/234983&start=276&end=336	2010 campaign videos of ads in California; other videos on the 2010 mid-year election
http://www.the-capitol.org/	Information about the Capitol
http://legacy.c-span.org/capitolhistory/interviews/	Capitol oral history project
http://www.c-span.org/Topics/111th-Congress/	111th Congress, contains votes by House and Senate; location, name, committee of officials
http://www.c-spanvideo.org/congress	Congressional Chronicle
http://www.house.gov/committees/ http://www.senate.gov/pagelayout/committees/d_three_sections_with_teasers/committees_home.htm	House committees Senate committees
http://www.c-span.org/Resources/Policy-Organizations/	Policy organizations
http://clerk.house.gov/member_info/	Member information
http://www.icivics.org/web-quests/making-rules?cck_pager_group_pages=1	Contains games, news, a forum, and more about civics and government
http://www.house.gov/ http://www.senate.gov/ http://ourcourts.law.asu.edu/legisvid/legis4.html	Making laws in the House and Senate

The Great Compromise at http://www.c-spanvideo.org/program/298275-27, which provides a historical view of the Capitol, Congress, and compromise that needed to take place to set up the Capitol.

In groups, students will:

- discuss what they learned from the documentary, what other compromises they are aware of, and would such a compromise be possible in today's Congress? Why/why not?
- complete a KWHL chart. As discussed in his keynote speech at the 2011 Curriculum Mapping Institute, Alan November, an international leader in education technology, takes the familiar KWL chart, seen in earlier chapters, a step further. The KWHL chart adds the "H"— How will we find answers to what we want to know? See Figure 10.15.

In groups, have students:

- research one representative or senator from their state (see Figure 10.16), with each student compiling one of the following:
  - List committees on which the person participates or holds office; describe the committee's purpose.
  - Identify total campaign contributions for a year, organizations/individuals who contributed, and the top three of each they represent.
  - Examine types of votes cast since the start of the present Congress. Discuss questions such as: How many times did the member vote yes or no? Not cast a vote? Vote along party lines?
  - Create a list of bills sponsored and their status and bills voted on and their status.

Figure 10.15. KWHL Chart

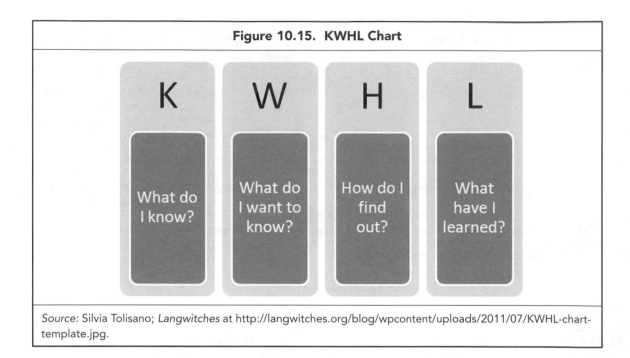

Source: Silvia Tolisano; *Langwitches* at http://langwitches.org/blog/wpcontent/uploads/2011/07/KWHL-chart-template.jpg.

Figure 10.16. Making Laws

Source: Congress for Kids; http://www.congressforkids.net/Legislativebranch_makinglaws.htm.

- Complete a chart similar to the one at http://www.c-spanclassroom.org/pdf/CSPAN_Classroom_Researching_My_Member_Handout.pdf. Place the chart on the class wiki.
- Identify relationships among committees, contributions, votes cast, and bills voted on and discuss the following questions: What kind of bills has their member of Congress introduced? Is there a relationship among the various committees on which the individual serves, the financial contributors, the voting record, and bills that are being proposed? Students will explain their reasoning in blog posts.
- Respond to blog posts of other groups identifying points they agree/disagree with.
- Create a glog poster (see Chapter 8) explaining why other students should vote or not vote for the person they have researched. Place it on the class wiki.
- The culminating task is an individual one—students must vote. They will evaluate all information they've collected about their representative or senator and review the glogs of all groups. Based on the information, they will select two candidates to vote for and explain in an evidence-based blog post or a podcast how their candidates will best serve their community and state.

Evaluation

The information gathered about their Congressperson, their blog posts, and their glog on the person they researched will demonstrate whether they have related knowledge about Congress and its applications to their community and state. Students will be evaluated on the content and persuasiveness of their presentation, as well as by teacher observations of how well they worked together in their groups. A group evaluation rubric (see Figure 10.17) will help in the evaluation process.

Extensions

To continue exploring this topic, students will:

1. take action on what they learned. In groups or individually, create their own documentary about the approaching 2012 election. Select a topic of particular interest such as major points

Figure 10.17. Group Evaluation Rubric

Student Group _____

Evaluator(s): _____ Peer _____ Teacher _____ Self

	Proficient	Developing	Emerging	Total
Researches and gathers information	Collects a great deal of the information—all related to the topic.	Collects some basic information—most related to the topic.	Collects very little information—some related to the topic.	
On task	Always does assigned work—without having to be reminded.	Usually does assigned work—rarely needs reminding.	Rarely does assigned work—often needs reminding.	
Listens to teammates	Listens and asks questions, offers ideas, never argues with teammates.	Listens but sometimes talks too much, rarely argues.	Usually does most of the talking—rarely allows others to speak; sometimes argues.	
Group work on final project	Works effectively as a group to organize, plan, and create a product.	Works well as a group to organize, plan, and create a product.	Sometimes works well as a group to organize, plan, and create a product.	

of contention on issues, differences between two candidates, or position of one political party. Use http://www.studentcam.org/getting_started.htm as a guide to create the documentary. Place completed videos on the class wiki or website.

2. create a presentation to the class using one of the Web 2.0 tools discussed in this book to present main points in the documentary, why they chose the topic, and what they learned. They will also present questions they still have.

Teachers might want to submit noteworthy student documentaries to C-Span's STUDENTCAM at http://www.studentcam.org/.

Summary

This lesson provides a series of activities for students at a middle- or high-school level who are studying government. It is important for students to gain critical-thinking skills to face problems outside the school environment.

Teacher Exercises: Now You Try It . . .

In each chapter, you have learned much about Web 2.0 and social networking tools and how to use them in the classroom to enhance student learning. Now is a good time to reflect on what you have learned throughout this book so far.

1. Prioritize the Web 2.0 and social networking tools you have learned about. Identify and write about each tool you:
   a. plan to try first in a lesson;
   b. think is the most useful for your students and why; and
   c. determine meets standards and objectives for your students.
2. List five new ideas you gained from information in this book you can employ in your lessons to enhance student learning.
3. Review your curriculum for the next month, and brainstorm places where you can incorporate one or more of the tools in this book.
   a. Select the tool you plan to include in your next lesson: write objectives and activities that include the tool to better teach and motivate students.
   b. Set up a rubric for the lesson that assesses content knowledge, students' abilities using the tool, and group work, if used.
4. In the next month, use at least two Web 2.0 and/or social networking tools that will help improve the learning of your students.
5. Continue to sign up for RSS feeds, use social bookmarking to identify more examples of new Web 2.0 tools, and share them on blogs and Twitter.

CONCLUSION

As a result of your continued participation with social networking and Web 2.0 tools, you should be comfortable enough to expand the use of these tools in your classroom and communicate with other educators who are doing the same. You might even take the leadership role in your school to encourage other teachers to try these new technologies.

REFERENCES AND FURTHER READING

Johnson, L., S. Adams, and K. Haywood. 2011. *The NMC Horizon Report: 2011 K–12 Edition*. Austin, Texas: The New Media Consortium. http://www.nmc.org/pdf/2011-Horizon-Report-K12.pdf.

CHAPTER 11

Creating Community with Web 2.0 Tools and Social Networking

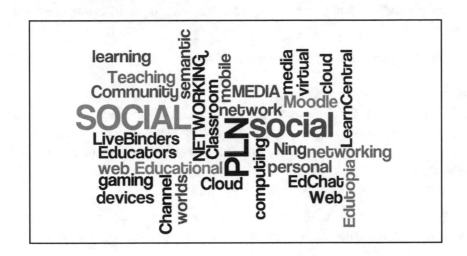

PART 1: IDEAS AND INSIGHTS

Are you a new teacher, feeling isolated and alone? Are you an experienced teacher looking for new ideas and inspiration? Are you interested in sharing ideas and collaborating with other educators? Are you unable to attend professional learning seminars because funding in your district is no longer available? Then you will want to read this chapter carefully.

Objectives of This Chapter

This chapter is different from Chapters 2–10 of this book, which focused on using Web 2.0 and social networking in the K–12 curriculum. Chapter 11 identifies social networking tools that facilitate communication, collaboration, and learning from other educators. After reading this chapter and completing the exercises, educators will be able to:

- create connections with other educators;
- set up their own personal learning network;
- identify social networking and productivity tools; and
- create a unit on copyright incorporating Web 2.0 and social networking tools

Glossary

The following words and phrases may be new to you, but you will see them in this chapter. Take time to familiarize yourself with them to better understand the material.

cloud: A term used to describe the vast collections of networked computers, typically housed in regionally distributed and redundant data centers that comprise the Internet.

cloud computing: A set of strategies that distribute data, applications, and computing cycles across the many machines in such data centers, and even across data centers.

LiveBinders: A website with educational resources in all subject areas and at different grade levels.

lurk: Following someone on Twitter, but not contributing to the conversation.

Moodle: An Open Source Course Management System (CMS), also known as a Learning Management System (LMS).

Ning: An online platform for educators, enabling them to create their own custom social websites, social networks, and communities.

personal learning network (PLN): A personal learning environment where a person interacts with like-minded individuals who share common interests and from whom one can derive knowledge.

Web 3.0 (or the semantic web): A term to identify changes and modifications emerging as a new Internet develops.

Glossaries in other chapters may also prove useful to help you understand new concepts in Chapter 11.

Advantages of Social Networking

Chapter 6 focused on how social networking can enhance student learning. However, it can also support educators in many ways. This chapter highlights a number of social networking tools that can help teachers and librarians continue to grow as educators by expanding their knowledge and assisting others.

Social networking can help educators by:

- acting as a communication tool—creating chat-room forums and groups to extend classroom discussion; posting assignments, tests, and quizzes; and assisting with homework outside of the classroom setting;
- fostering teacher-parent communication—parents can ask questions and voice concerns without having to meet face-to-face;
- supporting relationships between teachers and their students;
- enhancing educator professional development;
- bringing the world into the classroom;
- sharing content among colleagues;
- asking questions of an author or expert;
- engaging students in exploring real-world issues and solving authentic problems using digital tools and resources; and
- customizing and personalizing learning activities to address students' diverse learning styles, strategies they use every day, and abilities using digital tools and resources.

Educators are using personal learning networks (PLNs) as a means to interact with others on educational topics.

What Is a Personal Learning Network?

As stated on *Wikipedia*, a PLN consists of "the people a learner interacts with and derives knowledge from in a personal learning environment" (*Wikipedia*, 2011). Educators create connections and develop a network that contributes to their professional development and knowledge. They do not have to know these people personally or ever meet them in person.

Some characteristics of a personal learning network include the following:

- Making connections and building personal relationships with other educators and experts around the world. No matter where you are in the world, there's always someone online available to answer questions, share their expertise, and simply chat about what's happening in their lives and classrooms.

- Sharing ideas and resources through collaboration and learning. We may share our knowledge, ideas, and expertise in different ways, using different media and tools, but the essence is the same: the PLN is simply the best professional development you will ever participate in—and it's available 24/7.
- Enabling people to tap into and share diverse, global perspectives on teaching strategies, educational issues, and technologies.

Research shows that networking with fellow teachers is time well spent. In a recent survey, Teachers Network (http://teachersnetwork.org/) found that 80 percent of teachers said network participation encouraged them to remain in the classroom, while 90 percent said that networking improved their teaching practice. PLNs offer a powerful antidote for classroom isolation. Figure 11.1 shows a diagram of one educator's PLN at http://barbarabray.net/tag/pln/.

How to Build Your PLN

Learn to connect with a community of like-minded professionals, make contributions, have conversations, and make requests in your times of need. Powerful free tools and social media make this possible for you and your school. Here's how:

1. After joining a social network, complete your profile. People are going to want to know something about you to see if your interests and ideas are similar to their own.

Figure 11.1. An Educator's Personal Learning Network

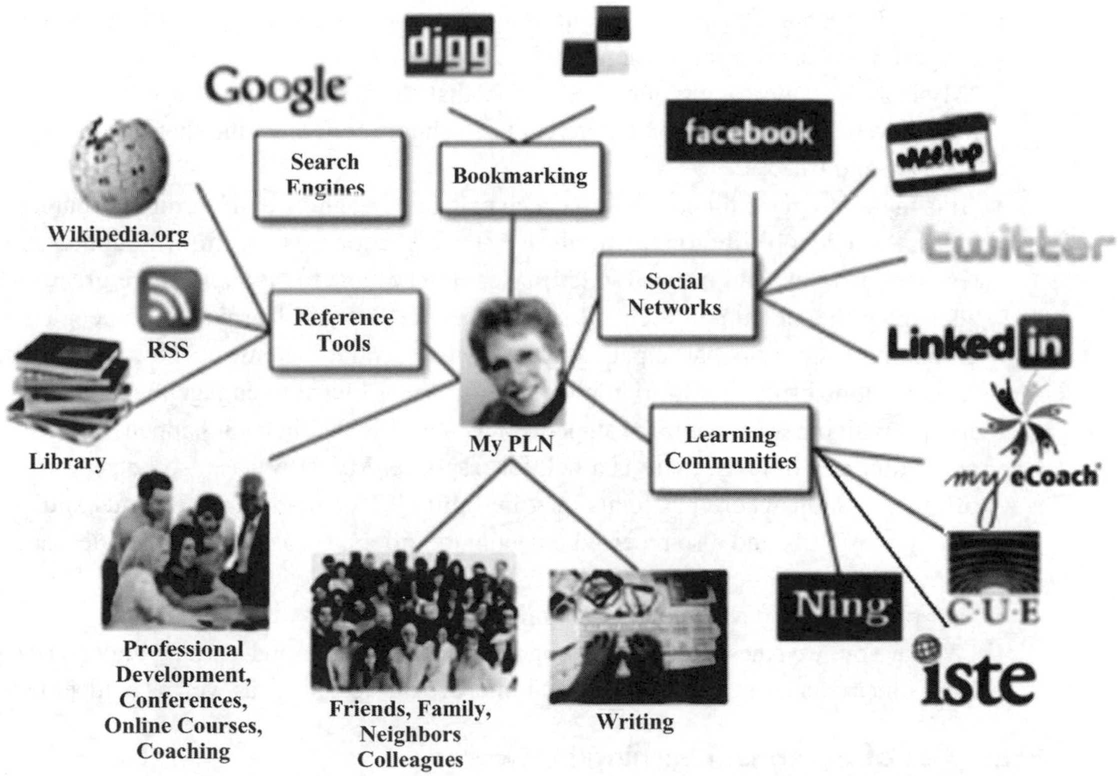

Source: Used by permission of Barbara Bray, Creative Learning Strategist at Rethinking Learning; http://barbarabray.net/.

2. Carefully select the people you want to follow based on their interests and backgrounds. Join multiple special interest groups. Use the site's search tool to find people talking about things you're interested in.

3. Follow recommendations from people you trust. Post responses to other peoples' messages. People expect to see new responses on these networks.

4. Start a conversation by posting a question, creating a poll, or posting a link to something useful or interesting.

5. Follow the same people your friends are following.

6. Check We Follow on Twitter at http://wefollow.com/twitter/, enter a tag of interest, and review some of the influential users. Twitter is about connecting with educators for personalized and ongoing professional development.

7. Search for content of bloggers you normally read. Most also have links to other social networks on their blogs.

Connections for Educators

Why a PLN? Why do I need to connect to other educators? What is the point? One educator uses a VoiceThread to solicit comments from teachers and librarians on why PLNs are important to them. Read and listen to their comments at http://web20classroom.blogspot.com/2010/03/why-pln.html. Here are a few sample comments from the VoiceThread on why these educators use a PLN:

- "My PLN is where I learn on a daily basis. I also try to share the information I have with my network to be a valuable contributor to the people who follow me."
- "Put out a question and have a number of responses from a global audience."
- "People I'm connected with through Twitter can help me solve problems, try new things, and celebrate successes. How productive, helpful, and kind my personal learning network is."
- "My PLN encourages me to step out of my box to learn, and see what other people are doing not just in my small rural community."
- "My PLN is an amazing group of educators that challenges, motivates, educates, and inspires me. If ever I need a question answered, I can shout it out knowing that the answers I receive are tried and true."
- "It is my go-to place for cutting-edge tech practices, teaching and learning resources, and new ideas. As a school librarian, I'm always sharing resources and information with students, teachers, parents, and peers. Twitter makes it very easy to find and share great resources. I also enjoy the global perspective I gain by networking and learning from people around the globe. In my opinion, participating in a PLN is essential to being a 21st century educator!"
- "It helped me bring the world to my students. When I want to engage my students in conversations with other educators or students, it is my PLN that helps it happen. I only have to ask on Twitter and quickly, there is a helpful response. My PLN has also helped me greatly by offering insight where my focus may be limited. I've made great friends and colleagues through my PLN and also received amazing job offers, speaking opportunities, and valuable learning opportunities that would never have been possible without my PLN."
- "For professional development, bar none, it's the best."
- "We have our weaknesses and by sharing with other educators and learning through best practices from other educators, we can grow and improve our teaching, as well as student learning."

Examples of Personal Learning Networks

Several examples illustrate learning networks for different groups of educators: librarians, classroom teachers, and technology specialists.

Example 1: Teacher Librarian Ning

Created as a community for school librarians and other educators, Teacher Librarian Ning (http://teacherlibrarian.ning.com/) contains many resources for librarians, including blogs, a forum, and a variety of groups—all for communicating with other members. An interesting group is Web 2.0 in the Library World, designed for those who wish to share about using collaborative Web 2.0 tools in their library instruction. Videos illustrate projects in libraries around the world. It's also a good place to learn about events for teacher librarians. Sign up and join the conversation (see Figure 11.2).

Example 2: The Educator's PLN

The Educator's PLN (http://edupln.ning.com/) provides a location for educators to join together and communicate on issues and ideas important to the educational community. Join and set up your own PLN page, view videos, join groups of interest, enter discussions, learn more about EdChat and propose questions for discussion, or write on the blog. There's plenty to support your interests, suggest new ideas, and more. Listen to podcasts on issues of importance to educators: learn what other educators think about issues such as iPads in the elementary classroom or whether mobile devices should be used in instruction. Build your own PLN on My Page. Classroom 2.0 also has a page where you can set up your PLN. Check it out at http://www.classroom20.com/profiles/ (see Figure 11.3).

Example 3: Personal PLN Page

A number of teachers and librarians have created PLNs, which are followed by educators at the secondary and elementary levels. Their PLNs contain a wealth of valuable information, from new Web 2.0 tools, to how to use them in classrooms, to lesson plans, to professional development ideas. Check out some of the following:

- http://bethstill.edublogs.org/2009/10/18/how-my-pln-saved-the-day/. Shows how her PLN saved the day during a workshop she was conducting. This is an excellent example of how a PLN works and why an educator should set one up!
- http://edupln.ning.com/profile/ShellyTerrell?xg_source=profiles_memberlist. Provides numerous ideas on Web 2.0 tools for educators, acts as guest presenter, and much more (see Figure 11.4).
- http://www.freetech4teachers.com/. Ideas on new Web 2.0 technology and how to use it in the classroom.

Figure 11.2. Teacher Librarian Ning

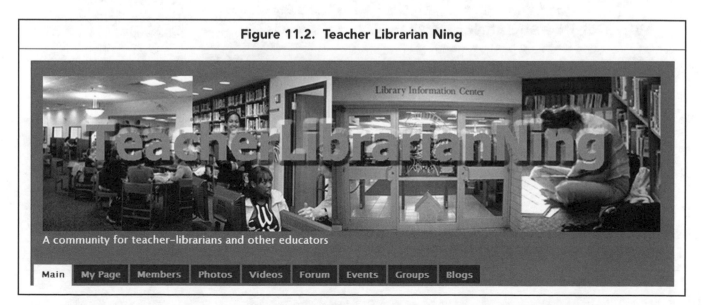

A community for teacher–librarians and other educators

Main | My Page | Members | Photos | Videos | Forum | Events | Groups | Blogs

Figure 11.3. The Educator's PLN

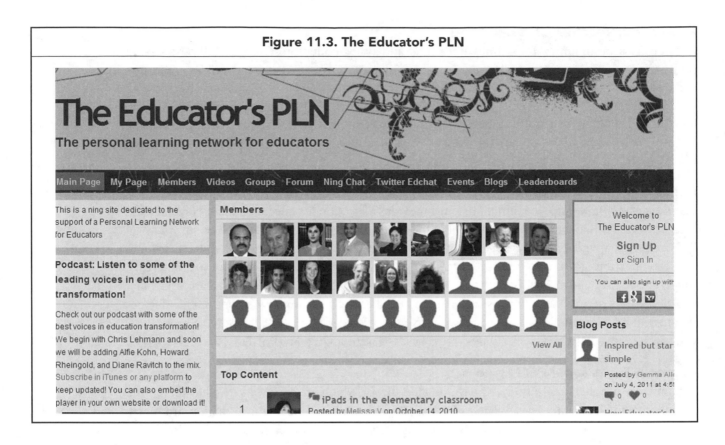

Figure 11.4. Page from Educator's PLN

Source: Used by permission of Shelley Sanchez Terrell.

PART 2: GETTING STARTED WITH SOCIAL NETWORKING FOR EDUCATORS

In this section you will learn more about social networking tools educators use to help them connect with other teachers worldwide, learn from them and other experts, and collaborate with classrooms on similar topics across the globe, as well as explore websites that will provide new ideas for integrating Web 2.0 into classroom lessons.

Social Media: Communicate and Collaborate

There are so many tools to connect educators with other educators, provide professional development right from their computers, and identify resources to motivate and teach students. Several were mentioned in earlier chapters, including Edublogs (Chapter 6). Here are a few more.

Classroom 2.0

Classroom 2.0 (http://www.classroom20.com/) is a social network for those interested in Web 2.0 and social media in education. Classroom 2.0 was started to create an environment where educators can experience community without having to create their own social networking site. With more than 7,000 members in 2008, the year after it started, it now has more than 422,000 members. From Web 2.0 for beginners to weekly reviews of new tools, educators can visit and participate quickly. They can create subgroups based on their own subject and grade level, for example, those teaching elementary students or a subject such as English or social studies. A Forum is the heart of the network where members post a question or comment and others respond. Because responses are indented under a question, they are easy to find. Other features are an RSS feed to bookmark the site, tags to help identify material, and a wiki to find Web 2.0 resources (see Figure 11.5). Classroom 2.0 LIVE!

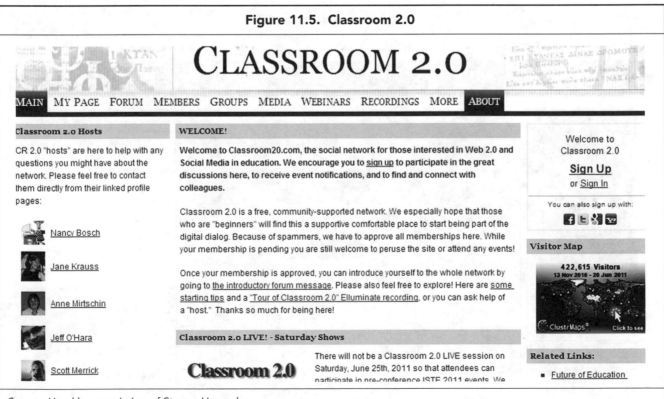

Figure 11.5. Classroom 2.0

Source: Used by permission of Steven Hargadon.

(http://live.classroom20.com/) contains a series of tutorials on educational topics, brought to you on Blackboard, where you can also hold webinars.

Edutopia

Edutopia (http://www.edutopia.org/) is an educational website designed to empower and connect teachers, administrators, and parents with innovative solutions and resources for better education. The website combines practical articles about teaching and learning, technology integration, blogging opportunities, resources by grade level, groups to help build and learn about community, examples of projects in schools, and much more. Sign up for free or join the community on Facebook or Twitter (see Figure 11.6).

edWeb.net

A professional social network for educators, edWeb.net (http://www.edweb.net) allows teachers and librarians to connect with colleagues or find new friends, create and join learning communities, collaborate on educational initiatives, and practice twenty-first-century skills. For example, librarians might want to attend a free webinar on emerging tech. Teachers might enjoy online sessions, such as global collaboration or digital citizenship. New teachers might be interested in game-based learning or how to implement core standards in math.

Once you have joined edWeb, you have a personal homepage and a Web 2.0 toolbox. You can select from a number of communities to join (see Figure 11.7). Each community has its own features, such as live chat, blogs, discussion forums, wikis, shared bookmarks, webinars, and more. You can also create your own community.

Figure 11.6. Edutopia Helping Teachers

Source: Originally published July 5, 2011 © Edutopia.org; The George Lucas Educational Foundation.

Figure 11.7. edWeb

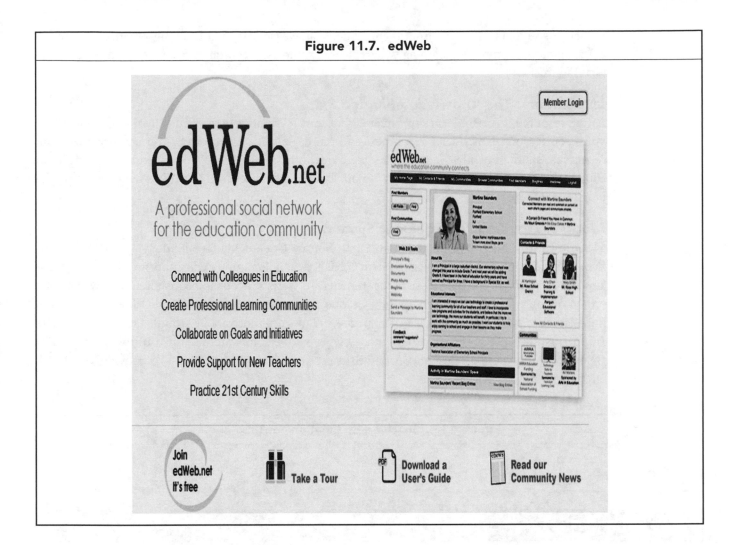

Productivity Tools: Collect, Instruct, and Share

The tools in this section are designed by teachers, librarians, and those creating some of the tools to help educators locate new ideas, lessons, tools, and more to enhance their teaching and students' learning. This section will be especially beneficial to new teachers. Bookmark many of these sites in your PLN.

Google for Educators

Google for Educators (http://www.google.com/educators/index.html) brings together tools for production and communication free to the K–12 classroom. The website supplies a wealth of instruction and examples so educators can make the best use of Google tools. From classroom activities illustrating the use of tools such as Google Docs or Google Calendar, to special events such as the Google Science Fair Project and Doodle 4 Google, to teacher institutes and workshops, Google for Educators illustrates how educators are using Google tools in the classroom and school library.

Teaching Channel

The Teaching Channel (http://www.teachingchannel.org/) is another innovation to bring best of class instruction to educators without their leaving their schools. Teaching Channel is teacher-focused. A community of teachers is sharing a wealth of teaching experience in all subjects and grade levels through videos that capture compelling teaching lessons and provide them to a wide audience so others can learn from them. Videos showcase inspiring teaching practices aligned to core standards, combining learning with real-life examples, techniques, resources, and lesson plans (see Figure 11.8).

LiveBinders: The Knowledge-Sharing Place

A free resource, LiveBinders (http://livebinders.com/) is similar to your educator's notebook where you keep lesson plans, ideas, resources, and more, only it's on the web. You can organize your resources, share your ideas and lessons, and view others' binders. Categorized by grade level or subject, binders can be shared through e-mail, Twitter, and Facebook, as well as put on a website or blog (see Figure 11.9).

Moodle: Learning Management System

Moodle (http://moodle.org/about/), an Open Source Course Management System (CMS), also known as a Learning Management System (LMS), is popular among educators around the world as a tool for creating dynamic websites for students. To work, it needs to be installed on a web server, either on one of your own computers or one at a web-hosting company. View the video at http://moodle.org/mod/forum/discuss.php?d=7899 to learn more about Moodle (see Figure 11.10). An interesting, entertaining video at http://www.youtube.com/watch?v=LhZCqFIwZl8 created by Bismarck Public Schools describes Moodle, its uses, and advantages. Table 11.1 provides additional URLs with productivity tools.

Figure 11.8. Teaching Channel on YouTube

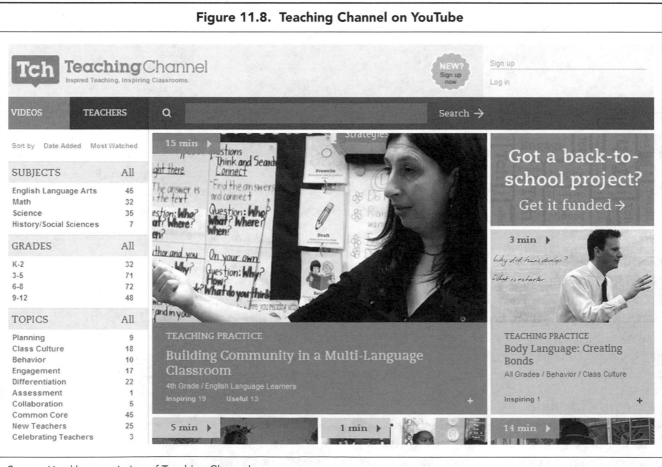

Source: Used by permission of Teaching Channel.

Figure 11.9. LiveBinders

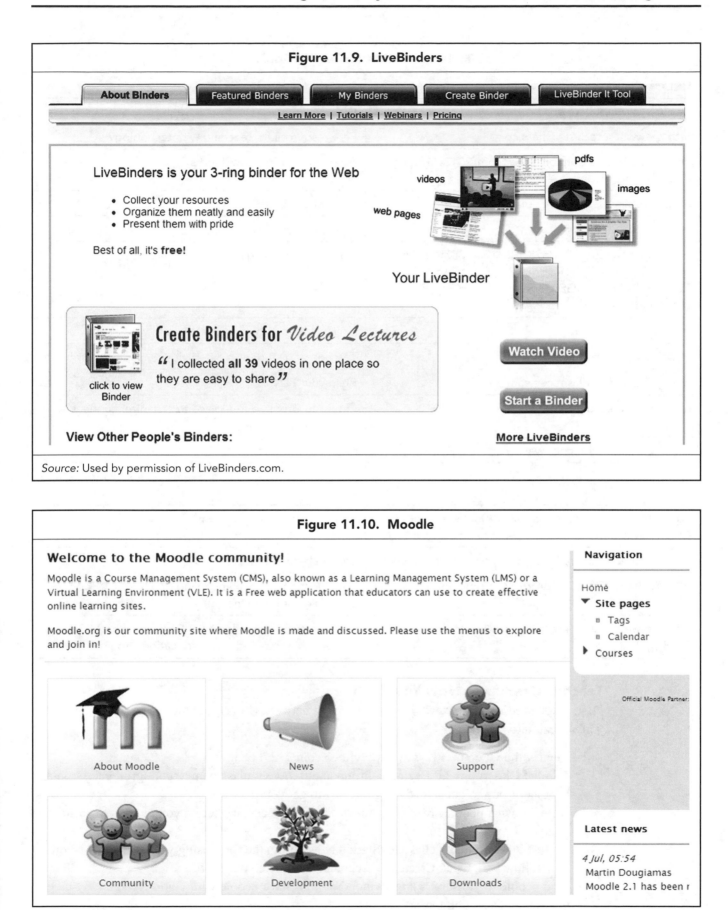

Source: Used by permission of LiveBinders.com.

Figure 11.10. Moodle

Welcome to the Moodle community!

Moodle is a Course Management System (CMS), also known as a Learning Management System (LMS) or a Virtual Learning Environment (VLE). It is a Free web application that educators can use to create effective online learning sites.

Moodle.org is our community site where Moodle is made and discussed. Please use the menus to explore and join in!

About Moodle   News   Support

Community   Development   Downloads

Navigation

Home
▼ **Site pages**
  ▫ Tags
  ▫ Calendar
▶ Courses

Official Moodle Partner:

Latest news

4 Jul, 05:54
Martin Dougiamas
Moodle 2.1 has been r

Table 11.1. URLs for Teacher Tools	
URL	**Description**
http://www.web20erc.eu/	Web 2.0 European Resource Center
http://www.freetech4teachers.com/	Free resources for teaching with technology
http://web20classroom.blogspot.com/2010/11/bring-those-boring-binders-to-life-with.html	A primer to using LiveBinders
http://livebinders.com/play/play_or_edit?id=120007	More about LiveBinders
http://edupln.ning.com/forum	The Educator's PLN
http://api.ning.com/files/p7KnHhXiGJl9B05RPhZjwH2w13CYXmn64iBRWRBHgHT7sqrGegcEbpUS-Pp6MGISMZWodpuGS0n3rRW6btSLcVHGc4yRFTct/NingGuidelines.pdf	Guidelines for Nings
tappedin.org/tappedin	Online community of educators with weekly activities
http://www.teachertube.com/	Teacher- and student-created videos, audio, and photos
http://suewaters.wikispaces.com/	Build your PLN
http://enterthegroup.com/	Enter the Group, a free place to organize, connect, collaborate, and learn
http://www.youtube.com/watch?v=LhZCqFIwZl8	All about Moodle
http://classtools.net/	Tools for the classroom to create quizzes, diagrams, and educational games.
http://www.scribd.com/doc/63331406/Twitter-in-K-8-Classroom-Globally-Connected-Learning	Twitter in the K-8 Classroom
http://open-tube.com/7-free-web-conferencing-tools/	Free web-conferencing tools
http://www.webjunction.org/technology/web-tools	WebJunction Social Networking and Web 2.0 Tools especially for librarians
http://id.webjunction.org/679/-/articles/content/93581141	WebJunction—compiled Web Resources for 2.0 Tools, content subjects, and other educational topics

Teacher Exercises: Now You Try It . . .

First, get started with your own personal learning network (PLN). Try these exercises to put what you've read into practice.

1. Review the video on PLNs at http://vimeo.com/11276683.
2. Join the Classroom 2.0 Beginner Group at http://www.classroom20.com/group/classroom20beginnergroup to get started—a good way to get your feet wet!
3. Listen to what people are saying. Ask questions if necessary before you jump in to participate yourself.
4. Go to Twitter.com and click Get Started Now. Fill in the form using your real name so others may follow you. Click Create My Account. Complete your profile.
5. Find people to "follow" using Twitter. You may have people with whom you already blog or interact on Facebook to start you out.

6. Use the hashtag # to focus your attention on a specific topic of interest (e.g., #special education). Then participate in a chat.

7. If you see people you are not following but who have similar interests to you, you may want to follow them, too. Choosing a hashtag directs you to a TweetChat room. This is a good way to build up your PLN. Review Twitter in Chapter 6 for more information. Take it slow!

8. Set as a goal a time daily or a few times a week to go on your PLN. Consistency is important.

9. Find other resources, for example, put the button for LiveBinders on your toolbar and start saving resources. Find a new resource and tweet about it.

PART 3: PRACTICAL APPLICATIONS

There's a lot of discussion among educators these days about plagiarism and adherence to copyright. This unit, designed for high school students, focuses on that issue and how to teach students about its importance, recognize when it is and is not a violation, and the various types of possible copyright options available, such as Creative Commons and fair use. Teachers need to make it their business to know about copyright, especially how it applies to digital media, so they can explain it to their students.

Collaborating on the Unit

This unit plan demonstrates to teachers how to create a unit that integrates Web 2.0 and social networking tools, illustrates to students how understanding copyright and plagiarism is important in a twenty-first-century technological environment, and describes how some of the concepts presented in this chapter can be used to create a unit plan. To get started:

- Send a tweet describing the unit on copyright you are interested in creating to other educators you are following. Ask those interested to contact you so that you can collaborate on the unit.
- Check with your PLN community and solicit ideas and other educators to help with the project.
- Divide tasks so participants contribute to different parts of the unit (e.g., standards, goals, and objectives; activities to use before, during, and following the unit; and assessment).
- Set up a wiki to receive and organize ideas for activities and provide a place for comments.
- Identify those teachers who are willing to use this unit with their students.
- Check in frequently on the progress of building the unit and set dates for conducting it.
- Tweet among one another during the unit to get advice, suggestions, and comments on what is going well and changes that are needed.
- Following the unit and after students complete self-evaluations, each participant does an evaluation of the unit and adds the information to the group wiki.

The following is an example of a collaborative unit that could be created on copyright and plagiarism.

Learning about Plagiarism and Copyright Unit

The activities in this unit let students discuss some of the issues surrounding plagiarism and copyright, illustrate how to avoid copyright infringement, and cite sources. This unit also emphasizes how teachers can create assignments that make it less likely for students to plagiarize.

Step 1: Connect to the Standards—What Should Be Taught?

Content frameworks and standards today encourage learner-centered classrooms, resulting in learning that is more active and less authority-dependent. Educational strategies that enhance student learning often include project-based activities. Technology standards both mandate active learning and assist it. In this unit, educators will:

- Teach students about copyright law, including the concepts of fair use, Creative Commons, and the public domain.
- Promote and model digital citizenship and responsibility, including ethical use of digital information and technology and appropriate documentation of sources as stated in NETS (see Chapter 1).

Step 2: Identify General Goals and Specific Objectives

Whether students are in elementary, middle, or high school, they should be made aware of definitions of copyright infringement and how to avoid the problem. They should also understand intellectual property and why it is important.

Goals

Use the goals and objectives that follow as a basis for content and skills covered in this unit. Goals for learning about plagiarism and copyright in general should include the following:

- Improve critical and creative thinking: brainstorm, analyze ethical and contemporary sources, and question group and individual assumptions.
- Communication: participate in group discussions, class projects, and role-play.
- Demonstrate comprehension by commenting (orally and in writing) on the material clearly and effectively.
- Research: collect, organize, and synthesize data from various sources (articles, commercial news sources, the Internet, and video).

Objectives

This unit provides content and strategies for students to achieve the following objectives. The unit will also emphasize the use of Web 2.0 and social networking tools. Students will:

- collaborate with peers, improving social skills;
- identify characteristics of plagiarism;
- learn how to use material without plagiarizing, including citing sources; and
- recognize and provide examples of plagiarism, fair use, and paraphrasing.

Step 3: Gather Materials

In this unit, each group will have some tasks that are similar and others that will be unique to their own group. Thus, material used may be somewhat different. All students will use the Internet and other sources for research on the issues surrounding copyright and plagiarism. These may include research articles, blogs, wikis, videos, discussion with other students, and more. Table 11.2 provides sources to help with the following tasks.

Step 4: Create Sample Activities

Procedures for this unit focus on show, tell, try, and do. First, students will understand the concepts of plagiarism and copyright. Second, they will see that working together with students in their own class enhances learning, and third they will understand how using Web 2.0 and social networking tools helps them communicate their message.

Activities to Introduce the Unit

Students should draw upon prior knowledge to indicate what they know about plagiarism, copyright, and citing sources. Teachers should start with the following:

Table 11.2. URLs for the Plagiarism/Copyright Unit	
URL	**Description**
http://school.discoveryeducation.com/schrockguide/referenc.html http://nausetschools.org/pdf/fairuse_slides.pdf http://www.cyberbee.com/copyrpln.pdf	Comprehensive list of sources for copyright and fair use, including lesson plans; slideshow put together by Kathy Schrock
http://www.cyberbee.com/copyrpln.pdf http://www.cyberbee.com/cb_copyright.swf	Q&A on copyright for elementary students
http://www.webenglishteacher.com/plagiarism.html	Sources to learn about plagiarism
http://www.aresearchguide.com/6plagiar.html	Links to citing, footnotes, and bibliography
http://www.noodletools.com/	Resources to teach citation styles, bibliography, and more
http://www.globalgridforlearning.com/	Global Grid for Learning—more than a million pieces of copyright-cleared digital information, including copyright-cleared images, video clips, audio files, and text documents ready for teachers to incorporate into their lessons
http://www.teachingcopyright.org/handout/trial-guide-educator	Mock trial based on copyright issue
http://www.teachingcopyright.org/download/handout/tc_trial_guide.pdf http://www.teachingcopyright.org/handout/trial-guide	Trial Guide for fictitious case
http://www.youtube.com/watch?v=zd89JpoHePE	Samples of mock trials by high school students
http://www.econedlink.org/lessons/index.php?lid=186&type=educator http://computer.howstuffworks.com/napster.htm http://en.wikipedia.org/wiki/A%26M_Records%2C_Inc._v._Napster%2C_Inc	Several sites on Napster case, how it worked, what happened
http://www.copyrightkids.org/cbasicsframes.htm	Copyright information for kids
http://creativecommons.org/ http://langwitches.org/blog/2011/07/09/creative-commons-kiwi/	Creative Commons

- Familiarize students with the following vocabulary:
  - **attribution:** Identifying the source of a work. For example, a Creative Commons "BY" or attribution license requires the second user of a copyrighted work to identify the original source of the work.
  - **copyright:** Form of legal protection given to the creators of "original works of authorship," including literary, dramatic, musical, and artistic works.
  - **copyright infringement:** Violation of the exclusive rights of a copyright holder, such as copying, distributing, or performing the copyright owner's work without permission unless the use is otherwise authorized by law.

- ◦ **copyright term:** Length of time the law allows copyright owners to hold the exclusive rights on their original works.
- ◦ **Creative Commons:** See Chapter 1 for more information.
- ◦ **fair use:** One of several legal limitations on the exclusive rights granted to copyright owners. Fair use permits a second user to copy part or all of a copyrighted work under certain circumstances, even when the copyright holder has not given permission or even objects to that use of the work (see Chapter 1 for more on fair use).
- ◦ **file sharing:** Practice of uploading and downloading digital files (text, audio, video, or image) to and from a computer network where more than one user has access to those files.
- ◦ **license:** Permission granted by the copyright holder to copy, distribute, display, transform, and/or perform a copyrighted work.
- ◦ **mashup:** Derivative works that are built by creatively reusing and combining various portions of music, film, audio, and graphics.
- ◦ **plagiarism:** The practice of passing off another author's work or ideas as one's own.
- ◦ **public domain:** Works not restricted by copyright that do not require a license or fee to use. Works can enter the public domain automatically because they are not copyrightable, be designated in the public domain by the creator, or become part of the public domain because the copyright term has expired.
- • Model an example of a student who plagiarized a research paper:
  - ◦ **Example:** The teacher explained the assignment to his students. They were to write a research paper based on a novel they had just completed. The teacher read a sample paper to show students an exemplary paper. When students turned in their final papers, one paper stood out: the exact same paper the teacher had read in class! This student had been absent that day and paid a student from a previous class for her paper—the same paper the teacher had read.
  - ◦ Discuss with the class whether this is plagiarism and who is at fault. Should both students be penalized, just the one who copied, or the one who gave away her paper? Why or why not? Have students write blog posts with their ideas.
- • Ask students to write blog posts about copyright and plagiarism questions they would like answered by the end of the unit. Here are some possibilities:
  - ◦ How do I cite content from digital sources in my work?
  - ◦ Does it violate copyright to find an image on the Internet and use it in my presentation?
  - ◦ Where can I find copyright-free images, audio, and video for a project I am working on?
  - ◦ If I absolutely want to use copyrighted content in my work, how do I ask for permission?
  - ◦ What does Creative Commons mean? Read more about Creative Commons in Chapter 1.
  - ◦ *Note:* For elementary students, use the following cartoon with questions and answers: http://www.cyberbee.com/cb_copyright.swf (see Figure 11.11).
- • Use a KWL chart placed on the class wiki to put what they know in the K column.
- • Give each group of five an example and have them discuss whether it is an example of plagiarism or not and why/why not.
- • Identify common characteristics from each group and add to the W column of the KWL chart on the wiki (see Figure 11.12).

Activities to Use during the Unit

A variety of activities based on copyright infringement and fair use principles will enable students to understand what is appropriate and what is not. Divide the class into groups that will do the following:

- • Select terms from the glossary to explain (e.g., fair use, Creative Commons, license, mashup, public domain). Find out the meaning of the term, create a visual representation of it (e.g.,

Figure 11.11. Cyberbee on Copyright

Source: Used courtesy of Cyberbee Learning, Ltd.; http://www.cyberbee.com/.

glog, video), and place it on the wiki. Sites students might use include: http://www.readwrite think.org/files/resources/lesson_images/lesson1062/checklist.pdf (fair use); creativecommons .org (Creative Commons); http://www.templetons.com/brad/copymyths.html (copyright myths). The sites in Table 11.2 (p. 239) are also good sources.

- Review the following videos or infringement cases and ask students if they think the videos qualify as fair use or infringe copyright. Each group should evaluate a case's copyright status using fair use standards or the *Best Practices Guide to Fair Use* (http://www.centerforsocial media.org/fair-use/related-materials/codes/code-best-practices-fair-use-online-video).
  - "Stop the Falsiness" (http://www.youtube.com/watch?v=sNHqX27hlz8).
  - J. K. Rowling copyright infringement
    (http://en.wikipedia.org/wiki/Legal_disputes_over_ the_Harry_Potter_series
    http://www.fantasybookreview.co.uk/blog/2009/06/16/bloomsbury-deny-jk-rowling-copyright-infringement-allegations/).
  - "A Fair(y) Use Tale" (http://cyberlaw.stanford.edu/documentary-film-program/film/a-fair-y-use-tale) by Professor Eric Faden, Bucknell University (see Figure 11.13).

Figure 11.12. KWL Plagiarism Chart

K—What I Know	W—What I Want to Know	L—What I Learned

Figure 11.13. A Fair(y) Use Tale

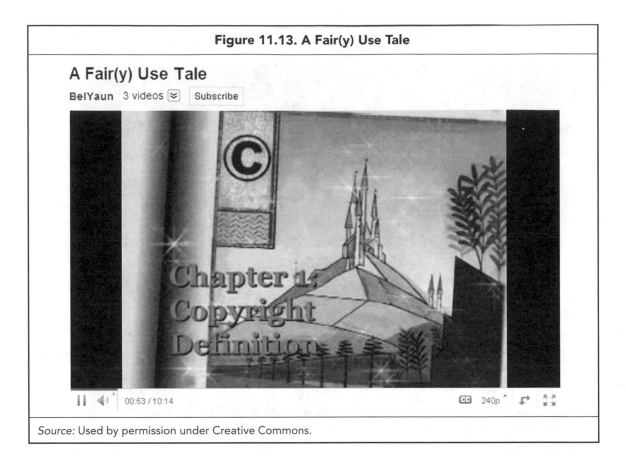

Source: Used by permission under Creative Commons.

- ○ Optional: "Remix Culture" (http://www.centerforsocialmedia.org/fair-use/videos/podcasts/remix-culture); *Best Practices Guide for Fair Use* (http://www.centerforsocialmedia.org/fair-use/videos).
- The final project to exemplify plagiarism issues will be based on one of several cases listed below or ones students make up. The following URLs provide background for these cases and samples of what teachers may want to put in their lessons.
  - ○ *Napster v. Metallica* in 2000—a music case. Possible sources include http://www.econedlink.org/lessons/index.php?lid=186&type=educator; http://www.readwritethink.org/classroom-resources/lesson-plans/copyright-infringement-debate-over-855.html?tab=4#tabs; and http://findarticles.com/p/articles/mi_qn4182/is_20000612/ai_n10136611/.
  - ○ *J. K. Rowling* (author of the Harry Potter novels) *v. another author.*
  - ○ *Walt Disney Studios v. Faden*, a fictional case at http://www.teachingcopyright.org/download/handout/tc_trial_guide_for_the_educator.pdf. This case has a number of handouts and activities associated with it.
  - ○ More infringement cases to choose from can be seen at http://www.benedict.com/Default.aspx, including music, movies, and more.
- Create a mock trial based on a copyright infringement suit. Some sites to use include: http://www.teachingcopyright.org/handout/trial-guide-educator; http://www.teachingcopyright.org/download/handout/tc_trial_guide_for_the_educator. pdf.
  - ○ Arrange your classroom into a courtroom and begin the mock fair use trial of *Company X v. Classroom*. Include the following:
    - Opening statements by plaintiff and defense attorneys
    - Testimony for plaintiff and cross-examination by the defense

- Testimony for the defense and cross-examination by the plaintiff
- Closing arguments by plaintiff and defense attorneys
- Jury deliberations—discussion and written verdict submitted to judge
- Post-trial debrief of student jury verdict with the class by teacher
  ○ Review mock trial videos created by high school students at http://www.youtube.com/watch?v=zd89JpoHePE.
  ○ Assign students to videotape the trial, edit it, and place the video on the wiki. See Chapter 8 for more information on creating videos.

Activities to Use as Follow-Up to the Unit
To keep students thinking about plagiarism, try the self-test at http://www4.caes.hku.hk/plagiarism/image/selftest.pdf. Two writing samples are given, as well as a number of student rewrites to the samples. Determine if the student has plagiarized, what is wrong, and how to fix the problem.

Step 5: Evaluate What You Learned
Evaluation is an important part of any lesson. Students will be evaluated based on completion of thoughtful blog posts, analyses of assigned roles, participation in class and group discussions, role-play in the trial, and participation in the video production.

- Complete the L column of the KWL chart (see Figure 11.12, p. 241) to answer questions students asked at the beginning of the unit. Post on the class wiki.
- Use the rubric in Figure 11.14 to evaluate participants in the trial.

Summary
The example cases in this unit and the trial enactment are ways for students to examine the controversy of fair use and copyright. Technology and innovation often challenge the rules of copyright. This unit helps to make clear the points about copyright and fair use so students know what is legal and what is not.

Figure 11.14. Trial Rubric			
	3 points	**2 points**	**1 point**
Viewpoint	Viewpoints are clear and organized.	Most viewpoints are clear.	Viewpoints are unclear and disorganized.
Use of facts and examples	Arguments are supported with facts and examples.	Most arguments are supported with facts and examples.	Arguments lack factual support.
Relevance of supporting arguments	All supporting arguments are relevant.	Many, but not all, supporting arguments are relevant.	Few supporting arguments are relevant.
Strength of arguments	All arguments are strong and convincing.	Some arguments are convincing.	Arguments are not convincing.
Voice presentation	Voice can always be heard.	Voice is heard most of the time.	Voice is difficult to hear.
Preparation	Student is well prepared.	Student needs more preparation.	Student is unprepared to defend argument.

Source: IRA/NCTE, 2005; http://www.readwritethink.org/files/resources/lesson_images/lesson819/rubric2.pdf.

Teacher Exercises: Now You Try It . . .

To get started using social networking and productivity tools for educators, complete the following exercises.

1. Select at least two or three blogs to read and sign up for Classroom 2.0.
2. Reflect on what you learned on a given day, and if you can't think of anything, go to Twitter or a blog or a PLN and write down one new idea.
3. Decide what social media works best for you and focus on those first. Set a goal of identifying at least one resource you want to follow each week. Remember you can always remove yourself.
4. Once you are comfortable on social sites, comment on a blog, send a reply tweet, or send an e-mail complimenting someone's work at least once a week. Next, add to the conversation.
5. Challenge yourself: Select a website mentioned in this chapter such as LiveBinders or Cyberbee. Explore the site, write a post providing an overview of the site, and describe your favorite resource and its applications for teaching. Send your post either to Twitter or put it on an educational blog.
6. Based on what you taught in the lesson:
   a. create a plagiarism policy for your school if one does not already exist; and
   b. create one writing assignment you think will be difficult to plagiarize (see Figure 11.15).

CONCLUSION

Professional development and networking are vital in any field, and that's especially true for educators. The tools discussed in this chapter provide you with the opportunity to learn from others, share your knowledge and ideas, and obtain support for your teaching. If you fail to connect to a network of learners, you miss out on this global conversation that can save you time and energy, and increase your reach beyond the classroom door. Connecting, contributing, conversing, and requesting should be the goal of every twenty-first-century educator. Building your own personal learning network (PLN) is the place to start.

FUTURE DIRECTIONS

"The Times They Are A-Changin'," a song by Bob Dylan from the 1960s, continues to resonate today. Three international organizations—the New Media Consortium (NMC), the Consortium for School Networking (CoSN), and the International Society for Technology in Education (ISTE)—compiled the collaborative *NMC Horizon Report 2011 K–12 Edition*, identifying the emerging technologies and key trends and challenges that will impact teaching, learning, and creative inquiry in the K–12 sector in the near future (Johnson, Adams, and Haywood, 2011).

Five trends may be realized in the next few years:

- **Cloud computing**, already used in many school districts, allows the school system to cut the costs of running district data centers, such as data storage, backups, and infrastructure maintenance. The reason cloud computing is so relevant is that it has more flexibility, space, collaboration, and ultimately, more creative uses of Internet resources for educators to incorporate in their classrooms. For example, Kerpoof, used mainly by elementary and middle school students, is a cloud-based application that enables children to make animated movies, artwork, and more. The site also contains downloadable lesson plans for teachers. Cloud-based applications and services are available to many school students today, and more schools are predicted to employ cloud-based tools going forward.

Figure 11.15. Plagiarism-Proof Assignments Checklist	
Read your assignments and use the checklist to see if you have considered these points when creating the assignment. Place a check next to items that need further review.	
Avoid open-ended topics.	
Create expectations or rubrics for the assignment together with students.	
Use class discussion(s) as a source.	
Require significantly revised multiple drafts.	
Add oral presentations.	
Break the assignment into parts requiring sources to be turned in at different stages of the process.	
Prohibit changing topics at the last minute.	
Require blog posts throughout the research process (e.g., comparing thoughts to what text presents).	
Source: Based on Burwell, Kibler, and Keir, 2003.	

- **Mobile devices**, especially smartphones and tablets, provide widespread access to information, social networks, tools for learning and productivity, and thousands of custom applications—all in one package that easily fits in a backpack. The age at which students in developed countries acquire their first mobile device is dropping, and by secondary school, nearly every student has one. With 24/7 Internet, mobiles combine several technologies that lend themselves to educational use, including electronic book readers, annotation tools, applications for creation and composition, and social networking tools.

    In the coming months, the vast potential of these devices for learning will begin to outweigh concerns about misuse that currently dominate most discussions about their use in school settings.

- **Educational gaming** spans the range from single-player or small-group card and board games all the way to multiplayer online games and virtual reality games. Games, simulations, and virtual worlds provide educators with an opportunity to engage learners in an immersive and interactive environment that requires knowledge, decision making, and information management skills.

    The National STEM Video Game Challenge encouraged middle school students to create their own games playable on open or free gaming platforms. The idea was to build both critical-thinking and creative-design skills. Another area of gaming that is increasingly interesting to schools is simulation-based games. For example, the game *Immune Attack* integrates key biology concepts about connective tissue and red and white blood cells into the plot. *Finding Identity*, a social science game, teaches K–12 students about history, culture, and life values using a twenty-first-century approach to storytelling and collaborative puzzle solving. A game design of high quality can deeply engage students in learning.

    Virtual worlds offer environments in which learners become central, important participants; a place where the actions of a ten-year-old can have significant impact on the world; a context in which what you know is directly related to what you are able to do and, ultimately, who you become, immersing learners in rich contexts where they apply what they learn. Gaming technologies and methodologies can be leveraged to establish worlds where children are transformed into empowered scientists, doctors, reporters, and mathematicians who have to understand disciplinary content to accomplish desired ends.

- **Web 3.0 or the semantic web** is being used as a term to identify changes and modifications emerging as a new Internet develops and has data integration as a goal. Educators currently spend much of their time trying to develop skills so that students can identify legitimate information, organize and synthesize the information, integrate it with other information from multiple sources, and produce new knowledge that can be applied directly to a real use.

  Knowledge construction and applied learning increase considerably when students spend less time locating and organizing information and more time constructing knowledge from the existing tagged information. Web 3.0 is continually evolving and can be shaped by those who use and develop new ideas and technology. Educators must step into the discussion and make sure education going forward is part of the Web 3.0 vision.

Get Started Now

The best Web 2.0 educators are a part of the web and social networking themselves. They have an RSS reader and subscribe to blogs in their subject areas, grade levels, and libraries. They have their own blogs and comment on blogs of other educators to stay abreast of real-time innovations in their fields. They are connected to other educators through their own personal learning network (PLN) and often share their best practices with others through Facebook and Twitter. They consider new technologies and try them, having recommendations from colleagues they respect most. In other words, they model what they teach.

Engaged educators have the following characteristics:

- They are connected.
- They are open-minded.
- They are vigilant.
- They hold students and themselves accountable.
- They have character.
- They are passionate about their subject.

But the most innovative educators don't stand still. They also look to the future. They know that in the next five years, education will continue to change along with the technology they will use. As I was writing the last chapter of this book, a blog post I saw on the *Langwitches Blog* from Sylvia Tolisano came to mind. Two new letters added to the familiar KWL chart used with students can also apply to educators:

1. "A"—What action will you take? Will you be leading the way, following experts in the field, or continuing to apply tired techniques from the 1980s? Will you apply what you've learned in this book?
2. "Q"—What new questions do you have? Once you've addressed what you currently know and have learned, what other questions are still unanswered? What else will you be learning in the next year? What new technologies will be available to help your students meet the challenges of the twenty-first century?

What does the future hold? Will mobile devices such as the iPad and smartphone flood the classrooms as they have the backpacks of your students? Will students be using e-books instead of the traditional textbook? Will a high school education include more online courses for a true blended learning environment? And, will cloud computing bring on-demand, shared resources to your classrooms? All of these questions and more will present challenges to innovative educators. What action will you take?

REFERENCES AND FURTHER READING

Burwell, Hope, William L. Kibler, and Jessica A. Keir. 2003. "Cheating and Plagiarism Using the Internet." PBS Teleconference (videotape). Dallas TeleLearning, April 2003.

Johnson, L., S. Adams, and K. Haywood. 2011. *The NMC Horizon Report: 2011 K–12 Edition*. Austin, Texas: The New Media Consortium.

Reynard, Ruth. 2010. "Web 3.0 and Its Relevance for Instruction." *THE Journal*. February 3, 2010. http://the journal.com/articles/2010/02/03/web-3.0-and-its-relevance-for-instruction.aspx?sc_lang=en.

Wikipedia. 2011. "Legal Disputes Over the Harry Potter Series." Wikimedia Foundation. Last modified October 8. http://en.wikipedia.org/wiki/Legal_disputes_over_the_Harry_Potter_series.

Wikipedia. 2011. "Personal Learning Networks." Wikimedia Foundation. Last modified April 10. http://en .wikipedia.org/wiki/Personal_Learning_Network.

Bev's Website and Blog

Using Web 2.0 and Social Networking Tools in the K–12 Classroom provides the basics to understand and get started using Web 2.0 tools in school libraries and content-area classrooms. One way to keep a book current is to have it constantly updating. Bev's Website allows *Using Web 2.0 and Social Networking Tools in the K–12 Classroom* to keep up with new teaching material, technology, and ideas. Look for the italicized boxed text in each chapter pointing out where to find these ideas on the website.

Here's what I'll put on my website at **http://www.neal-schuman.com/webclassroom** (see Figure A.1):

- **Models for Educators:** Descriptions of educators using Web 2.0 and social networking tools in subject areas at different grade levels. Educators are now really incorporating new technologies into their classroom lessons. I hope models will help those of you who have not

Figure A.1. Bev's Website

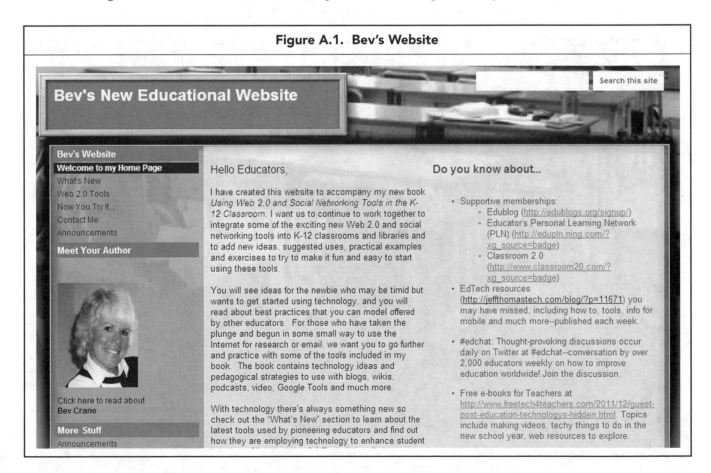

yet tried these tools. I also encourage contributions and commentary from teachers who are spearheading the use of these tools in their classrooms and libraries.

- **What's New:** New technologies and updates on Web 2.0 tools illustrated in *Using Web 2.0 and Social Networking Tools in the K–12 Classroom*. For example, I will look for innovative ideas, technologies that promote learning and are easy to use, ideas that motivate students, and much more.
- **Now You Try It...:** Additional exercises in different subject areas at elementary, middle, and secondary grade levels to challenge teachers and librarians not yet using Web 2.0 to take the plunge and incorporate technology into their lesson and unit plans.
- **Resources:** Articles, books you don't want to miss, lesson plans, conferences, projects, sites to see, free training, and more.
- **Special Topics:** More in-depth discussion of specific tools, for example, Skype and video, which have become quite popular with educators and students alike.
- **Features from Teachers:** Descriptions from teachers and librarians who have had special success with a project or lesson to motivate or teach students.

Bev's Edublog (http://bevcrane.blogspot.com): Updated weekly, Bev's Educational Blog (see Figure A.2) brings you:

- **Tips and Tricks:** I will tell you about ideas from other educators around the world. Also, I want you to submit ideas—tell us about a brilliant lesson you taught with technology, kids' reactions when using a blog, or a website that other educators might find interesting.

Figure A.2. Bev's Educational Blog

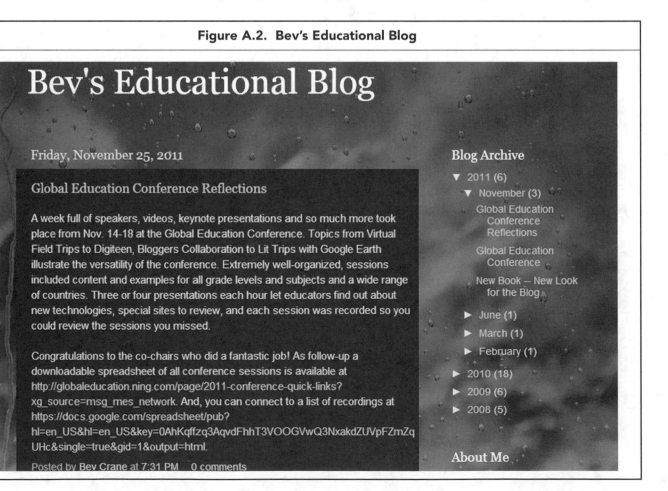

- **Links Galore:** I will provide links to articles about teaching practices, classroom blogs, technology conferences, teacher publishing sites, and projects.

I encourage you to add your ideas and examples of how you are using Web 2.0 and social networking in classrooms and libraries to the blog to make it useful to all K–12 educators worldwide.

Index

About the Author

Beverley E. Crane received a BS in Spanish and English and an MEd in Bilingual Education and English as a Second Language from Penn State University. She obtained an EdD in Curriculum and Instruction, with emphases in Language Arts and Educational Technology from Oklahoma State University. She has taught English/language arts and ESL at the middle, high school, and college levels.

While working on a grant for a five-state area multicultural resource center, she conducted workshops for K–12 teachers on such topics as literacy, writing and the writing process, ESL, and integrating technology into the curriculum. In addition, for 12 years at Dialog, she created educational materials and conducted workshops for K–12 library media specialists and teachers on using online searching in the curriculum. She presented throughout the United States across curriculum areas at conferences, such as the American Association of School Librarians (AASL), the National Educational Computing Conference (NECC), Computer-Using Educators (CUE), American Educational Research Association (AERA), National Council for the Social Studies Conference (NCSS), California Media and Library Educators Association (CMLEA), among others on topics such as using online searching in the elementary and secondary curricula, computers and writing, integrating online searching into social studies, and online research across the curriculum.

As director of the English Education Program at San Jose State University for five years, she worked closely with classroom teachers and administrators to provide guidelines for mentor teachers supervising English student teachers at SJSU.

Currently, she continues to write articles on using the Internet in the curriculum for the *Information Searcher*, as well as keeping up her website and blog. She also creates training materials for Dialog, including distance education online courses and self-paced modules on searching techniques, and is editor of the Dialog customer e-newsletters. Her books *Teaching with the Internet: Strategies and Models for K–12 Curricula, Internet Workshops: 10 Ready-to-Go Workshops for K–12 Educators*, and *Using Web 2.0 Tools in the K–12 Classroom* were published by Neal-Schuman in 2000, 2003, and 2009, respectively. She lives in Santa Fe, New Mexico, with her husband and dog Carmen.